ELI HASSIDOV
Government Licensed Guide

47a Einstein St.
Haifa, Israel
Tel. 04 - 24 16 14

To Dean

Mrs Koppenhaver.

From your
guide in ISRAEL
Eliagh.

March 8th. 1976.
Tel-Aviv.

THE

OF THE

MOUNTAIN LORD

Professor Benjamin Mazar

Assisted by **Gaalyah Cornfeld**

Professor D. N. Freedman, *Consultant*

Doubleday & Company, Inc.

Garden City, New York

1975

Library of Congress Cataloging in Publication Data

Mazar, Benjamin, 1906–
The Mountain of the Lord.

Translated and adapted from the Hebrew ms.
titled: Har ha-Bayit ve-'Ir David.
1. Temple Mount, Jerusalem. 2. Jerusalem – Antiquities.
I. Cornfeld, Gaalyah, 1902–
II. Title.
DS109.28.M38   956.94'4   74–5531

ISBN 0–385–04843–2

Library of Congress Catalog Card Number: 74–5531

Printed in Israel: By Peli Printing Works Ltd.

First Edition

Layout: E. Gilad

INTRODUCTION

When one considers what Jerusalem, the spiritual center of the monotheistic religions, has represented to countless millions of people, and then tries to assess whether these people had, or even nowadays have, any idea of what the city was like originally, it is clear that there is a major gap between imagination and reality.

For centuries no one had any real knowledge of what Jerusalem and the Temple Mount looked like, and all artistic representations were based on suppositions combined with a modicum of data rooted in old beliefs. The literary evidence for a topography of the city and the Holy Places up to their destruction by the Romans in 70 A.D. was preserved only in the books of Josephus Flavius and in allusions contained in the Mishna, the Talmud and a few other writings including the New Testament, and those dating to the days of the Crusaders and the Moslem Mameluke rulers who followed them. The physical remains, however, were buried under the ruins left by successive Roman and Byzantine occupations as well as by the Arabs. All that could be seen was a monumental pile of crumbling walls and debris — vast accumulations of earth and stone that blurred the outlines of the steep slopes that were the sides of the gigantic retaining walls erected by King Herod around the Temple Mount. Of the Temple Mount, the only visible remains were the top layers of the ancient walls and, surmounting them, the vast platform of the Haram es-Sherif on which stood the Dome of the Rock, the El-'Aqṣa mosque and other Islamic shrines.

With regard to the oldest settlements at the site (pre-Israelite and Israelite, but specifically the Ophel and the City of David, which lay immediately south of and below the Temple Mount), the endless sequence of building and destruction has left little evidence intact, and only traces of its periods of occupation. Because of the topography of Jerusalem with its precipitous slopes, the combination of erosion and quarrying has prevented the formation of a true tell (mounds composed of the remains of successive settlements). In fact, so much of the ancient city itself disappeared that the bedrock upon which it once stood was exposed. This bedrock, in turn, was itself quarried to provide building stone for new buildings, while parts of the hillside were cultivated or built over by Arab peasants. Despite all this devastation, however, tangible data has come to light that provides evidence of unbroken occupation of this historic site since the beginning of the third millennium B.C. (See Parts IV–V).

Remains of the Herodian city of two thousand years ago are more substantial. They include *inter alia* fragments of Herod's fortifications (the Phasael Tower on the western side of the city), the monumental tombs of the Kidron valley southeast of the Temple Mount, and the "Tombs of the Kings," which are actually the tombs of the converted

5

royal family of Adiabene and which lie north of the Old City. These ruins are the survivors of a long history, and the mystery of the ancient shrines that lie beneath them has challenged thoughtful and imaginative minds down through the centuries. Although many scholars have in the past attempted to reconstruct the different phases of the Temple Mount and its vicinity, they lacked scientific methods and validated data. Except for tantalizing clues in the ancient texts, they had mainly contradictory religious traditions, legends and folk stories to guide them, and their reconstructions were distorted accordingly.

Since the mid-nineteenth century, when systematic research was undertaken for the first time in Palestine, Jerusalem and the Temple Mount itself have been a principal attraction for archeologists. The fact that both were buried under layers of ancient civilizations and contained the sacred sites of the various religions made methodical research difficult. This was particularly true in the neglected area around the Temple Mount which is under Moslem control, as well as in the small exposed section of the Western Wall that is devoted to Jewish worship. Progress has been slow. Although many investigations have been carried out in the last hundred years, the resultant discoveries and insights were often mixed with mistaken impressions and ideas.

This, then, was the challenge we faced when we started our first excavations in 1968. Our purpose was and still is to learn as much as we can about the history of Jerusalem throughout the ages and to understand what was going on during the various periods.

The main excavations — and the main controversy stirred by Arab objections to our effort — have been centered on the area around the ancient Temple Mount, but close observation and various clues have also led us to take a fresh look at a number of obscure fields of investigation in other parts of biblical Jerusalem linked with developments in the Temple Mount area.

This book, then, is an attempt to depict Jerusalem as it emerges anew from the insights we have gained.

Benjamin Mazar

CONTENTS

PART I

GUIDELINES TO THE BURIED SANCTUARY

A. PROBING THE HISTORIC GROUND OF JERUSALEM

1. THE TEMPLE MOUNT IN THE BIBLE

Investigating the history of Jerusalem and its traditional sites began in the earliest times and has expanded considerably through the centuries. Evidence of this interest may be found, in fact, as far back as the Bible and is specifically expressed in the identification of ancient sites with names current in the days of the Israelite monarchy. For instance, the passage about "the stronghold of Zion, that is, the City of David" (II Samuel 5:7) explains that the pre-Davidic stronghold of Zion is identical with the City of David on the hill of Jerusalem south of the Temple Mount, and "the Valley of Shaveh [that is, the King's Valley]" in Genesis 14:17 indicates the area where King Melchizedek and Abraham met, or more specifically, the Ēn-Rogel spring in the King's Valley (see Part IV, A, 3: Ēn-Rogel, The Meeting Ground of Abraham and Melchizedek).

There was considerable confusion about the origins of the city and of its pre-Israelite population ('Amorite,' 'Jebusite,' and according to Ezekiel 16:3 "your father was an Amorite, and your mother a Hittite"). The history of the Temple Mount before the erection of the Temple was equally unclear, especially the reference to Abraham's hallowed High Place (Genesis 22:14): *"Yahweh Yir'eh"* which means "Yahweh sees," but is interpreted in the same verse as "Yahweh Yera'eh" ("Yahweh will be seen"). This applies also to the altars erected there by Abraham and, later, by David, on the threshing floor he had purchased from Araunah the Jebusite.

The biblical record has many references to the walls of the city in various periods, to its towers and gates, the different sections of the city and their principal structures including, in particular, the plans for the King's Palace and the work done on it. Interest also attaches to water supply projects and to cemeteries. Special attention, however, is paid to the Temple Mount. Detailed descriptions of the Temple and its furnishings are to be found, one in I Kings 6–7, the other in II Chronicles 3–4. The account in I Kings, in all likelihood, depicts the Solomonic Temple during its early stages, while II Chronicles describes it after it had undergone a number of repairs and some redecoration. The most thorough renovation of the Temple was carried out in the days of King Josiah (639–609 B.C.). In the

Taken in 1935 from the air, the photograph of the Temple Mount, center, poses the question of what historical and religious structures lie beneath the vast accumulation of debris, refuse and silt in the foreground and, to the left of the Islamic Haram es-Sherif esplanade, the agglomeration of hovels and cactus groves. This is equally true of the site of the Ophel on the following page. This question, for almost two millennia, has been taunting people of all the religions that center in Jerusalem

course of Josiah's repairs, an 'archeological' discovery was made: a scroll of the Law of Moses was found (containing the bulk of the present Book of Deuteronomy, in the opinion of most scholars), which caused a far-reaching reform in the religious life of Jerusalem and Judah (II Kings 22).

a. Blueprint of a Restored Temple

Besides these detailed descriptions of the Temple, the Bible also records the visionary plan or blueprint of the Temple as conceived by the priest-prophet Ezekiel (Chs. 40–45), then living in exile in Babylonia. His plan is a combination of accurate recollections of the Temple area during the period before his departure from the city in 597 B.C. with the exiled King Jehoiachin, and creative and imaginative ideas derived from a variety of sources and shaped by his mystical experience. It is presented as the blueprint of a restored Temple, established priesthood and sacred rites in the Holy City. It had a profound impact on later generations, partly in the learned discussions of its divergences from the directions given in the Pentateuch, partly in the practical matters of construction and orderly arrangement of furnishings and ritual procedures.

Considerable interest attaches also to descriptions and "glorification" of Jerusalem and the Temple found in liturgical poetry and prophetic literature dating from the period of the First Temple and the return from Babylon (e.g. Psalm 122). Noteworthy among these is the vision of the messianic age recorded in the books of two eighth-century prophets, Isaiah and Micah, in which Jerusalem and its Temple serve as a gathering place

12

Accumulated debris covered the site of the biblical Ophel and top of the 'City of David', shown below the walls, before excavations were planned

for all nations and peoples in an unprecedented era of peace and reconciliation, when "out of Zion shall go forth the law, and the word of God from Jerusalem" (Isaiah 2:3; Micah 4:2).

No less important from a practical point of view, the Bible contains details of various building projects and public works carried out by the kings of Judah. Such accounts constitute the principal source of useful information about the city and the Temple in pre-exilic times.

b. Nehemiah's Jerusalem Atlas

One of the most detailed sources is what may be called Nehemiah's Jerusalem Atlas, an invaluable source for the historical topography of fifth-century Jerusalem. It has provided vital clues to archeologists in their research, and given rise to lively debates about the identification of surviving remains and the location of certain landmarks. (See Part V, A: Nehemiah's Vital Evidence; New Archeological Insights into the Book of Nehemiah).

2. THE TEMPLE MOUNT IN HELLENISTIC SOURCES

Alexander the Great captured Palestine in the late fourth century B.C. Jerusalem and the Temple during the ensuing period are best described in the nonbiblical Letter of Aristeas, written in Greek, probably, by an Egyptian Jew and describing the travels of Aristeas, an official of the court of Ptolemy II (285–246 B.C.). It is a sympathetic account of life and times in Jerusalem, with valuable data on various places and structures and a laudatory description of the Temple. (See Part II, D: The Early Hellenistic Period;

13

Letter of Aristeas.) More information about the city and the Temple is to be found in the Apocryphal book of Ecclesiasticus and the two Books of Maccabees which reflect first-hand knowledge of Jerusalem before and during the stormy period of Maccabean dominance in the second and first centuries B.C.

3. JOSEPHUS

Joseph ben Mattityahu, a Jerusalem priest who was active in the second half of the first century A.D., wrote apparently first in Aramaic and then in Greek, several historical works that rank well above any other account which has come down to us concerning the history, topography, demography, social, political and economic life of Jerusalem.

Josephus was a gifted man of letters, deeply versed in the written sources of his own and former days. His principal works are Jewish *Antiquities* in twenty volumes covering the beginning of Jewish history to the start of the Great War with Rome in A.D. 66, and *The Jewish War* in seven volumes covering the period from Antiochus Epiphanes' conquest of Jerusalem in 170 B.C. to Titus' conquest of Jerusalem in A.D. 70 and some subsequent events of the Roman occupation. It is true that some of Josephus' statements cannot be taken at face value, and on occasion the opinions he expresses reflect his political leanings rather than his judgment as a historian, e.g. his pacifist and pro-Roman bias which made him unpopular in the days of the great revolt.

It has now become clear that we must draw a sharp line between Josephus as contemporary chronicler of events to which he was an actual witness, and Josephus as historian when he draws at his discretion upon outside sources and traditions. It must be remembered that he knew the city and the Temple thoroughly and was besides an eye-witness to and participant in many of the dramatic events leading up to and taking place during the Jewish revolt against the Romans, until the final destruction of the city and the state. Therefore, in spite of all discrepancies, ambiguities, contradictions and plain mistakes — which should not be overlooked — the fact remains that Josephus was a very reliable witness, not only with respect to Jerusalem in which he lived, but also, to a somewhat lesser extent, with regard to earlier times.

It is important, of course, to check his statements against data preserved in other ancient historical sources, such as the Letter of Aristeas and the Books of the Maccabees for the hellenistic period, and the New Testament, Mishna and Talmud for Roman times. We must also take into account serious problems arising from the interpretation of his record, more particularly in all that pertains to his descriptions of Jerusalem, its walls and important structures, especially the Temple and the Temple Mount. To interpret, appreciate and if necessary correct these accounts, it is necessary to check them against the result of systematic excavation.

Nevertheless, in spite of ambiguities and exaggerations, his is the most comprehensive account extant, and his works are our best guide to the understanding of the material data pertinent to the Temple Mount. The progress of archeological investigation highlights more than ever the great importance of Josephus as a primary source for the study of the topography and history of Jerusalem in Herodian times. *All this we were able to confirm on repeated occasions through our archeological investigations.*

4. THE TEMPLE SCROLL

A revealing source on religious concepts on Jerusalem is a parchment scroll discovered with other Dead Sea scrolls in Qumran, Cave 2, dating to Herodian times. It is the longest of the scrolls known so far and has not yet been published in full, though summaries and excerpts have been made available by the editor, Professor Yigael Yadin. It will be published in the near future. Among its contents is a detailed visionary description of the Temple of Jerusalem in the days to come, including its great courts and other structures which are laid out according to a definite pattern; the Temple stands in the middle of three square concentric courts, one outside the other, each with its chambers and porticos. From the innermost court out, their measurements are 250, 500, and 1500 cubits on each side, approximately 375, 750, and 2250 feet. As in Ezekiel and the New Testament book of Revelation, twelve gates are listed, one for each of the traditional twelve tribes of Israel. The author apparently based his plan on that of the Solomonic Temple as outlined in I Chronicles 28:11 ff., and on Ezekiel's blueprint, but he adapted and modified the latter in accordance with the special views of his cosectaries, the Essenes. The scroll also provides material concerning the ritual of the sanctuary and the celebration of the various festivals.

5. THE EVIDENCE OF THE MISHNA AND TALMUD

The Temple, with its priestly personnel, sacred rites, and festive observances, was the subject of continuous learned discussion and disputation among the informed priests and rabbis of late Second Temple days and some centuries after its destruction. The subject matter constitutes part of the code of Oral Law that deals with festivals, the Sabbath, ritual, and other laws preserved in the Mishna (which was completed about A.D. 200) and the Tosefta (supplements thereto). The Mishna formed the basis of academic discussions by generations of scholars, which were recorded and preserved in the Jerusalem and Babylonian Talmuds (up to ca. A.D. 500). The subject matter occurs also in Midrashic (homiletic) literature recorded from the first century B.C. to the tenth century A.D. This sums up the record of academic discussion. Especially valuable are the discussions which took place in the Temple precincts during the years before the destruction of Jerusalem. Many of them include descriptions of the Temple and its functions and can claim the authority of contemporary witnesses.

The Talmudic scholars were constantly absorbed in matters of Temple ritual.

Detailed expertise was necessary so that when Jerusalem would be restored the Temple could be rebuilt and full worship restored. We even hear of Jewish sages who visited the desolate site after the destruction and recorded their discoveries and observations. One such is ben Azzai, who discovered a genealogical scroll in Jerusalem (*Yebamot* 4:13). A wealth of material has been thus preserved dealing with Jerusalem, its gates, buildings, and marketplaces, as well as with the customs and experiences of the people in the years preceding the fall of the city.

6. THE APOCALYPTIC MYSTIQUE

While the Talmudic sages understood the biblical prophecies in a literal historical sense, and entertained the hope of returning to the land and rebuilding the Temple, there were others who interpreted these expectations in mystical, apocalyptic terms. That is, they applied them to what would happen upon the Day of Judgment. This tendency is illustrated in the vision of Baruch, which presents the ideal Jerusalem as a divine creation and perfect in every sense. The apocalyptic outlook took special form in the vision of the heavenly Jerusalem. Theological disputations about the Jerusalem of the last days and the relations between the earthly and the heavenly Jerusalem were common and reflected the importance of the subject.

These mystical views were adopted by early Jewish Christians and developed in a variety of ways. It has been observed that the prophecy attributed to Jesus, "There will not be left one stone upon another, that will not be thrown down" (Matthew 24:2) helped to enhance early Christianity's vision of a heavenly Jerusalem. The negative side of the Temple, and the emphasis on the heavenly vision, may have contributed to the neglect of the Temple Mount in the Christian tradition and during the years of Christian rule over the Holy Land in Byzantine times. However, it did not diminish in any way the holiness of Jerusalem itself in the eyes of the Christians. The prestige of the city reached its zenith with the discovery of what was thought to be the sepulchre of Jesus by Queen Mother Helena in the early fourth century A.D. and the erection of the Church of the Holy Sepulchre on the site by her son Constantine the Great. This one edifice marked the site of the crucifixion and the burial and resurrection as well. Here was the holiest place in Christendom, encompassing the core of Christian faith and piety.

B. THE ROMANS IGNORED THE TEMPLE MOUNT

The earnest hopes for the restoration of the Temple were never relinquished and remained a basic tenet of the Jewish faith. This confidence almost turned into reality on several occasions in Roman times. The first opportunity presented itself in A.D. 130 when the Emperor Hadrian decided to establish on the site of the ruins of Jerusalem a new

The crumbling slum inhabited by Algerian Moslems lay below the Jewish Quarter on the hill behind it. The slum ended in a narrow court facing the Western (Wailing) Wall, where Jews gathered for worship until the late 1940's, when they were refused access. This humiliating status quo could not endure forever. Added to this was the overriding necessity to clear away the millennial accumulation of debris on the slopes of the Temple Mount

Up to 1967, only a small portion of the Western Wall of the Temple Mount was visible. It faced a narrow court and was surrounded by ramshackle slums. Due to its proximity to the Temple esplanade, Jews had been worshiping there for the last fifteen centuries

Roman city called *Colonia Aelia Capitolina*. The Roman ruler celebrated the foundation of the new city with appropriate ceremony, in the course of which he plowed up the city. This sparked the Second Jewish Revolt, led by Simon bar Kochba. Between 132 and 135, the Jews were able to set up an independent government and Jerusalem was included in the Jewish state. Their determination to revive the glorious traditions of the Jewish Commonwealth found eloquent expression in the coins struck by Bar Kochba to commemorate the event. Some are inscribed "First Year of the Deliverance of Israel," and "Freedom of Jerusalem," or just "Jerusalem." One especially interesting coin shows the facade of the Temple. When the desperate efforts of the rebels under Bar Kochba had been quelled in A.D. 135, Hadrian deliberately blotted out Jewish Jerusalem and, in order to frustrate any further Jewish ambitions, he built on its site *Aelia Capitolina* and erected a tripartite temple in honor of Jupiter, Juno and Minerva on the Temple site. He set up an equestrian statue of himself on the site and his successor, Antoninus Pius (A.D.

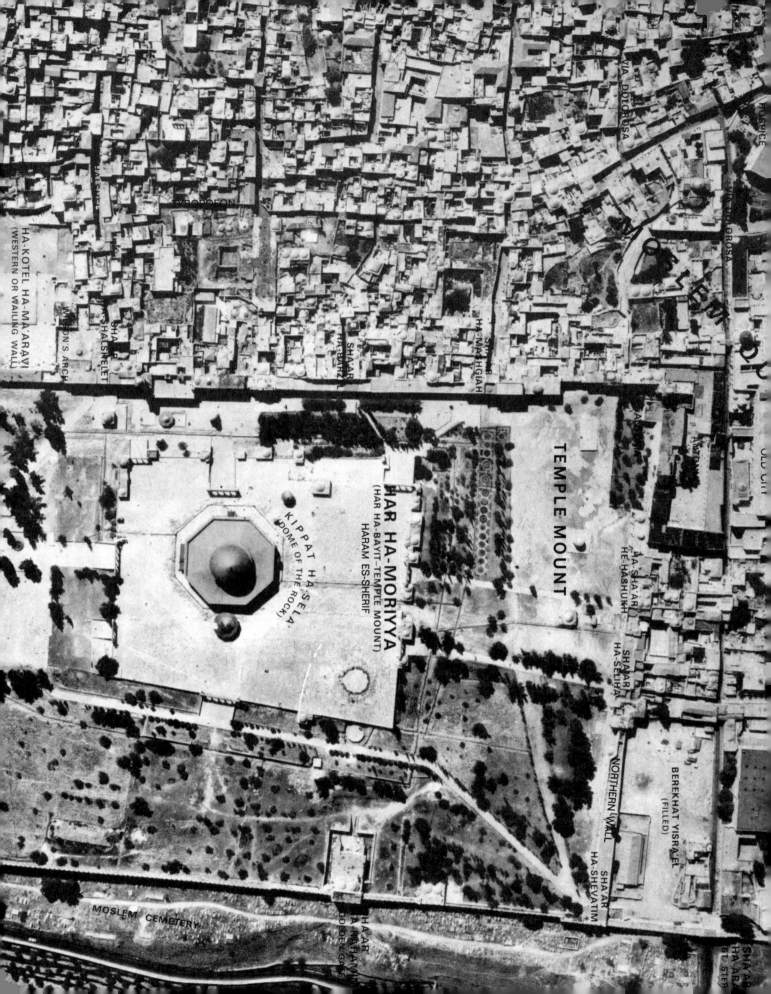

HA-KOTEL HA-MA'ARAVI
(WESTERN OR WAILING WALL)

WILSON'S ARCH

SHA'AR HA-SHALSHELET

SYROPOEON

SHA'AR HA-BARZEL

SHA'AR HA-MASHGIAH

VIA DOLOROSA

VIA DOLOROSA

HOSPICE

JERUSALEM — OLD CITY

ANTONIA

ANTONIA

HA-SHA'AR HE-HASHUKH

SHA'AR HA-SELIHA

TEMPLE MOUNT

HAR HA-MORIYYA
(HAR HA-BAYIT—TEMPLE MOUNT)
HARAM ES-SHERIF

KIPPAT HA-SELA
(DOME OF THE ROCK)

NORTHERN WALL

SHA'AR HA-SHEVATIM

BEREKHAT YISRA'EL
(FILLED)

SHA'AR HA-ARAYOT
6 L STEP

MOSLEM CEMETERY

SHA'AR HA-RAHAMIM
GOLDEN GATE

138–161) added another statue. The Jews were forbidden to return except to mourn on the Temple Mount on special occasions.

Historic circumstances offered the Jews two other opportunities to rebuild the Temple. They are described in Part II, H: Rebuilding Attempts.

1. EVIDENCE OF EARLY CHRISTIANS ON THE TEMPLE MOUNT REMAINS

The scant information covering this period may, however, be supplemented with other early Christian written traditions which add a note of strangeness to the historic scene: One is the interesting comment on Hadrian in the *Chronicon Paschale* dating from Byzantine times but based on earlier memories. While describing Aelia Capitolina, it attributes the destruction of the Temple of the Jews to Hadrian, who built there his tripartite pagan temple. The Roman historian Dio Cassius asserts also that Hadrian built his temple to replace the sanctuary of the god of Israel. It is assumed, consequently, that the Chronicon does not refer to the original temple destroyed by Titus in A.D. 70 (whereby the author replaced Titus by Hadrian) but to a partly restored sanctuary set up by Bar Kochba and his followers during the short few years of the commonwealth he ruled in Judea and Jerusalem before his defeat by Hadrian. This may be only guesswork as we found only two coins of Bar Kochba in the excavations on the Temple Mount. The only historic records which color the event are the coins struck by Bar Kochba dated 'Year 1' and 'Year 2' (between A.D. 132–135) of the revolt which bear a representation of the facade of this Temple.

2. WERE THERE ANY VISIBLE REMAINS OF THE TEMPLE

The ancient records provide the following information:
a. There is a reference in the Talmud (*Yoma* 5:2) to the 'Foundation Rock' upon which the Holy of Holies had rested (see below).
b. The Story of the "Pilgrim of Bordeaux": One of the earliest and best-known travelers, the "Pilgrim of Bordeaux," visited Jerusalem in the early fourth century. The *Itinerarium Burdigalense* relates that the Jews used to go up to the Temple Mount in his day: "There is a rock there with a hollow in it to which the Jews come once a year [probably on the ninth of Ab, the Jewish date of the Temple's destruction]; they anoint it with tears, while tearing their garments. Then they go back." This evidence supports references in the Talmud about Jews visiting the Temple Mount during the Roman and Byzantine periods. The "rock with a hollow in it" is not clearly identified, but it is assumed by many that the reference is to the *Eben hāštiyā* or Foundation Rock upon which the Holy of Holies was built.

20

On closer examination the Rock shows scars and markings which reflect the vicissitudes of the site over four millennia. There are marks of chiselling on its sides which may be foundation furrows supporting walls that were built around it. A Roman shrine to Jupiter Capitolinus was also built there (second century A.D.) and a Christian altar in Crusader times. A hollow is seen on the left; it runs through the rock to a cave underneath

A representation of the main entrance to the Temple on a coin struck by Bar Kochba ca. A.D. 132

c. Eusebius, the bishop of Caesarea (approx. A.D. 260–340) asserts that he could still see remains of the sanctuary and that its large stone blocks were hauled away and used in the building of theaters and sanctuaries.

d. Some of the early Church fathers (end of 3rd and early 4th century A.D.) refer specifically to visible remains. These reports may be related to the efforts of the Jews to rebuild the Temple under the protection of the emperor Julian ("the Apostate"), which finally were frustrated (see Part II, H). Chrysostomos (A.D. 354–407) relates: "The Jews began uncovering the foundations by removing masses of earth, intending to go ahead and build... You can see the bared foundations if you visit Jerusalem now." As to the sanctuary itself (naos), he remarks that "some of its parts are razed to the ground."

e. The church fathers often refer to the pilgrimage of Jews to the Temple Mount, and more particularly on the ninth of Ab (late July). A case in point is St. Jerome who lived in Bethlehem between 386–420 A.D. (where he translated the Bible into the Latin Vulgate). The pilgrims could tarry on the mount by bribing the Roman guards. At that time, the site of the Temple and the altar of sacrifices could be identified more clearly than in later times.

f. The Pilgrim of Piacenze (sixth century A.D.) mentions the "runas templi Salomonis" (ruins of the Temple of Solomon).

g. The 'Foundation Rock,' known to the Arabs as *Es-Sakhra*, assumed special significance when the Ommayad caliphs erected the Islamic sanctuary on the spot.

h. Repeated references since then to the 'Site of the Rock' under the Islamic 'Dome of the Rock' link the site of the Temple with the tradition that the sanctuary had been built there by King Solomon.

References c., d. and e. may be clarified by a recent observation of the ground (1972) which immediately surrounds the Dome of the Rock. This was made possible by the digging of trenches some 3 ft. (1 m.) deep for the installation of a new system of water

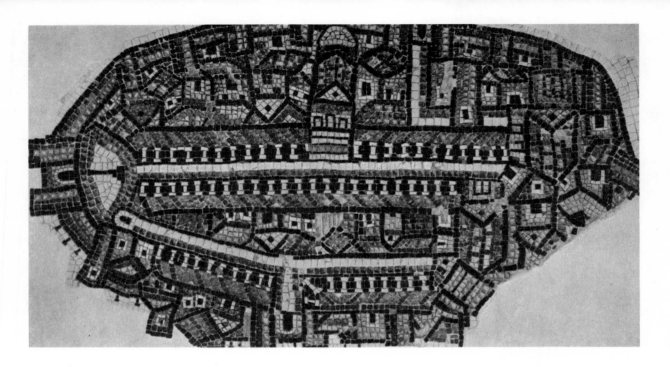

pipes. A section of the bedrock was laid bare south of the Rock and the ground on the other three sides of the Dome showed no accumulation of debris and stone fragments resulting from the destruction. This may plausibly suggest that various structures or parts of them may have remained undisturbed after A.D. 70, as recorded by the church fathers. Significant as this may be, the ground is held sacred by the Moslems and cannot be dug up, so the question of why there is no apparent evidence of destruction must be left in abeyance. Vast underground reservoirs, passages, halls, and ancient structures seem to have survived in one form or another under the Haram es-Sherif, the Moslem complex of sanctuaries, structures and courtyards overlying Herod's ancient projects (see Part III, E, 3).

3. THE MADEBA MOSAIC MAP

Christian religious literature of Byzantine times included guides intended for the use of pilgrims. The most important source of that period for the investigation of Jerusalem's past is the mid-sixth century Madeba map. A mosaic found in one of the churches of Madeba in southern Transjordan, east of the Dead Sea, this map is the only extant representation of ancient Palestine. It is the earliest in the series in which Palestine is placed at the center of the world, a convention adopted by later generations under the influence of the Bible. The map was found by J. Germer-Durand in 1896 and was published in the following year. Jerusalem and adjoining areas are depicted in great detail. The Holy City is shown as a walled metropolis in the form of an oval, as though seen from the air. Its towers, walls and gates, its streets, churches and monasteries are set forth carefully, and the Church of the Holy Sepulchre is at its center.

Jerusalem of the sixth century A.D. was actually a glorious successor to Aelia Capitolina (cf. Part VI, A). It was much larger in size than the Roman colony but in any case the Temple Mount was abandoned, following the practice of the Roman Colonia and the Church of Byzantium. In the Madeba map, a line of brown cubes already indicates an empty area, reflecting the fact that there was no building on the Temple area platform during the Byzantine period.

4. WHAT HAPPENED ON THE MOUNT?

Throughout the Roman and Byzantine periods and until the consolidation of Arab Ommayad rule over the Holy Land towards the end of the seventh century, Jerusalem was regarded as the Holy City of the Jews and the Christians. The dominance of the church in the Byzantine period led to a revival of interest in the holy places, especially those hallowed by the gospel tradition. Jerusalem became a magnet drawing Christian pilgrims from near and far; churches and monasteries were erected there between the fourth and sixth centuries, and many religious communities with their hospices for pilgrims flourished.

Jews regarded the abandoned ruins of the Temple and other remains, including the massive retaining walls and gates of the Temple Mount, as the central object and focus of their politico-religious dream. Some of the Hebrew inscriptions engraved on the walls of the Temple Mount may belong to this period, and they are evidence of the ongoing pilgrimage to Jerusalem by Jews from Oriental and south European countries. These travelers came to the site of the Temple in order to mourn over the destruction of the sanctuary and draw fresh hope for its eventual restoration.

5. A RUSH TO DISCOVER HOLY SITES

Christians, however, concentrated their interest on the Church of the Holy Sepulchre and a number of other shrines. No effort was spared by the Church to delve into the minutest details of Jerusalem's glorious past, and to identify holy places and buildings mentioned in the Scriptures. The various monuments were identified, though without a historical basis, and their conjectured history recorded. Attention was also paid to the remains of extant structures and the cave-tombs visible all around. No less avid was the search for relics related to the life of Christ and his Passion (the sufferings subsequent to the Last Supper, and on the Cross), as well as the gathering of local traditions and legends concerning biblical figures and later saints, which circulated among the people of both faiths. There are many stories concerning wonderful and extraordinary "discoveries": such was the vision granted to to Queen Helena, mother of Constantine the Great, which led her to carry out "excavations" over the site of Jesus' sepulchre. There she "uncovered" three crosses, and through a divine intervention was able to identify the "True Cross" on which Jesus had been crucified.

6. DEVOTION AND HISTORICAL TRUTH

It has often been said that the search of the ancients for holy sites and relics has been transmuted into the modern enthusiasm for archeology. Be that as it may, past examples of self-deception motivated by the desire to locate relics, inspired powerful religious bodies

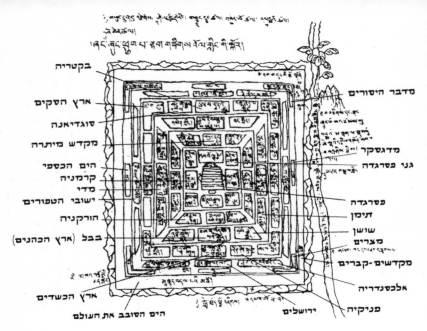

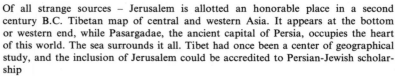

בקטריה

ארץ הסקים

סוגדיאנה

מקדש מיתרה

הים הכספי

קרמניה

מדי

ישובי הטפורים

הורקניה

בבל (ארץ הכהנים)

ארץ הכשדים

מדבר היסורים

מדגסקר

גני פסרגדה

פסרגדה

תימן

שושן

מצרים

מקדשים-קברים

אלכסנדריה

פניקיה

ירושלים

הים הסובב את העולם

Of all strange sources – Jerusalem is allotted an honorable place in a second century B.C. Tibetan map of central and western Asia. It appears at the bottom or western end, while Pasargadae, the ancient capital of Persia, occupies the heart of this world. The sea surrounds it all. Tibet had once been a center of geographical study, and the inclusion of Jerusalem could be accredited to Persian-Jewish scholarship

and their leaders, both civil and ecclesiastical, including kings, queens and other notables, to give proof of their devotion by immortalizing their "discoveries." They erected great shrines, churches, monasteries, mosques, colleges, hospices, and hospitals right over the ancient Jewish remains. The results are mixed: on the one hand they covered the ancient remains and sometimes preserved them; on the other, they prevented access to them, and so impeded the work of later archeologists. In the centuries that followed, these pious monuments raised by Byzantines, Crusaders and church orders entrusted with the preservation of the Holy Land, masked whatever antiquity had left behind by covering the remains with masses of stone constructions.

Insofar as the Temple Mount is concerned, it was just in this manner that its innermost Jewish elements were gradually destroyed and covered up, first by the Romans, then by the Moslem conquerors. A plethora of misinformation, traditions, and legendary tales mixed with prejudice, superstition, and error gradually filled the gaps in the ancient records. The resulting picture bore little if any resemblance to the real past.

7. ARAB RESTORATION OF THE TEMPLE MOUNT

A new era in the history of the Holy Land and the city of Jerusalem was inaugurated with the Arab conquest in A.D. 638. In particular, the Caliph Moawiya, founder of the Ommayad dynasty who established an Arab-Islamic empire in A.D. 660 had a completely different attitude towards the Holy City from that of his predecessors. Under his guidance, a third monotheistic faith, Islam, acknowledged the holiness of the city. Islam, however, stressed a different aspect of the picture: whereas the Byzantine rulers held to the traditional Christian view that the Temple Mount should remain in ruins as visible proof of the destruction of Jewish nationalism and the elimination of its ancient ties with the holy place, the Moslem conquerors restored the area and initiated Islamic worship there.

C. THE PIONEERS OF MODERN RESEARCH

The first modern scientific investigations of the geography and history of Palestine and its antiquities made their appearance in the eighteenth century. At that time, there was a revival of interest in the near east and the earliest centers of civilizations among western scholars. This new development is already reflected in the works of Bishop R. Pococke, who visited Palestine in 1738 and wrote a comprehensive description of its antiquities. In 1761–67, Carsten Niebuhr travelled through the near east; his published works, combined vivid descriptions and graphic illustrations, and aroused considerable interest. On his military expedition to Egypt, Napoleon was accompanied by French scholars, who opened a new chapter in the study of near east antiquities. The Holy Land is well represented in the "Description de l'Égypte," published in 1803–13. The multi-volume set is extensively illustrated and documented and contains a number of superb maps.

1. EDWARD ROBINSON'S SURVEY OF THE TEMPLE MOUNT

Modern topographical research and the location of historic and holy sites in Palestine was inaugurated in 1838 by Edward Robinson, the American biblical scholar. His great achievement was to establish scientific principles and methods for the identification of sites in the Holy Land, combining meticulous topographic observations with solid training in Semitic philology and careful consideration of biblical and historical data. In the course of identifying many biblical sites correctly, he exploded many hallowed traditions derived from earlier visitors and enshrined in popular piety. Robinson was tireless in investigating the entire area of the Old City and the Temple Mount; he aroused special interest by pointing out the presence of a section of a wide arch, which protruded from the southern section of the Western Wall. In his honor it is known as the Robinson Arch (see Part III, F, 1, a: The New Significance of the Robinson Arch).

Among other observations, Robinson seriously questioned the location of the tomb of Jesus at the site of the Church of the Holy Sepulchre, which goes back to early Byzantine times. He also identified the Third Wall of Jerusalem, described by Josephus, with sections of a huge wall located north of the present walls of the Old City.

Following in Robinson's footsteps, other students of the topography and monuments of Jerusalem made substantial progress. They concentrated their efforts on locating and identifying the city's main sites and buildings, always attempting to connect them with reliable historical data and, as far as conditions permitted, to support their conclusions with tangible evidence. In addition to Robinson, three figures stand out as pioneers of topographical and archeological research in the middle of the nineteenth century: the Marquis de Voguë for his investigations of the Temple Mount (1852; 1861); Titus Tobler for the vast extent of his studies and his keen observations (published in 1853); and

Charles Wilson for his comprehensive survey and mapping (published in 1865). He was responsible for the discovery of the arch leading to the Western Wall, and called in his honor the Wilson Arch (see Part V, D, 1). He also planned the work of his brilliant successor, Charles Warren.

2. AN EARLY EXAMPLE OF EXCAVATION

A direct outgrowth of the topographic surveys just described, but different in character, were the excavations in Jerusalem beginning in 1863 with the work of the French scholar F. de Saulcy. He uncovered the burial site known as the Tombs of the Kings which was believed to be the royal necropolis of the First Temple period. It proved to be a royal burial place after all, but of the House of Adiabene, which had converted to Judaism in the first century A.D. (see Part V, E, 5: The Mausoleum of Queen Helen of Adiabene). De Saulcy held firmly to his belief that the tombs belonged to the Davidic dynasty, even after he discovered a number of magnificent sarcophagi, one of which bore a double inscription in Aramaic and Syriac (obvious evidence of their later origin). However, the excavation was not carried out systematically, and was more a treasure hunt than a scientific exploration. Since de Saulcy mistook the Aramaic script for ancient biblical Hebrew, he had no hesitation in identifying a female skeleton buried in one of the sarcophagi as none other than the 'wife of King Zedekiah'! Here we have a striking example of the way in which 'folklorist' data had influenced and misled the many diligent seekers after truth in earlier times. It also illustrates how deficient they were in basic knowledge of ancient architecture and art and, above all, in Semitic epigraphy. De Saulcy transferred the sarcophagi to the Louvre Museum, where they are to this day. Furthermore, the gate to the monumental burial site of the royal family from Adiabene still bears the now familiar if erroneous title: "Tombeaux des Rois."

3. CHARLES WARREN AND THE PALESTINE EXPLORATION FUND

A generation after Robinson's pioneering work, much more serious archeological research was undertaken in Jerusalem, under the aegis of the British Palestine Exploration Fund. Its first systematic exploration was carried out in 1867–70 by Charles Warren, along the lines established by the earlier research of Charles Wilson. Warren was a very competent engineer whose main efforts were concentrated on the Temple Mount area and the Ophel (the ancient core of biblical Jerusalem). One of his important achievements was the discovery of the ancient underground water works connected with the Gihon spring. A striking feature of this system was a shaft leading into the spring from above, which is named in honor of the discoverer (see Part IV, B, 1: The Ṣinnōr).

His main accomplishment, however, was the systematic work all along the great

retaining walls of the Temple Mount. He dug perpendicular pits and horizontal tunnels towards the walls, with a view to determining the nature of Herod's walls and the topography of the area which lay east, south and west of the Temple Mount. The undertaking was marred, nevertheless, by his method of excavation, and by antiquated and erroneous sequence-dating he employed in relating the various levels in which artifacts were found. As a result, many of the finds were misdated. He did not believe that the 'Robinson Arch' was the surviving remnant of a series of arches supporting a high causeway over the Tyropoeon valley which linked the Temple to the opposite Western hill. (This widely held view was shown to be erroneous as a result of the present excavations). But we must express full appreciation, even a century later, at the extraordinary quality and scope of the work he carried out, the large number of drawings including accurate diagrams and stratigraphic charts, all of which were published in his "Recovery of Jerusalem," 1871, and in the Warren-Condor "Survey of Western Palestine, 2" (Jerusalem, 1884). Indeed, the Palestine Exploration Fund conducted the first systematic survey and mapping of Western Palestine between the years 1872–78, a historic achievement in itself, in which General H.H. Kitchener of later Khartoum and Boer War fame took an active part.

In the course of the following decades, many other scholars conducted serious investigations of the remains of ancient Jerusalem and its tombs, probing into the mysteries of the Temple Mount and its environs. One important study of the topography of the city was conducted over a long period of time by the German architect Conrad Schick; his reconstruction of the Temple complex is well-known, though fanciful. Another notable scholar was the French scholar C. Clermont-Ganneau, who *inter alia* deciphered the famous Greek inscription originally placed in the Outer Courts of the Herodian Temple, warning gentiles against entering the Inner Courts (Part III, D, 3, b: The Balustrade).

4. OBSTACLES TO TANGIBLE PROGRESS

Systematic excavation in the southern part of the Ophel was started only at the end of the 19th century, but it proved of considerable value in the ongoing study of ancient Jerusalem. A dig was carried out between 1894–97 by F.J. Bliss and A.C. Dickie, in the area of the Siloam Pool and to the south of it (see Part V, B, 1). They uncovered some remains of the southern walls of the city, and a gate of as yet undermined date. In the light of our present knowledge, these probably formed part of the First Wall of the Second Temple period. Also of interest were the remains of city streets, discovered at the southern end of the Ophel hill, as well as architectural materials in the Siloam Pool area, among which were remains of a Byzantine church attributed to Queen Eudokia. These and other discoveries did not help to solve the basic topographic and historic problems of Jerusalem, and as a consequence it was widely believed in those days that it would never be possible to resolve them by means of excavation. Other formidable obstacles had to be reckoned with: the vast extent of destruction and the huge mounds of accumulated debris from later periods; the resistance of religious authorities to archeological probes and excavations (chiefly in and around the Temple Mount area, the Haram es-Sherif); the density of population within the Old City proper; and finally, the difficulty of determining the relative chronological age of the uncovered remains and artifacts. In combination, these obstructions seemed to be insurmountable.

5. DARING PARKER AND DILIGENT FATHER VINCENT

Captain Montague Parker led an archeological mission in 1909–10, which boldly excavated areas not explored by earlier expeditions. He dug into the area adjacent to the Siloam Pool, clearing the subterranean caves and opening trenches in the Ophel hill. He failed in his objective of discovering the famed Temple 'treasures', but he managed, nevertheless, to uncover interesting remains. Captain Parker was not content with mere archeological research. He had an even more ambitious project to excavate within the inner area of the Temple Mount. Although he managed to penetrate into holy ground by night, his secret plot was soon discovered, arousing tremendous excitement among the Moslems. He and his associates were forced to flee to Jaffa and to escape on board their yacht before the gendarmes, armed with a warrant of arrest, caught up with them.

Parker's various finds were carefully studied and described by his archeological adviser, Father L.H. Vincent O.P. of the École Biblique of Jerusalem. The diligent Father Vincent resumed the excavation near the Gihon spring and discovered galleries and caves cut in the rock which contained, among other things, pottery dating to the beginning of the third millennium B.C. (Early Bronze I). He found also one utensil dating from the beginning of the second millennium B.C., which had originated in Cyprus. It was on the basis of these finds that Father Vincent was able to prove that the southeastern ridge or Ophel hill was the original site of ancient Jerusalem, and that the Gihon spring played an important role in the establishment of the settlement. He was also able to investigate thoroughly the primitive though intricate hydraulic system by means of which the people of the ancient city had procured water from the Gihon spring.

It was Vincent's merit to have saved for posterity the discoveries made by Parker and other scholars, and to collate systematically all the archeological data available from

Jerusalem excavations (published in a monumental work, "Jerusalem Sous Terre," 1911). This was followed by another masterful book authored jointy by himself and the eminent historian and historical geographer, Father V. Abel.

6. RAYMOND WEILL'S DISCOVERIES IN THE OPHEL

A new era of discovery was inaugurated by Raymond Weill, leader of the Rothschild Mission which started its work in 1913. This was the first Jewish archeological expedition in Palestine, which was still under Turkish rule at the time. He met with success in excavating the southern section (called el-Dahurah) of the Ophel hill. Of particular interest was a series of curious rock-tombs shaped like long, vaulted tunnels which could be reached from above by means of shafts cut in the rock (see Part IV, E: Royal Tombs in the City of David). Also significant was Weill's discovery in the Ophel of an inscription of Theodotos, who was head of a synagogue in the days of the Herodian dynasty (see Part II, F, 5, d).

D. THE OLDER AND MORE RECENT ARCHEOLOGICAL TECHNIQUES

It must be underlined in our survey of archeological research conducted in Jerusalem up to the end of World War I, that no scientifically accepted standards had been followed until then, at least none that could be relied upon to solve basic problems relating to the character, development and dimensions of the city in ancient times. Notwithstanding this limitation, considerable archeological material had been gathered, dating to the various cultural periods of the past. Moreover, extensive research had been done in historical topography, and this activity resulted in numerous scholarly works, including the writings of outstanding figures such as George Adam Smith, Father Vincent, and Gustav Dalman.

1. A WAVE OF RESEARCH AFTER 1920

As might have been expected, archeological exploration took a leap forward when the backward Turkish rule over Palestine was replaced by a British administration. New scientific institutions made their appearance, to join existing societies, and they were staffed by capable and imaginative scholars who developed new and effective methods to the excavating of the many tells and ruins in the country. One of these institutions was the American School of Oriental Research, headed by W.F. Albright. The Old City of Jerusalem, however, became the center of attention in the year 1923, when the pioneering Palestine Exploration Fund renewed its excavation of the Ophel hill for a period of three years, under the leadership of R.A.S. Macalister (the Irish archeologist who had won fame for his dig of Gezer in 1920–5), assisted by J.G. Duncan. They concentrated mainly on uncovering the remains of the ancient walls on the higher Ophel slope overlooking the Kidron valley. The discovery could not fail to arouse widespread interest. This is described in Part IV, D, 1: The Myth of the Jebusite Wall. The J.W. Crowfoot expedition in 1927–28 revealed in the area remnants from the days of the Second Temple and Byzantine period.

No further excavations were undertaken in the City of David after 1928, and archeologists restricted themselves to re-examining the remains and artifacts turned up in earlier digs, and reassessing them in the light of other materials found elsewhere, thus leading to an improved understanding of the history and topography of ancient Jerusalem. Extensive research was carried out in the areas adjoining the Old City. New clusters of tombs were discovered, including a large number dating to the Second Commonwealth, and particularly to the first century A.D.

Widespread interest was generated by the discovery by E.L. Sukenik of a carefully dressed stone slab which was found in the Russian Church on the Mount of Olives, describing the transfer of the bones of King Uzziah from his former place of burial (see Part IV, E, 3: The Burial Ground in the Tyropoeon.)

In the course of excavations north of the present Old City wall in 1925–27, L.A. Mayer and E.L. Sukenik uncovered the massive foundations of a tremendous city wall, the Third Wall, over close to a third of a mile (500 m.). (See Part II, F, 4, c: The Third Wall.)

2. THE CITADEL OF HASMONEAN (MACCABEAN) AND HERODIAN DAYS AND THE WESTERN CITY WALL

Significant progress was made in the excavation of the Citadel area, close to the present-day Jaffa Gate, by C.N. Johns (1934–40), who uncovered its lower Hasmonean and Herodian levels. Three prominent Herodian towers, Hippicus, Phasael and Mariamne, once dominated this area, all of them lying north of Herod's Palace. The Tower of Phasael, today miscalled "Tower of David," is built in typical Herodian style and has been preserved to a height of 66 feet (20 m.). Its dimensions are 71×56 feet (21.5×17 m.). The excavation proved that the tower had been built into a more ancient wall of the Hasmonean era, in which Johns could distinguish three stages, each of a different building style and date. A fourth stage may be attributed to the days of the war with Rome. John's excavation not only helped to uncover the original wall at the northwestern angle, but proved that it had already been in use in Hasmonean times and moreover, that this Hasmonean wall encompassed the Western hill (Mount Zion) from the west. Its southern extension consists of the wall remains which Bliss and Dickie had uncovered in 1894, whose eastern angle lies south of the Siloam Pool. Bliss had been able to distinguish at least two stages of this wall's history. It was only in 1962–63 that Kathleen Kenyon was able to assume, on the basis of further investigation, that the gate and the adjacent wall section should be dated to Herodian times or, more precisely, to the time of Agrippa I.

In summary, it has become evident that the foundations and earliest phase of the wall line are Hasmonean, while the second phase is Herodian. It is also clear that Bliss and Dickie had uncovered sections of an early wall which bore a strong resemblance to the wall uncovered in the Citadel. The latter, which is now covered by Herodian remains, has been attributed to King Alexander Jannaeus. (See description of the Ophel and the City of David in Part IV, B, 7: The City Wall and Structures on the Eastern Ridge.)

3. KATHLEEN KENYON'S EXCAVATIONS IN THE CITY OF DAVID

This British archeologist inaugurated her excavations in 1961, on behalf of the British School of Archeology in Jerusalem and the Palestine Exploration Fund, and carried them out intermittently until 1968. Her primary aim had been to clear up basic problems involved in the history and topography of ancient Jerusalem by means of modern methods of research, going over the results achieved in former digs on the spot. She laid special stress on Ophel hill, paying particular attention to the eastern border of the City of David.

a. The Battle of the Terraces and the Weather

Another factor brought into sharp relief by K. Kenyon was the influence of climate and weather on the City of David. Throughout the more ancient periods, the Bronze and Iron Ages (first and second millennia B.C.), the houses of the small town were built on terraces buttressed by supporting walls, which were constantly being affected by weather conditions. It is no wonder, therefore, that the structures could not last very long. Some were allowed to erode, while others were maintained through a continuing process of repair and renovation. As a consequence, most of the remains of the early period which have survived belong to the last days of the Monarchy, when maintenance work ceased. Certain structures, solidly and attractively built on the terraces at the top of the Ophel ridge, may be assigned to this period. There are remains of a tripartite building whose sections are set off by pillars resting on bases, an architectural style reminiscent of the latter phase of the Monarchy.

b. *Identity of the Millo*

One of K. Kenyon's insights provides a basic foundation for understanding the city plan of ancient Jerusalem: She identified the supporting walls and the terraces on the eastern ridge with the Millo, a landmark of central importance in the Scriptures. It will be discussed in Part IV: Remnants in the City of David. Kathleen Kenyon's excavations, reported in "Jerusalem: Excavating 3,000 Years" (1967), gave impetus to the archeological study of the Ophel hill, the site of early Jerusalem. She defined more accurately the nature of the site in the biblical period, and she helped to dispel a number of erroneous ideas which had previously been taken for granted by the archeologists who preceded her. On the other hand, her study of the Western hill is considerably less rewarding. Her small digs in certain areas of Mt. Zion, the Muristan (near the Church of the Holy Sepulchre) and other sites were compromised in large measure by her own acceptance of faulty conclusions drawn by earlier scholars to the effect that the Western hill of ancient Jerusalem had not been occupied at all in the days of the Judean Kingdom. Discoveries in the past few years have shown this view to be in error. (See below, G,2: Expansion over the Western Hill).

E. THE PRESENT ARCHEOLOGICAL EXCAVATIONS SOUTH AND SOUTHWEST OF THE TEMPLE MOUNT

After the Six Day War in 1967, the two parts of Jerusalem were reunited as a "city which is bound firmly together." New opportunities for the systematic exploration of the ancient city were presented by this unexpected development. Therefore, on February 28, 1968, the author initiated extensive excavations south and southwest of the Temple Mount on behalf of the Hebrew University and the Israel Exploration Society. This work has been maintained and expanded without interruption until the present time, and is scheduled to continue indefinitely into the future. (See details in Parts III, IV, V and VI.)

Professor Benjamin Mazar addressing an archaeological conference held in October 1974 on the stairway leading up to the Hulda Gate. To Professor Mazar's right is Professor Yigael Yadin and Mr. M. Kol, Minister of Tourism, to his left is Yitzhak Rabin, the Prime Minister, Seated at the far left of the dais is Teddy Kollek, Mayor of Jerusalem

1. THE MAIN PURPOSE AND PLAN

The primary objective in the excavations was to lay bare the huge Herodian supporting walls of the Temple Mount: the Southern Wall throughout its entire length and the southern half of the Western Wall. We also planned to clear the adjacent area, uncover all architectural remains, and recover all significant artifacts dating from the time of Herod until the destruction of the Temple. We were largely successful in discovering the major components of the Herodian complex, and have been able to reconstruct in all its essentials the master plan of the area (see Part II, F: Herod's Period).

2. THE OPHEL AND CITY OF DAVID

The plan of excavation, worked out by the author with the able assistance of M. Ben-Dor, J. Abiram and a permanent staff, is also to conduct a systematic investigation of the upper reaches of the Ophel hill as it descends southward from the Temple Mount, and of the slopes of the City of David leading eastward to the Kidron valley and westward to the Tyropoeon valley.

The organization and layout of the area as a whole, one of the main city centers for many centuries, was determined to a great extent by the massive public building projects, undertaken there throughout the Herodian period and, centuries later, by the Arab Ommayad rulers. Other important projects were also carried out in the Roman and Byzantine periods, preceding the Arab Conquest. As a result of our excavations, it was possible to assess properly the great changes that had taken place in the area from the end of the Judean Monarchy (First Temple) until modern times (see Parts, III, IV, V and VI).

3. IN THE STEPS OF HEROD'S ACHIEVEMENT

The basic aim of Herod and his architects was to enlarge the area at the top of the Temple Mount. The slopes of the western valley (Tyropoeon) were filled in, then the top of the Temple Mount was levelled and around it was erected a great belt of supporting walls (see Part III, E, 1: Discovery Bears out Contemporary Ancient Writings). In the process, they destroyed all the buildings that formerly had stood on the upper (northern) part of the Ophel, obliterating almost all traces of any structures that could be attributed to earlier times. Nevertheless, some isolated remains of the period of the First Temple were found *in situ*, south of the Southern Wall. One of these survivals is a plastered cistern located near the Eastern (Triple) Hulda Gate; it dates from the eighth-seventh centuries B.C.

4. RECONSIDERING CERTAIN CURRENT THEORIES

The excavations have established certain basic facts, shedding new light on the data handed down by Josephus, which, for the most part, were found to be accurate. A striking example is the so-called Robinson Arch, which, as a result of the new excavations is now seen to be a huge arch supporting a monumental stairway which ascended from the paved street running along the Western Wall to the upper Western Gate leading into the Royal Portico (see Part III, E, 2, a: The Royal Portico). Moreover, this arch was not part of a causeway spanning the Tyropoeon valley, as mentioned above (cf. Charles Warren). This discovery fits in perfectly with Josephus' description of the four gates of the Western Wall of the Temple Mount (*Antiquities* XV, 410). He states specifically that the descent from the southernmost gate to the Tyropoeon valley was by "many stairs" (see Part III, F, 1 a: The New Significance of the Robinson Arch).

5. THE UNEXPECTED COMPLEXITY OF THE SOUTHERN AREA

The excavation of the area which faced the two gates of the Southern Wall, known from the Mishna as the 'Hulda Gates,' uncovered a variety of installations, and with them a series of problems. We discovered that a paved street ran the whole length of the Southern Wall, while beneath it were underground chambers with vaulted roofs. In addition, two wide stairways led up to the gates. The more impressive of the two was 210 feet (64 m.) wide and led from a plaza below to the upper paved street and thence up to the Western (Double) Hulda Gate. (See Part III, F, 4, b: The Monumental Stairway.)

F. THE PRESENT EXCAVATIONS

While the main digging was aimed at the Herodian remains, serious attention was also given to the other periods of occupation in the areas uncovered, to thus record the many major changes and developments which took place during the long history of the city and its holy places. For example, after the terrible destruction of A.D. 70, nothing was left standing except the remains of the supporting walls of the Temple Mount platform. The adjoining areas were occupied only by army barracks for short periods, beginning with the establishment of the Roman colony of Aelia Capitolina by the Emperor Hadrian.

1. LATER PROFILE OF THE TEMPLE MOUNT AREA

Other developments, however, took place in Jerusalem proper as its population increased spectacularly in Byzantine times (fourth-seventh centuries A.D.), particularly in the latter part of this period. A new age was inaugurated by the Emperor Constantine who built the Church of the Holy Sepulchre; physical expansion and general prosperity continued under his successors. In the light of our excavations, it is reasonable to infer that some Roman buildings of the fourth century built near the Western Wall, were destroyed by Jews in the turbulent days of Emperor Julian the Apostate who had encouraged them to restore the ruined Temple (see Part II, H). Building in this area in the Byzantine era was resumed, and reached its peak in the fifth and sixth centuries A.D. These data, derived from the Temple area, and this profile complement and amplify the picture and conclusions previously reached on the basis of earlier excavations conducted in the Ophel hill and is also consistent with excavations conducted more recently on the Western hill and Mount Zion.

a. *The Byzantine Structures at the Foot of the Temple Mount*
Many of the Byzantine structures we uncovered were well preserved, and testify to the prosperity Jerusalem enjoyed in that period. Most of the Byzantine buildings were either destroyed or abandoned in the Persian invasion of A.D. 614. (See Part II, H: Rebuilding Attempts.)

b. *The Ommayad Compounds*
A group of palatial structures uncovered during the course of excavations, bear witness to a resurgence of building activity which took place close to the Temple Mount in the heyday of Ommayad Arab rule (A.D. 660–750). West and south of the Temple Mount walls, there was a large and well-planned cluster of great buildings, provided with all amenities, as well as an extensive sewage system (see Part VI, C: The Early Moslem Period).

In subsequent years, the area south of the Temple Mount was gradually abandoned. Still later, the Crusaders walled up the two Hulda Gates situated in the Southern Wall.

An oil press built on the bedrock of the
earliest level of habitation in the *Mishneh*
quarter of the Upper City, dating from the
late Judean Monarchy period
(eighth-seventh centuries B.C.)

2. EXPLORATION OF THE DIVIDED CITY BETWEEN 1948–1967

The progress of excavation slowed down considerably during the years of Jordanian occupation. Nevertheless, resident Catholic scholars were responsible for a number of notable discoveries in the area of the Notre Dame de Sion Monastery and the nearby Bethesda Pools. On the basis of excavations at Bethesda since 1956, Father Pierre Benoit, the eminent New Testament scholar at the Ecole Biblique, has shown that both pools date back to Hasmonean times, but were abandoned for many centuries, when the higher 'Israel Pool' was carved out of the northern edge of the Temple Mount. Furthermore, the cave situated east of the Bethesda Pools was the only site that could be connected with an early Christian tradition about the healing powers of its waters, as related in John 5:2–4.

3. THE DISPUTED EXTENT OF THE ANTONIA

P. Benoit tried to demonstrate, moreover, that the lower ancient pavement within the grounds of the Notre Dame de Sion Monastery (along the 'Via Dolorosa' and therefore of special interest to pilgrims) could not be identified with the famous Lithostrotos pavement of John's gospel (19:13) nor with the actual court of the Antonia Fortress, traditionally connected with Pilate's Praetorium (see below, The True Site of Pilate's Praetorium). He proved that, instead, it had its origin in the Aelia Capitolina of Hadrian's time after A.D. 135, when the emperor erected a triumphal arch on a new pavement, which covered the underground cistern (see Part VI, A, 8: Aelia's Plan). P. Benoit also challenged the generally accepted reconstruction of the Antonia; according to Father Vincent, it extended over a wide area, spreading across the Via Dolorosa and reaching into the precincts of Notre Dame. Rather, Benoit argued, the fortress was confined to a less extensive area on the rocky scarp at the northwestern end of the Temple Mount, within the grounds of the Arab Omariya school which occupies the site. During the same period, the Franciscan archeologists had the good fortune to discover clusters of cave tombs in the area of the Dominus Flevit church on the lower slopes of the Mount of Olives. Among them was a group dating to the end of the Middle Bronze and Late Bronze Age (16th–14th centuries B.C.), which contained a rich collection of pottery and other artifacts.

G. INTERESTING DISCOVERIES IN THE UPPER CITY

The scientific bodies of Jerusalem had, since 1969, expanded archeological exploration of the hill within the Old City. The Jewish Quarter of the Old City which overlooks the Temple Mount had been overrun by the Arab Legion during the fighting in 1948, and

View of an excavated building of the Hasmonean period, found in the Upper City

all the major buildings, both civil and religious, had been destroyed. After the Six Day War an elaborate plan was adopted to restore the Jewish Quarter in its entirety, and to reconstruct its historic religious buildings. At the same time, a rare opportunity presented itself to carry out excavations throughout the area, penetrating into the older strata, and at the same time, preserving the quaint and charming structures above ground of the medieval and later periods. Actual digging had to be restricted to areas which were not encumbered by some buildings and other structures still standing gauntly along the narrow twisting lanes. Excavations on the hill overlooking the Temple Mount were conducted by Professor Nahman Avigad and his assistants and contributed greatly to our knowledge of the western section of ancient Jerusalem, dating to the period of the Judahite monarchy, which had been buried under accumulated debris for more than two millennia. Substantial information was secured concerning the city, not only in the last centuries before the destruction of the Temple, but also during the latter period of the monarchy.

1. HEZEKIAH'S WALL

Totally unexpected and of the greatest importance was the discovery in the Jewish Quarter of a section of a massive city wall 23 feet (7 m.) thick, when some of the foundation layers made of large untrimmed stones came to light. It is attributed to King Hezekiah and is described in Part IV, C, 2: Hezekiah's Great Wall. It may also be noted that it was during the reign of the same Judean king that the great underground tunnel was constructed linking the Gihon spring to the Siloam Pool, and thus insuring a constant supply of spring water for the city (Part IV, C, 1: A Remarkable Hydraulic Engineering Feat).

2. EXPANSION OVER THE WESTERN HILL

It may therefore be assumed that from the time this city wall was built, the Mishneh (second) Quarter grew steadily as an important part of the capital city. This may have been the district in which King Jehoiakim built his new palace (Jeremiah 22:13–14). No

37

Large paving stones in the Lithostratos, showing games, carved by Roman soldiers

Plaster fresco fragments bearing a depiction of a menorah, found in a building of the Herodian period in the Upper City. It is the earliest detailed representation of the Temple candelabrum so far known

traces of such a structure have been discovered there up to the present time, only private residences dating from the eighth-seventh centuries B.C. and down to the destruction of the First Temple (586 B.C.). Further excavation in this area has produced additional evidence of the expansion of urban occupation over the Western hill during the last phase of the Judean Monarchy — not only within the confines of the Mishneh, but also beyond it. Several remains of this period were uncovered earlier in the excavations undertaken by C.N. Johns in the Citadel (see above D, 2) and, in more recent years, by Ruth Amiran and Abi Eitan at the same site, by Magen Broshi on the grounds of the Armenian Saint Saviour Church, just outside the Zion Gate, and by a group of German scholars at the Muristan near the Church of the Holy Sepulchre. As a result of all these activities, the contours and structural configurations of ancient Jerusalem are emerging from long-standing obscurity and confusion (see Part II, F, 3, b).

3. THE PATRICIAN LIFE-STYLE

Excavations in this sector have shown that following the destruction in 586 B.C. there was no new occupation of the Western hill before Hasmonean times (second and first centuries B.C.). During that period there were extensive building operations, and by the end of it a substantial community had settled there. It continued to grow and prosper in the time of Herod the Great and his successors, right up to the final disaster in A.D. 70. This proved to be a wealthy residential part of the city, characterized by spacious luxurious houses filled with expensive furnishings of every kind. One of these private homes (close to the ruins of the Tiferet Israel Synagogue) covered an area of approximately 2152 square feet (200 square meters), including its inner court, rooms, ovens, mikveh (ritual bath) and cisterns, in a good state of preservation, along with a rich collection of objects. It provides invaluable clues to the life-style of a patrician family in Herod's time.

Another large two-story home (on Misgav Ladach Street) was severely damaged by fire in the general destruction of A.D. 70 (see Part II, F, 5, a: Discovery of the House of Kathros).

Recent archaeological investigation indicates that the ancient pavement (Lithostratos) underlying the Notre Dame de Sion Monastery along the Via Dolorosa indeed formed part of the Roman garrison area near the Temple, but it cannot be identified with Pilate's Praetorium mentioned in the Gospel of John 19:13 (see below, G, 4: The True Site of Pilate's Preatorium)

4. THE TRUE SITE OF PILATE'S PRAETORIUM

Of prime interest are the new data relating to Herod's great palace and the vast platform on which it stood. While remains of the Palace have been obliterated by later reconstruction on the site, the excavations south of the Citadel nevertheless determined that an elevated platform had been constructed there, similar in many respects to the platform erected by Herod's architects on the Temple Mount. Its dimensions were about 984–1149 feet (300–350 m.) from north to south and 198 feet (60 m.) or more from west to east. To some extent the archeological evidence supports Josephus' description of the Palace in his book, *The Jewish War* (V, 175). In addition, it has helped to establish that the palace served as the official residence of the Roman Procurators, and that here indeed was Pilate's Praetorium referred to in the story of the Passion of Jesus Christ (see Part II, F, 3, a: Herod's Palace).

5. CONCLUSION

With all the recent archeological activity in Jerusalem and its environs, the secrets of the ancient city and its history have gradually been uncovered. Thanks to refinements in the associated disciplines of stratigraphy and pottery chronology, not to speak of the analysis of wall and gate and building construction, the meticulous classification of coins and other artifacts, it is now possible to organize and interpret varied data even of the most fragmentary kind in the continuing quest for a satisfying synthesis and recovery of the life-experience of the city in all its multitudinous incarnations and historical phases.

At the very center of popular interest and scholarly research is the Temple Mount, the appropriate target of the most massive archeological undertaking in this area in the history of the discipline. For a number of years, the work has been carried on without significant interruption, and the time is ripe for a comprehensive report on this activity: the essential findings about the history of the sacred precinct, and especially the incredible planning and achievements of Herod the Great in rebuilding the monuments, restoring and redecorating the Temple and the approaches of the Temple Mount, in constructing a panoply of service buildings and living quarters for all those who had official business, duties and obligations in the Temple area.

PART II

HISTORICAL STAGES OF THE TEMPLE MOUNT, THE HILL OF OPHEL AND JERUSALEM

A. BIBLICAL JERUSALEM UNTIL THE TIME OF DAVID*

Jerusalem, focus of the spiritual, creative powers of the Jewish people in their native land, has been woven into their psyche since the days of David. Its image is embedded not only in Scriptures, but in Jewish inspirational literature throughout the ages to this day. It is central in the documents discovered at Qumran, in the works of Josephus, the first century A.D. historian of priestly lineage, and in Talmudic literature. The Prophets' devotion to the site of Yahweh's presence among His people lends peculiar poignancy to their warnings that the city will be destroyed and its people exiled by God's anger, though the exiles will return through His mercy and love. The priests of Israel have meticulously preserved the traditions and the sacred rites related to the worship at the Temple. Jerusalem has inspired the finest of the Psalms and other biblical poetry, and is enshrined in both classical and modern Hebrew literature. The concept of Jerusalem as the focus of redemption, moreover, has carried over into the spirit of Christianity.

1. ITS NAMES

The city's history and its exalted position are reflected to a marked degree in the names and titles it has borne. Its present official name, "Yerushalayim," pronounced Yerushalem in ancient parlance, is rooted in its earliest origins, and "Shalem" may well have been its abbreviation (see below: B, 1: David in Jerusalem). It appears that Shalem derived its name from an ancient tradition that the city was the cultic center of the God Shalīm. The name Shalīm occurs elsewhere in a remote Canaanite source: ancient

---

*The following historical survey serves to introduce the crucial Parts III, IV, V, and VI which deal with our archeological discoveries and their significance. It offers the background material directly connected with the areas uncovered and with the objects discovered there, thus helping the reader to establish their mutual relationship. For instance, we have mentioned above (Part I, E, 5) one example of the unexpected complexity of the southern area now being excavated. The background of this particular area is rooted in Herod's building program (see Part III, D, 2) and in its continuing significance for the people of Jerusalem (Part III, F, 4).

40

The pre-Israelite city called Urusalim and later, the City of David, lay on the slopes of the southeastern ridge (center) below the Temple Mount walls shown at top right. The historic ridge is bounded on the east (below, along lower road) by the Kidron valley and on the west by what is left of the silted Tyropoeon valley (shown at top left among the trees). Ancient sites can be discovered on the right (above the flat-roofed house) and on the left (white spot showing tombs and quarries). A detailed description is given in Part V

Ugaritic mythology refers to two deities: "Shahar," god of the rising sun and "Shalīm," god of the setting sun.

The name "Zion," on the other hand, could have designated from the start the eastern hill of Jerusalem, the hill called Mount Zion which included the Temple Mount and the Citadel guarding its southern extension. These names, as well as "Mount Moriah" and the "Land of Moriah," the hill sloping north from the Temple Mount, predate the days of David by far. From about 1200 to 1000 B.C. it was called "Jebus," 'ir hayebusī, meaning "town of the Jebusites." This was an ethnic-geographic name identifying it with its inhabitants in the period of the Judges, before its capture by King David who transformed this citadel of Zion into the City of David, a Jewish city and the capital of the United Kingdom of Israel. Later, the "City of Judah" designated it as the capital of the Judahite Kingdom. It was also called, simply but significantly, "The City," for it is indeed unique. Titles such as "City of God," the "Holy City," "Ariel," the "City of Justice," and others are rooted in the national and religious consciousness of the people, for they exalted it as the seat of the Temple.

2. ITS ORIGINS

The biblical record, extrabiblical literary sources, and archeological research combine to present, with historical veracity, the genesis and growth of Jerusalem, and to trace its location and earliest settlement. Topographical and archeological excavations, which began as early as 1867 when the British engineer Charles Warren led the first dig in the holy city, indicate that ancient Jerusalem was a small town, which lay isolated on the

41

eastern flank of a ridge known as Zion, south of the Temple area. It owed its origin in the main to an abundant underground water source, the Gihon spring, which lay at the foot of the ridge of Ophel above the Kidron valley. This made the ridge of Ophel a valid site for a settlement in the harsh mountain area, even though it lay slightly east of the main watershed and below it. The watershed was the dividing line between the Mediterranean to the west and the wilderness of Judea facing it on the east. The hill of Zion is bounded by two steep valleys: the Kidron to the east, and the Vale of Hinnom *(Gē-Hinnom)* to the south. The valleys converge near the lower spring of 'Ēn-Rogel, making a V-shaped end to the hill. Another valley, the Tyropoeon, separates the eastern part of the hill of ancient Jerusalem from its western hill which was the site of the Upper City in the period of the Second Commonwealth. The steepness of the contours of the Tyropoeon is masked by the age-long accumulation of debris. The ancient site on the lower ridge was thus strongly defended by nature except on the upper saddle joining it to the higher ground of the Temple Mount and the ramparts of the Old City. Ancient Jerusalem was fed by the perennial spring mentioned above.

The southeastern town was in the form of an elongated narrow oval covering some ten acres, an average size for a Canaanite town of the Bronze Age, in the second millennium B.C. Despite its small size, it was situated in a good defensive position on the watershed of the central mountain range of Palestine, close to the only convenient north-and-south route of the hill country leading from Shechem to Hebron, the important cities of the central range. A road dipped east from Jerusalem to the Jordan Valley, forded the Jordan (a route used by the Israelites in the opposite direction when they invaded the country) and ran up to the rich plateau of Transjordan. In addition, there was a choice of passable routes down to the coastal plain and the seacoast.

3. THE RAVAGES OF TIME

Despite the strength imparted to the historic hill by the valleys bordering it, especially the steep Tyropoeon Vale, most of the latter valley was filled in and could not be discerned on the surface in later times. The skilled eye of the archeologist could still determine that its original slope had once been almost as steep as that of the Kidron valley to the east. The combination of violent military assaults upon the city and repeated rebuildings over the older ruins throughout the millennia helped to blur the traces of the ancient biblical metropolis. This is evident from the first pictures in Part I above. In many parts of the southeastern ridge of Ophel vast quantities of debris, containing pottery fragments and other artifacts beginning from the Early Bronze Age settlement in about 3000 B.C. to recent times, have thus been thrown together into a tumbled, confused heap, instead of accumulating in layers in the gradual manner of a tell, a man-made hill. Bronze Age shards discovered in 1974 near the Southern Wall of the Temple Mount seem to confirm the date (see Part IV, A, 5, b: Earliest Defenses of Jerusalem).

The Ophel, which was the site of the original settlement, continued within the city walls until the Middle Ages of our era, when a new plan for the city was adopted that left the hill outside the walls. As a result of severe erosion, along with the other factors mentioned, the late renowned archeologist, G. Ernest Wright *(Biblical Archeology,* Philadelphia: Westminster, 1957*)* believed not many years ago that "not a single discovery has been made in Jerusalem which can be dated with any certainty to the time of David or Solomon." Nevertheless, various remains dating to the days of the Judean monarchy have been discovered there in the last fifteen years (see details in Parts III-IV).

It should be noted at this point that the biblical record and extra-biblical literary sources give only scant information about the extent and character of buildings in Jerusalem in any period of history. Furthermore, archeology has revealed singularly little about the Temple Mount and its neighborhood until recent times. This failure was largely due to the fact that exploration met with many religious taboos, and that whatever was done took place largely before the development of modern methods. The discoveries were poorly recorded and interpreted, the multitudes of shards and other finds not sorted and dated properly.

4. THE FINDINGS OF ARCHEOLOGISTS

Nevertheless, before we began exploring the terrain, we were able to refer to some tangible data relating to the beginnings of continuous habitation in Jerusalem. A deep shaft to the Gihon spring was discovered by Charles Warren, the pioneer excavator appointed by the British Palestine Exploration Fund to lead an exploration into underground Jerusalem between 1867–1870. Most notable is a collection of unbroken ware and shards which were discovered in shafts and caves close to the Gihon spring in 1909. They were carefully examined and catalogued and the findings published by Father L.H. Vincent in his work, *Jerusalem Sous Terre.* Most of these artifacts belong to an early stage of the Early Bronze Age, that is, the beginning of the third millennium B.C. This was one of the positive proofs that early Jerusalem lay on the southeastern hill popularly known as Ophel. These indications, together with later, scant discoveries of pottery lying on bedrock, as determined by subsequent digs in the Ophel hill layers of the Early Bronze Age offer evidence that the southeastern hill of Jerusalem was occupied some 5000 years ago, and had the Gihon spring as its core.

We have described above (Part I, C, 4: Obstacles to Tangible Progress) the slow progress of archeology between the days of Sir Charles Warren and those of F.J. Bliss and A.C. Dickie in the past century. The excavations in the early years of the present century were carried out by more modern methods, and though time seemed ripe for further excavations, they were deterred by the resistance of religious authorities and other obstacles in the days of Turkish rule. But ever since, there has been accumulation of knowledge on the dating of pottery and other objects.

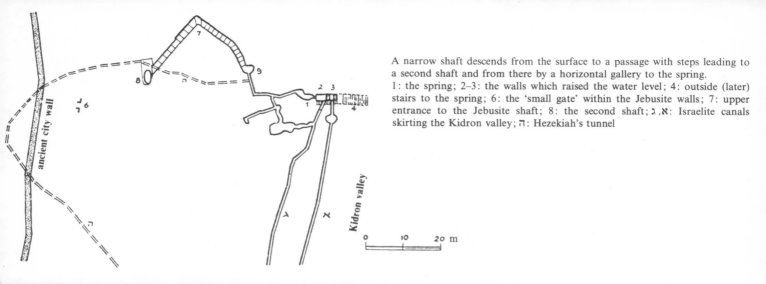

A narrow shaft descends from the surface to a passage with steps leading to a second shaft and from there by a horizontal gallery to the spring.
1: the spring; 2–3: the walls which raised the water level; 4: outside (later) stairs to the spring; 6: the 'small gate' within the Jebusite walls; 7: upper entrance to the Jebusite shaft; 8: the second shaft; ג,א: Israelite canals skirting the Kidron valley; ה: Hezekiah's tunnel

Early natural gallery giving access to the Gihon spring prior to the digging of the Hezekiah water tunnel leading the water to the Pool of Siloam

a. Ancient Fortification and the Warren Shaft

Outstanding among the preserved ancient fortifications are the remains of a wall and bastion fairly low down the eastern slope of the Ophel uncovered by Kathleen Kenyon in 1961. This stronghold was traced between the Gihon spring and the Warren shaft (see Part IV, A, 5, b: Earliest Defenses of Jerusalem on the East). Kenyon attributed the beginning of the erection of the fortifications to the first phase of Middle Bronze II, i.e. the first quarter of the second millennium B.C. They were to remain in use for another millennium. If this premise, based on the evidence of shards found in the debris, is correct, it is quite probable that the defenses built on the slope of the hill were intended not only to protect the structures standing over the terraces which had been raised on the higher ridge of the slope, but also to guard the precious source of water in time of war and siege. The ingenious entrance to the underground Gihon spring is described as follows: "From an opening in the surface of the rock, a tunnel descended obliquely by a curiously circuitous route and then plunged in an almost vertical shaft, the construction of which was aided by a slight natural fissure. To the foot of this shaft, water from the spring was brought by a horizontal tunnel" (K. Kenyon, *Archeology in the Holy Land* [Tonbridge: Bonn, 1960; New York: Praeger, 1960], p. 242). From this opening, jugs and pitchers could be lowered down the shaft to the water in the tunnel. An earlier attempt during the second millennium to sink a shaft down to spring level failed because the hard limestone strata proved too much for the bronze tools used then. The planning and engineering of a system of access to the spring within the limits of the fortified city was a remarkable achievement of the pre-Israelite people of Jerusalem, and provided the inhabitants with a secure water supply inside the city in times of danger.

b. Urban Development

The assumption that Jerusalem started to develop as a fortified and comparatively well-populated city early in the second millennium B.C. gains support from a similar growth of contemporary urban centers in the central mountain range, notably Shechem and Bethel. Jerusalem is first mentioned in epigraphic sources of the nineteenth and eighteenth centuries B.C., the two groups of Egyptian Execration Texts. They were a special feature of Egyptian foreign policy during the Middle Kingdom (Eleventh and Twelfth Dynasties, 2160–1500 B.C.). The names of rebellious officials or other enemies of the crown were inscribed on clay bowls or figurines with appropriate curses, referred to now as execration texts. The piece of pottery was then smashed in a ritual of sympathetic magic to indicate the certain fate of those rebels or enemies in accordance with the curse. The more ancient of the two lists includes two governors of Jerusalem *(Rushalimum)* who are referred to as rebels and cursed as enemies of the Egyptians. The names of the culprits, Yqr'm and Shas'an, testify to the West-Semitic character of Jerusalem's population. The later texts are inscribed on clay figurines and mention only one governor whose name has not been preserved. It may, therefore, be inferred that by then Jerusalem had become an urban center of some importance in the central range, as was evidently the case with Shechem, also mentioned in the later execration texts.

Egyptian clay execration figure of a bound prisoner, dating from the eighteenth century B.C., inscribed with a curse upon a governor in Palestine who refused allegiance to Egypt. For the curse to take effect, the figure had to be smashed in a magical rite. Twelve centuries later this practice was echoed in Jeremiah 19:11: "So I will break this people and this city, as one breaks a potter's vessel, so that it can never be mended."

This El-Amarna tablet records the turmoil which prevailed in Canaan during the decline of Egyptian power in the first half of the fourteenth century B.C., and the infiltration of the *Apiru*, early Hebrews

King Akhenaten (Amenophis IV) in whose court at El-Amarna were found the El-Amarna tablets. The king and his beautiful queen, Nefertiti, had abandoned Memphis and its all-powerful priestly hierarchy, to institute in the new city, Akhet-Aten, the worship of the sun-god Aten. Above the king are the radiating hands from the sun-disc. (Painted limestone fragment from Tell El-Amarna, fourteenth century B.C.)

46

Nevertheless, remains of ancient Jerusalem in this hill are disappointingly scarce. This disappointment is offset to some extent by interesting finds in a Middle-Late Bronze cave-tomb on the nearby western slope of the Mount of Olives, in the grounds of the Dominus Flevit Church. The tomb contained over two thousand vessels. Its rich cache of pottery includes imported Cypriot ware as well as some Egyptian ornamental objects including scarabs, dating from the sixteenth-fourteenth centuries B.C. (see map 1). Another large hoard, mostly imported Cypriot and some Mycenean pottery was discovered in a rock-cut tomb near Rehavia (western Jerusalem), and still another collection in a pit in the United Nations Headquarters grounds near Talpiot (southern metropolitan Jerusalem). According to early burial customs, the dead were buried with offerings as they would require the same nourishment and daily objects which they used while alive. These tomb finds not only provide tangible evidence of Jerusalem's commercial contacts with the outside world, but also point to lively and extensive activity among the people of the city.

c. The El-Amarna Tablets

The most important extrabiblical source of information about ancient Jerusalem in the era during which the Canaanite city-states owed allegiance to the Egyptian eighteenth dynasty are the *El-Amarna Letters* dating from the first half of the fourteenth century B.C. The letters are in the form of clay tablets inscribed in cuneiform characters representing the Akkadian (Assyro-Babylonian) language, which was the official medium of international diplomacy during that period. The story of how these tablets came to light is reminiscent of the later discovery of the Dead Sea Scrolls.

In 1887, while digging up the earth before planting, an Egyptian woman accidentally found a number of tablets at El-Amarna in Middle Egypt, near the Nile, some 190 miles south of Cairo. The local inhabitants hunted out many more of the tablets, concealing them until dealers or scholars would buy them. Eventually, several institutions including the Berlin Museum, the British Museum and the Cairo Museum purchased large numbers of them. J.A. Knudtzen published 377 of these documents in Berlin in 1907–1915, and since then several more have been published by various scholars. About a dozen more tablets and additional fragments were recovered in the excavations of Tell El-Amarna.

The tablets, most of them letters, come from the royal archives of Amenophis IV (King Akhenaten, 1379–1362 B.C.) and his father, Amenophis III. Some of the letters were despatched by various kings of Western Asia to Pharaoh, while others are copies of Pharaoh's replies. The great majority, however, were written by the vassal kings of Canaan to their Egyptian overlord. Similar documents were discovered in Palestine in the excavations, among others, of Tell el-Hesi, Ta'anach, Shechem, Gezer and even Jericho.

About a hundred and fifty letters originated in Canaan. They reveal such a confused political situation under Egyptian domination, such a web of plots, counterplots, and contradictory accusations, that it is hardly possible to tell truth from falsehood insofar as the facts stated are concerned. Nevertheless, they vividly reveal the conditions of life

Victory celebration in the palace of the king of Megiddo. He is seated on a throne decorated with a sphinx and is drinking from a goblet, while a courtier, behind, serves him with food. His queen stands in front of him accompanied by a musician plucking her lyre. The right side of the picture depicts the king in his chariot, to which two naked captives are tethered (fourteenth century B.C. ivory inlay from Megiddo)

and the social structure of the population in Palestine in the Late Bronze Age (fifteenth-thirteenth centuries B.C.).

(1) *Abdi-Hiba of Jerusalem.* Six of the El-Amarna Tablets were sent to Egypt by Abdi-Hiba, governing prince of Jerusalem, who declared, "Pharóah has impressed his name on the land of Jerusalem forever." He entitles himself the "Officer of the King" (of Egypt), a position inherited from his father. He swears his loyalty to his suzerain, and clamors for help against the king's enemies in Canaan in those days of the sharp decline of Egyptian sovereignty over the land.

Two passages from the El-Amarna letters are most important: One, letter, 287, from Abdi-Hiba reads, "and now *Urusalim* [Jerusalem]... if this land does belong to the King, why, as [is the case with] the city of Gaza, does it not concern the King?" Another letter is from Shuwardata, a prince in Southern Palestine, who writes, "The *'Apiru* chief [the chief of an *'Apiru* band] has risen in arms against the lands which the King gave me, but thy servant has smitten him. Also let the King, my lord, know that all my brethren [kings of Canaan] have abandoned me and that it is I and Abdi-Hiba who fight against the *'Apiru* chief." (Standard translation in J.A. Knudtzen's *Die el-Amarna Tafeln*, Leipzig, 1907–14.) The chief of Canaan referred to is probably Labaya, who ruled over the territory of the central mountain range which included Shechem.

Besides the information on Abdi-Hiba's intrigues against the other city-kings of Canaan, his correspondence casts important light on the situation in central Palestine. His difficulties with Cushite troops (Nubian garrison) who tear up his roof in order to rob his house emphasize the now familiar state of affairs, that the inadequate supplies and pay made it necessary for Egyptian troops and mercenaries to sustain themselves by ravaging the already depleted land. There has been a suggestion that the "breaking through the roof" is descriptive of the manner of building on stepped terraces rising from the Kidron valley, as discovered by Kathleen Kenyon. At one point Abdi-Hiba pleads for troops, but suggests that they be quartered at Gezer or Lachish or Ashkelon; he obviously did not wish to be burdened with any more hungry men (the numbers involved were quite small, certainly not more than one or two hundred soldiers). His letters reflect the combination of self-justification and recriminations against one's enemies characteristic of the unsettled conditions in Canaan. At the same time, they indicate that every local prince was anxious to get as much as he could out of Egypt at the least possible expense to himself. The game was to seek and keep as much power and freedom as possible for oneself at the expense of one's neighbors, but at the same time to remain on good terms with the overlord.

The letters of Abdi-Hiba and others from the El-Amarna collection reveal that since Jerusalem occupied a key location in the central mountain range, it was one of the leading city-kingdoms in Canaan, and was regarded as especially loyal to Pharaoh. However, in

Ivory carving of the fourteenth century B.C., found at Megiddo, shows Canaanite *marianu* (knights) driving their chariots over wounded enemies on the battlefield

the course of the El-Amarna period, Semitic adversaries from the west and north had already encroached on the territory of the 'Land of Jerusalem,' i.e. the land *around* Jerusalem, captured some of its towns and villages, and seriously interfered with its caravan trade. The letters written by Abdi-Hiba, or rather his scribe, although ostensibly in Akkadian, abound in Northwest Semitic words and constructions (which are closely akin to biblical Hebrew). In any case, Jerusalem's mention in written history precedes the earliest biblical records by many centuries.

(2) *Insights into the Biblical Narrative.* The background material furnished by the El-Amarna Tablets helps to explain certain points in the biblical account of Joshua and Jerusalem at the time the Israelites invaded the central hills of Benjamin and Ephraim (Joshua 10). It may be inferred from the biblical data that at the time of the Israelite Conquest (thirteenth century B.C.), Adoni-zedek, king of Jerusalem, headed a confederacy of Amorite kings of southern Canaan, and claimed authority over a consortium of Hivite cities situated northwest of Jerusalem, headed by Gibeon, then considered an important town, "like one of the royal cities." Adoni-zedek attacked Gibeon when the latter concluded a covenant of peace with Joshua. The Israelites rushed from their camp in Gilgal on the Jordan to the aid of Gibeon, inflicting heavy losses upon the king of Jerusalem. Jerusalem's fortunes suffered considerably, but it was not captured by Joshua. In contrast to this account, chapter one of the book of Judges relates that "after the death of Joshua" Jerusalem had been destroyed and burned by the men of the tribe of Judah, an event which apparently occurred at the end of the thirteenth century B.C. and resulted in the annihilation of the city's former population.

5. THE JEBUSITES AND THE OPHEL

A possible result of this radical change was the appearance of a new ethnic group in Jerusalem. These were the Jebusites, possibly allies or vassals of the Hittites, many of whom had been forced to migrate south from Asia Minor and northern Syria after the destruction of the Hittite empire at the beginning of the twelfth century B.C. An elusive evocation of this remote occurrence may be found in Ezekiel 16:3: "Thus says the Lord God to Jerusalem: Your origin and your birth are of the land of the Canaanites; your father was an Amorite, and your mother a Hittite." It is also significant that one of David's officers was Uriah the Hittite, a citizen of Jerusalem. The new arrivals could easily have exploited the weakness of the Hebrew tribes in the area between Judah and its southern tributaries on the one hand, and Benjamin with the Hivites living in their midst on the other. This weakness is clearly attested in the book of Judges. They entered the border area on the ruined and depopulated hill and erected fortifications there, in

The substructures uncovered in past years in the course of excavations on the eastern slopes of the City of David and the terracing, consisting of unmortared stone walls rising from below, could be the '*millo*' terraces referred to in I Kings 9: 15 and 24

particular on the stronghold of Zion. They ruled over a small territory which separated the tribal area of Judah from that of Benjamin and constituted a foreign enclave in their midst. Very few structures of the Jebusite period remain, as explained above (The Ravages of Time): some foundations on the eastern slope of the hill and remains of supporting walls on the higher slopes (see Part IV, A, 5, b: The Earliest Defenses of Jerusalem on the East).

Retaining walls on the hill had served to strengthen the terraces upon which the city's houses were built. Some scholars believe that these terraces, taken together, are designated by the biblical term "millo" (II Samuel 5:9; I Kings 9:15; etc.), and I am inclined to support this view in the light of recent explorations (see Part IV, B: The Millo). The finds dating from the Bronze Age and the beginning of the Iron Age, including more particularly those discovered in the tombs, attest to continuous occupation during the third and second millennia B.C., and rather elaborate urban development during several periods of its existence.

B. IN THE DAYS OF THE MONARCHY

JERUSALEM ENTERS HISTORY

David had been anointed king over Judah at Hebron, presumably "before Yahweh" i.e. at the site of an Israelite sanctuary (II Samuel 2:4), and he ruled from there over the southern territory. After defeating Ishbaal, his rival and son of King Saul, David planned to capture the city of the Jebusites, a territorial corridor which divided the southern from the northern tribal area (see below). From there he could reign over the united people of Israel. In order to spiritually consolidate his position, David brought the Ark of the Covenant to Jerusalem in a great ceremony, described in II Samuel 6:1–19, thereby establishing his royal residence in the 'City of David.' This represented a decisive develop-

An imaginary representation of the Holy Ark of God, brought by David to Jerusalem, in a carving from the fourth century A.D., synagogue of Capernaum in Galilee

ment in the history of Israel and the land of Israel in the days of the United Kingdom. It raised Jerusalem to the prestigious status of the "royal city" and the metropolis and religious center of the new integrated state, unlike Hebron which had not been a formal cultic center though it possessed its sanctuary.

1. DAVID IN JERUSALEM

The capture of the Jebusite stronghold through a strategem initiated by Joab ben Zeruiah is described vividly in the biblical record. A dramatic account is given of Joab's entry into the city by the ṣinnōr (pronounced tzinnōr), creating a diversion and thus enabling David to break in. Its archeological background in given in Part IV, B, 1: The Ṣinnōr and Capture of the Jebusite Stronghold. The Jebusite fortress appears to have been captured during the initial years of David's reign at Hebron (approximately 1000 B.C.). The Bible indicates that the Jebusite enclave was liquidated, but Joab "repaired the rest of the city" (I Chronicles 11:8), while Araunah the Jebusite, apparently the last native prince, was permitted to hold on to his estates outside the Citadel, including the threshing floor on Mount Zion. After consolidating his sovereignty over all Israel, he transferred his seat from Hebron in the eighth year of his reign, to the stronghold of Zion and changed its name to the City of David making it the King's royal domain, the capital of the realm. He thereby achieved several goals at once; by centralizing government authority and tightening his grip on the kingdom, an indissoluble bond was established between David and his dynasty and Jerusalem. It became indeed the City of David. At the same time, it was outside tribal boundaries and hence not subject to territorial claims or other tribal pressures.

David conferred on the city the considerable prestige of his own name. He also built it up in the course of his reign. He restored the 'millo' terraces, and with the help of Sidonian and Tyrian master builders he initiated a vast building program which included

51

Pottery from the days of the Judean Monarchy (eighth century B.C.) found in a pit near the Hulda Triple Gate

David's Tower, apparently the New Citadel, his royal palace (the 'House of Cedars') as well as the 'House of the Mighty Men' and the royal acropolis. He assembled his warriors in Jerusalem where he had set up a centralized administration, and brought the Holy Ark of God from its temporary resting place at Kiryat-Yearim to the City of David, where he set it up in a sanctified Tent, an elaborate version of the wilderness Tabernacle. However, his most significant accomplishment at the end of his reign was the erection of an altar to the God of Israel at the top of Mount Zion, on the threshing floor he had purchased from Araunah the Jebusite (II Samuel 24:16–25). The threshing floor had probably served as a pagan field sanctuary over a long period, even before the time of David. The story of the altar and its locus became intertwined with other traditions which enhanced the sanctity of Jerusalem, within whose walls was the holy place, Mount Zion. Other traditions identified the site as Mount Moriah, associated with the patriarch Abraham and the near sacrifice of his son, Isaac (see Part III, A: The Temple Mount).

The belief in the permanance of the House of David or its restoration is faithfully expressed in the pronouncements of the prophets in the liturgical poetry of Israel, and the narratives of the biblical annalists. The confident hope in the present and future was based on the conviction that the covenant between the Lord and David was everlasting. A striking illustration of this buoyant faith can be found, for example, in Jeremiah 33:19–22 on the permanence of the House of David.

2. SOLOMON IN JERUSALEM

The sanctification of the summit of Mount Zion, which is called Mount Moriah, by virtue of the altar erected there in David's time, paved the way for his son Solomon's dedication of the Temple, an awe-inspiring event that was to take place some years later on this elevation north of the City of David. By the reign of Solomon, it was included in the

52

This eighth century B.C. Assyrian wall relief from the palace of Sargon depicts the shipping of logs on rafts or on the upper deck of light Phoenician coastal craft. In the same way, Solomon brought home the cedar logs of Lebanon, intended for the Temple. The logs were landed at the mouth of the Yarkon river (present-day Tel-Aviv), then carried overland to Jerusalem

expanded precincts of Jerusalem. Solomon began the construction of several magnificent buildings on Mount Moriah in the fourth year of his reign (probably the year after David's death). First he erected the Temple, then the royal palace. It is not unlikely that the general plan had originated in the last years of David's reign, when Solomon was coregent of the kingdom. The entire project was carried out under the guidance of Tyrian master builders and took twenty years to execute. (See Part III, B, 2: Analogies with Other Temples.)

The Temple and Palace: The Temple was erected on the summit of Mount Moriah. It was "an exalted house, a place for thee to dwell in for ever" (I Kings 8:13, see description in Part III, B, 3: The Plan of the Temple).

The terms used in the Bible to designate the Temple are *bēt YHWH* or *bēt elohim*. This is strikingly verified by an inscribed shard from the Israelite temple of Arad, dating to the period of the Judean monarchy, which mentions *"bēt YHWH"* (as reproduced in our picture).

The Palace, with its impressive architecture and elaborate decorations, was set up south of the Temple, and was planned as a royal residence and center of administration. Its structures included the palace itself, which housed the king and his family, the House of Pharaoh's Daughter (one of Solomon's wives), the House of the Cedars of Lebanon (possibly the arsenal), and the House of the Throne (Hall of Judgment, the main ceremonial hall). He lavished equal care on the Ophel, the original site of Jerusalem, whose *millo* he repaired. This is attested to by the discovery of the new retaining walls which replaced the former ones guarding the lower slopes of the hill and, very likely, a few remnants of a casemate wall (along which stand blind rooms filled with rubble) which Kenyon discovered on the upper reaches of the eastern hill. It seems certain that the city expanded considerably in Solomon's time, embracing the City of David and Mount Zion which were both surrounded by the city walls. It is significant that "Zion" had become Jerusalem's main title and a poetic designation of the metropolis, while the name City of David designated specifically the Ophel.

Seal, dating to the late period of the Judean Monarchy (eighth century B.C.), bearing the griffin-beetle symbol. It was discovered west of the Temple Mount

3. JERUSALEM, THE "CITY OF JUDAH"

After Solomon's demise and the division of the United Kingdom into Judah in the south and Israel in the north (ca. 930 B.C.), Jerusalem ceased to be the sole center of the country's political life. It remained the capital of Judah and the center of the faith, but it suffered many vicissitudes thereafter. Nevertheless, the sanctity of Mount Zion, secured by the Temple which Solomon had built there, persisted and was never forgotten. Jerusalem did not cease to be the "City of God," the "Holy Habitation of El-Elyon" (the Most High, Psalm 46:4). David's dynasty endured for many centuries. The House of David became rooted in the hearts of the people as a permanent symbol of the eternal bond between God and people, land and city. In the same way, David's descendants never relinquished their claim to the throne of a united Israelite Kingdom. The biblical record preserved many references to the varied works undertaken by the kings of Judah to defend and expand Jerusalem, to maintain and repair the Temple, and thus enhance the city's prestige. Henceforth, the history of the Temple and of Jerusalem cannot be examined separately.

The reforms of the gifted King Jehosaphat in centralizing the administration of the land and setting up the highest court of justice in Jerusalem are described in detail in II Chronicles, as are the vast building plans of King Uzziah and his son Jotham, intended to reinforce the city's defenses. In line with these plans, a new citadel was constructed south of the Temple Mount and entitled the Ophel; an upper gate to the Temple area was added. Developments of this nature were the natural accompaniments of periods of military success and prosperity. It should be pointed out that the Hebrew term "Ophel" as a city stronghold came into use in the ninth century B.C., for example in Samaria (in the Hebrew of II Kings 5:24), at Dibbon (the Mesha Stone of Moab, lines 21–22) and in Jerusalem itself. This stronghold stood as a fort between the king's residence and the City of David.

4. KING HEZEKIAH IN JERUSALEM

Jerusalem's fortunes rose even higher during the reign of King Hezekiah, after the Northern Kingdom had been destroyed by the Assyrians and the city of Samaria was reduced to the status of an Assyrian provincial capital (721 B.C.). In the aftermath of the liquidation of the independent Northern Kingdom, the stature of Jerusalem as the metropolitan focus of national life was strongly enhanced and the centrality of the Temple on Mount Zion received new emphasis. It symbolized and concentrated the spiritual and religious life of the nation as a whole. A scion of the Davidic dynasty, Hezekiah, promptly made plans to reunite all the tribes of the north and south, thus reasserting the claims of the House of David to rule a united Israel stretching "from Dan to Beersheba." The more favorable political climate during the reign of the Assyrian

54

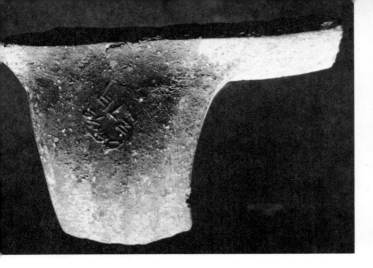

Jar handle bearing seal impression with four-winged scarab; above it appears the word *lmlkh* ("belonging to the king"), and below, the place-name *Socoh*. Such an impression, as well as others bearing the place-name of an administrative centre, were stamps by royal officials guaranteeing the capacity of the jar or standard-sized container of oil and wine taxes

Clay pottery and vessels of the Herodian period

emperor, Sargon II (705–702 B.C.), enabled Hezekiah to expand Judah's sphere of influence and thereby improve the status of Jerusalem, which enjoyed a favored position in international trade and gained extensive economic privileges as a result. Consequently, high hopes were entertained in Jerusalem of restoring the ancient glory of the Davidic dynasty and enlarging the Judean Kindom into a powerful state able to hold its own between the two great empires, Assyria and Egypt. The possibility emerged at the time that Sargon was actively promoting peaceful international trade relations under the aegis of Assyria, and even setting up a commercial outpost at the border of Egypt populated by both Assyrians and Egyptians. This background illuminates the ringing prophecy of Isaiah: "In that day Israel will be the third with Egypt and Assyria, a blessing in the midst of the earth, whom the Lord of hosts has blessed, saying 'Blessed be Egypt my people, and Assyria the work of my hands, and Israel my heritage.'" (Isaiah 19:24–25).

The great prophet expressed ultimate confidence that peace would reign in the land: God would redeem Israel and Judah, and unite the divided people into a single nation with Jerusalem as the metropolitan center and the Temple on Mount Zion as its cultic and spiritual locus, ruled and defended by an anointed king of the House of David. Isaiah affirmed another dream of universal salvation: a future in which a divine light would be shed upon Israel and all the peoples of the earth, and all the nations would come to the Temple Mount to worship and proclaim: "For out of Zion shall go forth the law, and the word of the Lord from Jerusalem" (Isaiah 2:3). This vision of the last times has been bound up permanently with the real city of Jerusalem and its destiny.

5. JERUSALEM EXPANDS TO THE WESTERN HILL

The westward expansion of the capital apparently began in the time of Hezekiah, when two new quarters emerged: the *Mishneh* (Second Quarter) situated on the Western hill which faces the Temple Mount, and the *Makhtesh* (Hollow) in the Tyropoeon valley; cf. Zephaniah 1:10–11 (see Map 1 and Part I, G: Interesting Discoveries in the Upper City).

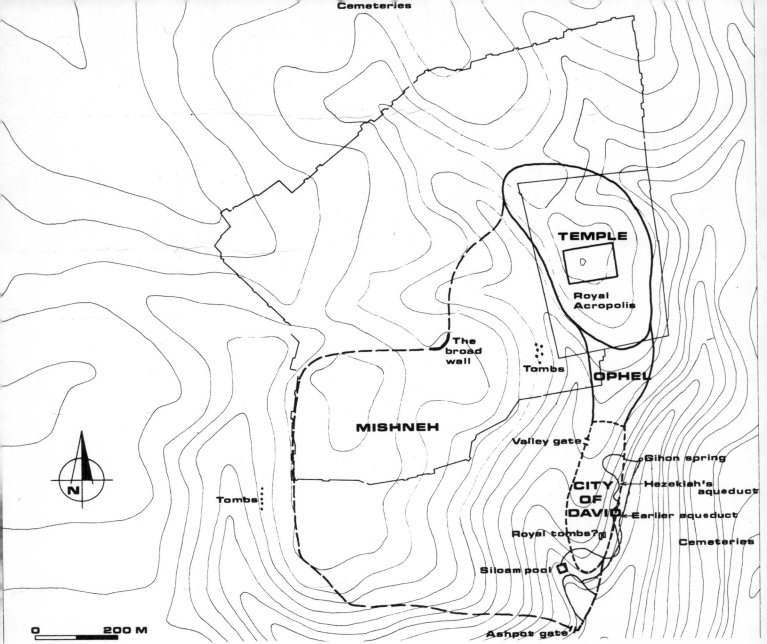

Cemeteries

TEMPLE

Royal
Acropolis

The
broad
wall

Tombs

OPHEL

MISHNEH

Valley gate

Gihon spring

CITY
OF
DAVID

Hezekiah's
aqueduct

Earlier aqueduct

Tombs

Royal tombs?

Cemeteries

Siloam pool

Ashpot gate

N

0   200 M

The building boom in Hezekiah's time kept pace with the growing prosperity in the land and in the capital; it may have been a consequence of an extensive migration of northern Israelites from the Assyrian 'Province' of Samaria. The developments in the later years of King Hezekiah's reign are echoed in Isaiah's optimistic prophecies. The developing political entity which had been envisioned, a neutral and prosperous Israelite state expanding between Assyria and Egypt, failed to materialize after all. Assyria's former conciliatory policy was changed by Senacherib, Sargon's son, mainly due to the aggressive stand of Egypt and her allies.

When Senacherib acceded to the throne (702 B.C.), Hezekiah became involved in political plots and a search for new allies among neighboring nations, including Egypt. This involved the planning of new defenses throughout the land and in Jerusalem, among them the tunnelling of the underground water conduit from the Gihon spring to the Siloam Pool, a most remarkable water engineering feat; and the erection of the new broad city wall (see Part IV, C: Hezekiah's Achievements).

Hezekiah's defenses in Jerusalem were nearly complete and a substantial military force was concentrated there when the city was besieged by Senacherib's army as the climax of the Assyrian invasion of Judah in 701 B.C. It was at this time also that the prophet Isaiah bolstered the people's courage by saying: "I will defend this city to save it, for my own sake and for the sake of my servant David" (Isaiah 37:35). Hezekiah's success in saving Jerusalem even at the cost of an enormous tribute (recorded both in the Bible, II Kings 18:13–16 and in the royal Assyrian inscriptions) was an event of historic importance. Embellished by legendary accretions, it strengthened the popular view of the impregnability of the city, and the ultimate sanctity and inviolability of Mount Zion and the Temple. This confidence remained intact through subsequent generations down to the last years of the monarchy, until the day that the city walls were breached, the defending forces overwhelmed, and the city itself destroyed by the armies of the Babylonian king Nebuchadnezzar.

6. MANASSEH IN JERUSALEM

The reign of Manasseh, Hezekiah's son and successor, witnessed a new stage in the annals of Jerusalem. Towards the end of his rule, national and religious hopes were revived in Judah as Assyria's hold weakened. The Bible states that Manasseh diligently buttressed Jerusalem's battlements and, more particularly, the Ophel citadel: "He built an outer wall for the City of David west of Gihon, in the valley" (II Chronicles 33:14). This may be the wall discovered by K. Kenyon to the west of the very ancient wall on the western slopes of the City of David. By the time of Manasseh, in the early seventh century B.C., the new quarters on the Western hill and in the Tyropoeon valley had expanded considerably. An unexpected discovery occurred in the course of our excavations. On the eastern slope of the Western hill (facing the Western Wall and Robinson's Arch of the Temple Mount), we uncovered a sizeable cemetery which had been in use in the eighth century B.C., and had been abandoned during the first half of the seventh century, apparently in the days of Manasseh (see Part IV, E: Royal Tombs in the City of David).

The initial decades of Manasseh's long reign (698–642 B.C.) were marked by his subjugation to Assyria and his paganization of the kingdom, which prospered nevertheless.

7. JOSIAH'S ERA OF REFORM AND INDEPENDENCE

Jerusalem reached its zenith during the reign of King Josiah, when Judah once more became independent of Assyrian tutelage, following the decline of the empire. The kingdom prospered greatly, expanding over large areas of southern Palestine, including the Negev. The Mishneh (Second) Quarter had become one of the most populous sections

King Josiah, as related in II Kings 23:4, purged Judah of foreign cults. The vessels mentioned were incense stands, such as the one above, found in Megiddo (thirteenth century B.C.); the *asherah* (left) was a pillar like those found in the Canaanite temple at Hazor (seventeenth century B.C.)

of the capital. The Bible notes that "Hulda the prophetess, the wife of Shallum... keeper of the wardrobe" made her home there (II Kings 22:14). This is significant as Jerusalem's important southern gates in Second Temple times and until their destruction, were called the Hulda Gates (see Part III, F, 3: The Monumental Southern Gates).

Josiah followed through with his revolutionary religious reforms, relentlessly purging foreign cults from Judah's worship, burning "all the vessels made for Ba'al, for Asherah and for all the host of heaven; he burned them outside Jerusalem in the fields of the Kidron" (II Kings 23:4). He deposed the idolatrous priests who had been "ordained to burn incense... to Ba'al, to the sun, and the moon, and the constellations and all the host of the heaven" (II Kings 23:5).

It has been suggested that one of the places into which the "abominations" were cast was the cave discovered by Kenyon on the lower slopes of the ridge toward the Kidron valley. The crux of Josiah's reform was the renewed centralization of all Israelite worship in "the place Yahweh chose," i.e. the Temple Mount. The unification of the cult exclusively in the Temple exalted Jerusalem as the sole center for all the faithful to Yahweh, "the site Yahweh had chosen among all the tribes of Israel" and the place where the nation as a whole was to assemble for the prescribed yearly pilgrimages. The territories of Judah and the southern region of Samaria had by that time been reunited, and the capital city once again served an enlarged nation-state as its politico-religious center.

8. IN THE SHADOW OF BABYLON

The high hopes for the resurgent State of Judah, nurtured by the early successes of King Josiah, faded away. Jerusalem's position became critical as the war between Assyria, supported by its ally, Egypt, and Babylon engulfed Judah. The death of King Josiah in his

This clay prism from the annals of the Assyrian King Senacherib gives an account of the siege of Jerusalem in 701 B.C. The king lifted the siege when his army was afflicted by a plague

Jewish prisoners and spoils taken away from Lachish by the Assyrians

encounter with the Egyptians at Megiddo (609 B.C.) foreshadowed the tragic outcome. Five years after the death of Josiah, in 605 B.C. Nebuchadnezzar acceded to the Babylonian throne, thus ushering in the final struggle between Babylon and Judah. In 598 B.C. he led a military expedition to Judah and laid siege to Jerusalem. The new king, Jehoiachin (who succeeded King Jehoiakim), reigned only three months, just long enough to surrender the city in March of 597. He and the royal family, palace officials and thousands of prisoners "and all the craftsmen and the smiths" (II Kings 24:14) were exiled to Babylon. The prophet and priest Ezekiel was also among the exiles.

The Revealing Babylonian Chronicle: The counterpart to the biblical tale is related in the Babylonian Chronicle (tablets of which are now in the British Museum): "The king of Akkad [Babylonia, i.e. Nebuchadnezzar]... laid siege to the city of Judah [Iāhūdū] and the king took the city on the second day of the month Addaru. He appointed in it a new king of his liking, took heavy booty from it and brought it into Babylon." The 'new king' was Zedekiah.

Nebuchadnezzar started his siege of the city in the spring of 587 B.C. He employed

59

the most advanced military techniques of the time, including the circumvallation of the city by earthen dykes, the raising of ramps against the city walls and the use of ramming engines. The city fell after the collapse of the northern walls which had no deep valleys below to protect them. The desperate attempt of Zedekiah, the remaining son of the great Josiah and last king of the Davidic dynasty to rule in Jerusalem, and his men to escape through the King's Garden by "the Gate between the two walls" near the Siloam Pool, failed dismally, for the Babylonians captured them when they reached the plains of Jericho. Jerusalem was captured and destroyed in the month of Ab (August 586) and the Temple burned down. We find some scanty evidence of this destruction in the City of David, for example the remains of homes destroyed by fire in that period. These were discovered mainly over the eastern slopes of the ancient hill of Jerusalem, among them a structure of three halls, divided by partitions made up of monolithic pillars resting in their sockets. An abundance of shards and other artifacts discovered on both the eastern ridge and the Western hill can be dated to the last years of the Judean Monarchy.

The intense hope for the restoration of Jerusalem which lay in ruins, is reflected not only in biblical literature, but also in Hebrew inscriptions recently found. One of the most revealing is carved on a tomb at Khirbet-Beit-Lei, about 5.5 miles (8 kms.) east of Lachish, and dates from the sixth century B.C. It reads: "I am Yahweh thy God, I will protect the cities of Judah and will redeem Jerusalem." It is interesting to compare it with the words of the unknown sixth century B.C. prophet, found in the Hebrew of the book of Isaiah 52:9: "...For Yahweh has comforted his people, he has redeemed Jerusalem" (see also Isaiah 44:26).

C. JERUSALEM IN POST-EXILIC TIMES

The destruction of Jerusalem and the Temple, along with the mass banishment of its inhabitants, including the aristocracy and the priesthood to Babylon, had effectively shattered the Judahite kingdom. But the disaster did not weaken the love and reverence for Zion among the exiles, nor among those who stayed behind in Judah and its adjoining districts. For example, the Bible states that eighty mourning pilgrims from Shechem, Shiloh, and Samaria came to Jerusalem after the disaster "with their beards shaved and their clothes torn, and their bodies gashed, bringing cereal offerings and incense to present at the temple of the Lord" (Jeremiah 41:5).

The contemporary prophets, especially Jeremiah and Ezekiel, held fast to their faith in the restoration of Zion, looking ahead to days of glory for the city which would be suffused in bright light. The memory of Jerusalem was kept alive by the poets of the Babylonian exile, in the fervent hope that redemption would not be far behind (see Part III, B, 5: Ezekiel Plan). Towards the end of the period of the Babylonian exile, there appeared the great prophet whose name is unknown to us, but whose oracles of comfort and hopes of restoration are recorded in the latter part of the book of Isaiah, namely Chapters 40 to the end of the book. Commonly designated as Second Isaiah, he lived

Cyrus, king of Persia, gives an account of his capture of Babylon in 536 B.C. He permitted the return of the Judean prisoners from Babylonia to their own land, and aided them in restoring their Temple. Cyrus' edict promulgating these rights is duplicated in the words of Ezra 1.

in Babylonia about a century and a half after Isaiah, the son of Amoz of Jerusalem, and it was mainly this later prophet who infused into the hearts and minds of the exiles the unique and majestic vision of the return from exile and the restoration of Zion.

1. RESTORATION OF ZION AFTER THE EXILE

A great turning point in the annals of Jerusalem came after the conquest of Babylon by Cyrus, king of Persia (538 B.C.). It was he who translated into political action the great awakening among the Babylonian exiles, and their first attempts to return to Zion. (See Part III, C: The Second Temple.)

The first wave of repatriated exiles, headed by Sheshbazzar, prince of Judah and purportedly, at least, a scion of the Davidic dynasty, were not successful in establishing their position firmly in the desolated land, or in carrying out the great plan for a new exodus. They barely managed to lay down foundations of the Temple. But in the following generation, during the second year of the reign of Darius I, Zerubbabel, a grandson of Jehoiachin and head of the House of David, was repatriated, together with a large group representing the various clans of Judah, and they proceeded to settle in and around Jerusalem. This gave impetus to a genuine restoration, eloquently expressed in the messages of the contemporary prophets, Haggai and Zechariah.

a. A Modest Second Temple and Beginnings of the Second Commonwealth
Zerubbabel, whom Darius had appointed governor (Peha) of Judah, and the high priest Joshua resumed the building of the Temple in the second year after Darius' accession (520 B.C.), but it was only completed in the sixth year of his reign, precisely on March 3, 515 B.C., according to Ezra 6:15 (see Part III, C: The Second Temple). Jerusalem itself, however, was still underpopulated and its fortifications lay in ruins (see

The letters "YHWD" (Province, or City of Judah) stamped on the handle of a jar used in trade

Nehemiah 1:2–3 and Part V, A: Nehemiah's Vital Evidence on the City of David).

When Ezra, the priest and scholar, arrived there in 458 B.C., after a hiatus of more than fifty years, he found a sanctuary town of modest proportions, its small population huddled around the Temple. It was not fortified adequately against the neighboring inimical communities, and the community of Jewish repatriates had become embroiled in strife with the inhabitants of the adjacent provinces, chiefly Samaria, north of Jerusalem. The population of Samaria consisted mainly of immigrants of mixed origins who had been settled there by the Assyrians after the conquest of the Northern Kingdom in 721 B.C. and who had adopted the religion of the land, plus remnants of the old Israelites. Both these and the pagan neighbors now claimed rights of precedence over the repatriates who nevertheless formed close relations with neighbors. Intermarriage was common among the Jewish and Samaritan upper classes and even among the priesthood. The Samaritans built their own temple on Mount Gerizim overlooking Shechem as they were estranged by the priests from the Temple of Jerusalem (see below: Four Jewish Temples). This set them apart as a powerful sectarian community whose policies ran contrary to those of the Judean commonwealth.

Ezra had come to Jerusalem in the seventh year of the reign of Artaxerxes I, then the Persian emperor, with his explicit permission to establish the Torah (Law of Moses) as the normative guide for Israel's faith and rule of life among all Jews living in Jerusalem and Judah. His first concern was to unify the people and to purify the status of family life as well as their religious conscience. But he was unable to overcome the opposition of the neighboring population to the project of rebuilding the ruined city and its fortifications. Moreover, the repatriates were poorly organized as a community and lacked the executive ability as well as the means to carry out public works or even to protect the city with new walls.

b. Nehemiah

A more effective program of physical and political restoration was actually carried out by Nehemiah, a high officer in the Persian court (see Part V, A, 1: His Place in the Revival of Jerusalem, which underscores the real nature of Nehemiah's achievement). No evidence has been found to prove that the city rebuilt in Nehemiah's time encompassed the Upper City (the Western hill) in addition to the Ophel. In fact no other remains of the Persian period have been found in Jerusalem so far. Even isolated finds such as coins or jar handles inscribed *YHWD*, meaning the Province of Judah or the City of Judah (Jerusalem) are few and far between (see Part V, A, 2: New Archeological Insights into the Book of Nehemiah).

A new concern was added to the situation of the pre-exilic remnants and the repatriates, as expressed in Nehemiah's basic plea to the Persian emperor: "Send me to

Aramaic papyrus from the Jews of Elephantine, who were serving as mercenaries in the Persian garrison in southern Egypt, to Bagoas, Persian governor of Judah, and to Johanan, the high priest, requesting aid in rebuilding their local temple which had been destroyed by their neighbors. The aid was granted

Judah, to the city of my fathers' sepulchres, that I may rebuild it" (2:5). The returning exiles and the Jews who had never left the land attached the greatest importance to their old cemeteries and above all to the ancient tombs of the Davidic dynasty in the City of David (see Part IV, E, 1: The Ancient Royal Burial Ground in the City of David). It is significant that ever since Nebuchadnezzar had exiled the royal family and its entourage to Babylon, together with the priests, nobility and skilled craftsmen of the capital, the tombs of their ancestors occasioned great concern among the expatriates, and was a central factor in their longing for Zion. In this connection, the priest-prophet Ezekiel voiced a protest against the tendency to link palace and temple, royalty and religion too closely, and the institution of a cult of the dead kings. Thus he complained about the proximity of such tombs to the Temple Mount, claiming that "the corpses of their kings" near the Temple "defile my holy name" and he insisted "Now let them put away their idolatry and the corpses of their kings far from me, and I will dwell in their [the people's] midst for ever" (Ezekiel 43:7–9). However on the basis of comparative materials in Ugarit (a North Canaanite city which flourished in the fourteenth-thirteenth centuries B.C.) it is now considered that the Hebrew *pigrē* is not to be understood as 'the dead bodies' but as monuments or funeral stelae.

Jerusalem prospered in the following decades as the site of the sanctuary and the seat of provincial government. This was owing in no small degree to the events of the period corresponding with Nehemiah's second appointment as Governor of Judah (422–421 B.C.). Among other reforms, normal to a theocratic community, he initiated strict measures against the intermarriage of Judeans with neighboring foreign communities; he reorganized ritual practices in the Temple in line with ancestral traditions, and he prohibited buying and selling by Tyrian tradesmen at the city gates on the Sabbath.

2. THE PERSIAN PERIOD

There is but little information about the governors of Jerusalem after Nehemiah's time. Foremost among those of whom some record remains is the *Peha* (Governor) Bagoas and the High Priest Yohanan. Both names have been preserved mainly because of an Aramaic papyrus found in Elephantine in southern Egypt, where Jews were serving as mercenaries in the Persian garrison. Their community head wrote to Bagoas and Yohanan asking for aid in restoring their temple which had been destroyed by Egyptians (408 B.C.).

3. CONTEMPORARY ARTIFACTS

Archeology has provided interesting evidence of the Persian rule in the *Pahva* (Province) of Judah, which eventually became a semi-autonomous community within the framework of the Fifth Persian Satrapy of *Eber-Nahara* (Beyond the Euphrates River). The community was granted the right to levy taxes and strike coins. Coin currency first appeared in the near east in the wake of Greek commercial activity, and the Athenian owl struck on the drachma became a common symbol. The Judeans took the Attic coin as their model, adding at the top the letters *YHWD* (Province or City of Judah). They stamped these letters on the handles of jars used in commerce, as well.

Throughout the restoration of Zion in the fifth and fourth centuries, Jerusalem maintained close ties with the Jewish Diaspora, in particular with the communities in Babylon and Egypt. The Jews of the Diaspora regarded Jerusalem as their own metropolitan center and holy city, and felt both a need and desire to visit the Temple for worship. As a consequence, a steady stream of pilgrims used to come from those countries to the Temple of Jerusalem, as ordained by ancient tradition.

D. JERUSALEM IN THE EARLY HELLENISTIC PERIOD

While Jerusalem was being restored as a Jewish city under the benevolent Persian rule, a new conquering power was growing in the west. The Macedonian conquest of Syria and Palestine by Alexander the Great in 333–332 B.C. inaugurated not only a political change, but a cultural revolution as well. The opening of the near east to western influence was followed by an economic growth and the expansion of trade throughout the whole area, as well as the world-wide spread of the hellenistic way of life. The Jewish people thus came into contact with the hellenistic world. It affected them deeply and involved them by force of circumstance in current political developments from the earliest days of Macedonian rule.

Judea retained and even strengthened its internal autonomy. This status did not change to any serious extent throughout the strife which raged for years among the generals who succeeded Alexander, the Ptolemies in Egypt and the Seleucids in Syria, who divided this segment of his empire. According to Josephus' account, the conquest of Jerusalem by Ptolemy I, founder of the dynasty in Egypt, was accomplished without bloodshed and without opposition, as it occurred on a Sabbath when the Jews would not defile the holiness of the day by fighting (*Antiquities* XII:1). A tolerable situation prevailed, in fact, until the time of Antiochus III, ruler of Syria, who wrested Palestine and Jerusalem from the Ptolemies in about 200 B.C.

Jar handle bearing the stamp impression YRŠLM dating to early hellenistic times

1 THE LETTER OF ARISTEAS

A contemporary literary source, the Letter of Aristeas, an Alexandrian, recounts the journey of Philadelphus (285–246 B.C.), an official of the court of Ptolemy II, from Alexandria to Jerusalem. Aristeas describes Jerusalem and the Temple in glowing terms, as well as the fortress known as the Birah. This citadel, known since the time of Nehemiah (2:8), stood at the northwestern end of the Temple Mount and protected the sanctuary. It contained a garrison which, according to Aristeas, consisted of five hundred men. The citadel was called *Baris* by Josephus (*Antiquities* XV:403); Herod would transfrom it into a massive stronghold and rename it the Antonia in honor of his patron, Mark Anthony.

Little is known about the fortunes of Jerusalem in the third century B.C. Despite the constant tensions between the Ptolemaic and Seleucid kingdoms, the country was fairly prosperous. Jerusalem was one of the important cities in the region, due mainly to the Temple, religious focus for both local Jewry and the Diaspora. Many pilgrims were drawn to the city, and the country enjoyed general prosperity under a stable government headed by a high priest, Onias II, a direct descendant of the great high priest, Zadok, who first presided over the Temple of Solomon. The high priest was supported by the Council of Elders recruited from the aristocratic families who owned considerable estates.

It is to this period that certain inscribed jars discovered in Jerusalem and Judea are attributed. The jar handles bear the seal impression YRŠLM (Jerusalem), rather than YHWD as had been the case in the preceding period, suggesting that with the demise of Persian rule and its system of governors, the country was permitted by Alexander to consolidate its internal administration under the leadership of the high priests. (See also Part V, D, b: A Startling Archeological Find.)

Another contemporary Hellenistic writer, Hecateus of Abdera (third century B.C.), who wrote about the Jews, perhaps as part of his larger history of Egypt, also discussed Jerusalem. He dwells with admiration on the large outer and inner courts of the Temple, on the Sanctuary proper, and on the high status enjoyed by the Jerusalem priesthood, numbering some one thousand five hundred, and on the august position occupied by the high priest who was the representative of the people and, at the same time, their leader (reported by Josephus in *Against Apion* I:22).

The Temple was the focal point of Jewish worship and the symbol of Jewish solidarity, but in addition it served as an instrument of great political and financial power to a degree unknown heretofore. It controlled not only the income accruing from all taxes and donations, but also the funds placed there in trust. The hellenistic writers, however, may have been inclined to exaggerate, or they may have been uncritical in accepting traditional figures (which tend to increase in the course of transmission). The same may be true of Hecateus, who estimated Jerusalem's population at a hundred and twenty thousand (quoted by Josephus in *Againt Apion* I:22). We know, however, that the effects of the quickening of trade and industry in the near east and Palestine were felt from the early days of hellenistic rule. Moreover, the Ptolemies did not maintain a tight economic grip on Palestine, which was at the remote northern end of their dominions.

2. FOUR JEWISH TEMPLES IN EXISTENCE

In the days of the Second Temple four other sanctuaries modelled ultimately on the Temple in Jerusalem, served Jewish communities outside Judea. Two of them were erected in Egypt: one at Elephantine (Yeb; see above: The Persian Period) and the other in northern Egypt; it was built by the high priest Onias, who left Judea during the troubles preceding the Maccabean revolt, and was intended to rival the Jerusalem shrine. The third temple was built by the Samaritans on Mount Gerizim (see above: A Modest Second Temple). The fourth was built early in the second century B.C. by Hyrcanus, son of Joseph the Tobiad, in the valley of 'Arāq-el-Emīr, west of Amman in Transjordan (see below: The Tobiads and other Hellenizers).

The construction of these temples was undertaken in large part to meet the needs of a large Jewish population already widely dispersed from its homeland, and to fulfill the ambitions of the leaders of these Jewish communities outside Judea. Although they were inspired by the Second Temple of Jerusalem, built during the Persian Period (see Part III, C, 1: What Did the Second Temple Look Like?), the new structures were significantly different in architectural plan and execution, showing the influence of contemporary styles.

3. CONFLICT BETWEEN THE HIGH PRIESTHOOD AND THE ARISTOCRACY

Towards the end of Ptolemaic rule, the first portents of the strife between the high priesthood and the Jerusalem aristocracy became visible. The aristocracy had attained a prominent position because of its wealth and connections with the royal court at Alexandria. Josephus gives a graphic description of the clash between the high priest and the heads of the House of Tobias (*Antiquities* XI:4). His account is supported by another document of the Ptolemaic period, the Zenon Papyri, which describe the purchases of oil, wine, slaves, and other commodities, made by the Egyptian authorities through the agency of Greek and Egyptian officials in the country. One of Zenon's prominent correspondents was Tobias, a Jewish prince in Transjordan and a descendant of 'Tobias the Ammonite' mentioned in the annals of Nehemiah. The prince was a powerful personality who wielded great authority in the public affairs of Jerusalem, ruling at the same time over his own principality, a district in the Land of Ammon east of the Jordan, which he had inherited from his forebears.

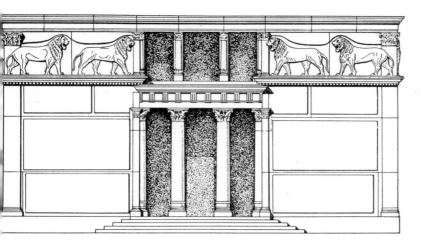

a. The Tobiads and other Hellenizers

The influence and power of the Tobiads were very great in the Ptolemaic era, both in Jerusalem and across the Jordan River; they were also leading hellenizers. These pro-hellenists comprised an elite group of cosmopolitans intent on maintaining a conciliatory attitude to hellenistic rule and culture. The higher classes saw in hellenization a useful and effective instrument in their drive for greater wealth and power, so they adopted Greek speech, names, and manners.

The confrontation between the high priests and the aristocracy, headed by the Tobiads, began in the second half of the third century B.C., when Joseph the son of Tobias was appointed chief tax farmer, responsible for the gathering of taxes from the Asiatic countries under Ptolemaic dominion. The tax farmers would pay a large sum to the central authorities for the concession or lease on the taxes of a province of the empire, then proceed to extract as much as possible from the populace. Joseph's son, Hyrcanus, became the virtual ruler of Jerusalem due to the backing of the Ptolemies. He eventually fell out of favor in Jerusalem, whereupon he built himself a splendid castle called *Tyros* (in Greek — Tsor in Hebrew) in the heart of the Land of Tobias (as described by Josephus in *Antiquities* XII:280). The castle's remains at *Khirbet es Şār* are situated on a high eminence some 10.5 miles (17 kms.) west of Amman on the way to Jericho. Excavations in nearby *'Arāq el Emīr* in 1961–62 have confirmed that the ruins of the large building on top of a hill, called *Kasr el-'Abd* by the Arabs, are those of a Jewish temple erected by Hyrcanus early in the second century B.C.

b. The Tobiads and the Priesthood

The increasing power of the Tobias family, supported by the Ptolemies, rendered it a rival center of authority in Jerusalem, which challenged the traditional status of the high priest. This was probably one of the reasons why the high priest Onias II (a scion of the Oniad priestly clan) favored the Seleucid kings of Syria who were then preparing to wrest Palestine from the Ptolemies. Indeed, after the Seleucid Antiochus III fought the Egyptians and drove them out of Palestine (c. 200 B.C.), the high priesthood gained in honor and prestige under royal sponsorship, and received considerable assistance in developing the city and fortifying it.

Internal rule was not concentrated solely in the hands of the high priests, however. Their rivals, the Tobiads, had regained a considerable share of their former authority and power by shifting their allegiance to the Seleucids and heading the hellenizing movement.

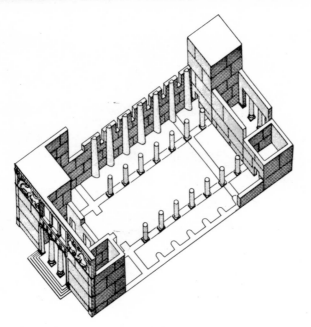

In the days of Antiochus III and to an even greater extent after he was succeeded by Antiochus IV Epiphanus, the Jerusalem population and the Temple in particular were called upon by the Seleucid empire to enrich the imperial treasury.

E. THE HASMONEANS

1. IMPACT OF HELLENIZATION ON URBAN JERUSALEM

The next step was the designation of Jerusalem's citizens as 'Antiochians', that is, citizens of the capital of the Seleucid empire, Antioch, with corresponding privileges and obligations. This included the erection of a gymnasium for athletic games in the shadow of the Temple, on the same spot where the Xystos plaza was to be situated in the days of Herod, close to the Tyropoeon and south of the causeway known as the Wilson Arch of today (see Part V, B, 2: Architectural Achievements of the Hasmonean Kings; and Part V, C: Rediscovering the Lower City of the Herodian Period).

The consequences of these revolutionary innovations, abetted by the pro-hellenist and worldly Tobiads, were soon felt: Jerusalem was being transformed into a hellenistic *polis* (free city, Greek style), to be called "Antioch in Jerusalem." Thus far, the hellenizers' program had not affected Jewish religious practices or the Temple ritual. But their eventual aim was to do away with the exclusiveness of the Jews, and to open the way to Jewish membership in the commonwealth of hellenistic communities of the empire. Hellenist culture had actually reached the countries of the eastern Mediterranean about two centuries earlier. The seafaring Phoenicians had adopted the Greek language which had become the *lingua franca* of this part of the world. In fact, the true connotation of hellenization was a westernizing trend in the broadest sense of the word which the oriental pagans did not actively resist. Though the Jews of Palestine shunned its influence, the more worldly elements regarded it with favor. In short, hellenization had become the avowed policy of the ruling factions of the city, its aristocracy and its priesthood, fully encouraged by their Seleucid overlords. The "true believers" and diehards in Jerusalem and Judea, however, regarded all these developments as a calumny of the true faith which debased the exalted nature of the Temple priesthood and betrayed the ancestral religious

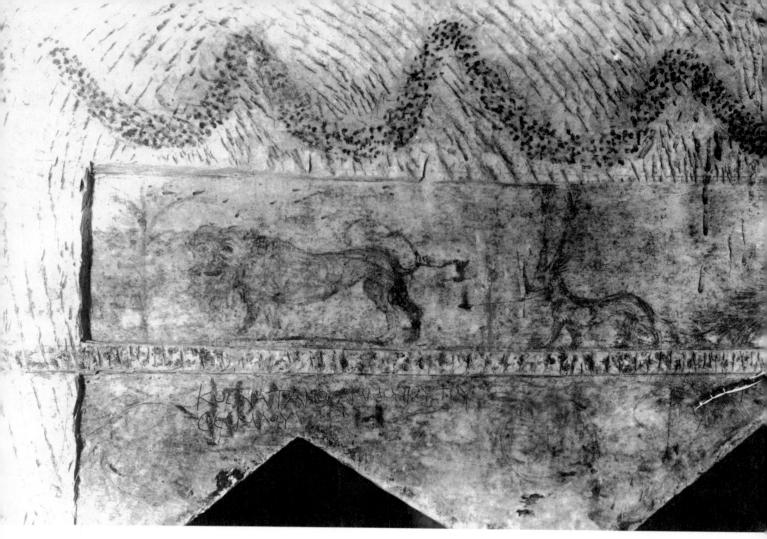

Wall carvings in the catacombs of Maresha in southern Judah, a center of the Judaized Idumaeans, of whom Herod was a descendant

values and hallowed traditions of the nation. The reaction was not slow in coming: A powerful nationalist and religious movement arose spontaneously, spearheaded by the Hassideans, a puritanical and ascetic sect who clung tenaciously to the pure Mosaic faith. They formed the backbone of the populist uprising led by the Hasmonean priestly family, popularly known as the Maccabees.

2. THE TEMPLE IS PLUNDERED AND DESECRATED BY ANTIOCHUS

The tension in Jerusalem reached a critical stage following the usurpation of the high priesthood by Menelaus who, though related to the high priest's family, was an extreme hellenizer. Backed by the Tobiads, he obtained Jason's post as high priest by bribing the Syrian officials and was able to appropriate money from the Temple treasury and generally exploit his position for political and material gain. His unbridled behavior in the Temple matched the recklessness of King Antiochus. The calamitous denouement was reached in 168 B.C. when Antiochus came to Jerusalem on the way back from his luckless war with the Ptolemies. At a time when Jerusalem was torn by the strife between the factions of Jason and Menelaus, Antiochus seized the city and plundered the rich Temple treasures, including the wealth that was being held in trust. The situation became still more ominous when Antiochus erected the *Akra,* a great, powerful citadel, south of the Temple Mount at the top of the Ophel ridge, and garrisoned it with his own troops. In this way he clearly intended to dominate and intimidate the whole population of Jerusalem.

Antiochus was not content with military measures only. He wanted to uproot the Jewish faith together with its focus in the Temple of Jerusalem, and thus completely hellenize the holy city and Judea. His next steps were to set in motion a new era in Jerusalem's long history. He first abrogated the community's rights, hallowed by long tradition and many precedents, "to live in accordance with the ancestral faith."

His next step was to desecrate the Temple by sacrificing a pig, the epitome of the unclean animal, on the great altar of God. This awful act, which was followed by the installation of a statue of Zeus Olympius in the Temple, reverberated throughout the community as the greatest national calamity of all time, filling the Jews with grief and horror. The universal execration is expressed eloquently in the Book of Daniel (12:11) where the desecration is described as "the abomination that makes desolate." The expression in Hebrew (Ba'al Shamaim) which links the name of the chief deity of the pagan Phoenicians is a play on the title of Zeus as the Lord of Heaven, in subtle defiance of the pagans. Moreover, the Akra had been transformed into a stronghold of foreign rule and of the hellenizers who lived under its protection. It was like a dagger striking into the flesh of Jerusalem, for it faced the Temple Mount and commanded a strategic position over it.

3. HASMONEAN LIBERATION OF JERUSALEM

The attempt to transform Jerusalem into a hellenistic 'polis' with all that this entailed in a mixed population, the hellenization of the ruling class, aristocracy and priesthood, in addition to the introduction of foreign rites — all these factors built up gradually to give powerful impetus to the popular movement, initiated by the Hassideans and led by Judah the Maccabean and his brothers, scions of a priestly family from Modi'in in northwestern Judea. The revolutionary movement swept Judea following Antiochus' edict forbidding the Jews to "live in accordance with their ancestral laws" and then spread to the rest of the country. The movement grew into a national rebellion which had far-reaching consequences: Jerusalem was captured by the rebels in the month of Kislev, 164 B.C., the Temple was purified, the ritual resumed and the sanctuary rededicated in a joyous ceremonial including the kindling of lights which lasted for eight days (Hanukkah).

This did not end the war, however, for Judah the Maccabean had not managed to capture the Akra stronghold, still garrisoned by foreign troops. The turn in the political tide came later, when the Seleucids were ready to compromise and to recognize Judah's brother, Jonathan, as High Priest and in effect the virtual ruler of Judea (152 B.C.)

Autonomous rule under the Hasmoneans (Maccabeans) was consolidated beginning with the rule of Simon (142–135 B.C.). He destroyed the Akra and in so-doing abolished the hellenistic 'polis'. Jerusalem once more became a city with a homogeneous Jewish population, the metropolis of an autonomous Judea, no longer subject to Syrian rule. It expanded steadily and prospered, serving again as the national and religious center of world Jewry. Progress was even greater in the days of Simon's successors, the princes of the Hasmonean dynasty. It reached its zenith during the reign of Alexander Jannaeus (103–76 B.C.) who completed the unification of the entire Holy Land north and south (called Judea from that time on), with Jerusalem now the capital of a small but powerful and well-organized state located at the cross-roads of the near east. The transition from hellenistic to independent rule was marked by tangible changes in the appearance of the city and the environs of the Temple Mount.

4. THE MAUSOLEUMS IN THE KIDRON VALLEY

Jerusalem's splendors are attested in the Books of the Maccabees and in Josephus' writings; their reports are confirmed by the remains of buildings and fortifications uncovered to date. Further imposing evidence are the underground family tombs, cut into the bedrock, and the monumental mausoleums surmounting them. One of the most imposing funerary monuments of Hasmonean days is the Bnei Hezir mausoleum of the illustrious priestly family, located in the Kidron valley (next to Absalom's Monument

71

dating to Herodian times). It consists of a porch and sepulchral chambers characteristic of the Hasmonean and subsequent periods, decorated with motifs borrowed from the Greco-Oriental art of the time and sufficiently removed, due to native patterns, from Greek classicism (as shown in the illustrations accompanying section F, 5, b, below: Contemporary Art Designs). The facade of the mausoleum is decorated with Doric columns, resembling the simpler Greek style and distinguished especially by its shaft without a base and its saucer-shaped capital. Its identification with the House of Hezir in the second century B.C. is derived from the Hebrew inscription on the architrave (upper panel) stating that the people buried there, whose names are given, are priests of this distinguished group, and that the adjoining monument *(nefesh)* belongs to this mausoleum. A flight of stairs and a tunnel on the right connect it with this monument, known as the Tomb of Zechariah (see below), a cube-shaped structure cut from one single rock. Its sides are decorated with Ionic columns and it is topped by a pyramidal roof (see Part V, E: The Necropolis of Jerusalem).

Josephus mentions two splendid mausoleums of the Hasmonean period outside the city, one of the Hasmonean ruler, John Hyrcanus, and the other of his son, Alexander Jannaeus. The official title of the ruler was high priest, and he was supported by the Great Assembly *(Haknesseth Hagedolah)*, made up of priests, heads of the community, and elders (I Maccabees I:14, 18; the Letter of Aristeas). In the course of time the ruling body came to be known more specifically as *Heber Hayehudim* or Community of the Jews, a legend stamped on late Hasmonean coins. It is believed by many that this council was later transformed into the well-known Sanhedrin of the period of Herod and afterwards. From the time of the Hasmonean high priest Aristobulus Judah (104–103 B.C.), the Hasmonean rulers designated themselves also as king, a title taken over from them by the usurper Herod and his dynasty. These royal titles bring out in bold relief the increasingly worldly nature of Hasmonean rule.

5. THE HASMONEAN COINS

Great historic interest attaches to the coins stamped by the Hasmoneans in Jerusalem. Such coins, discovered in large quantities throughout the land, illuminate the background and careers of the Jewish rulers and their new status. It is now apparent that Alexander Jannaeus (103–76 B.C.) was the first member of the dynasty to stamp his coins, though it is known that Antiochus VII had granted the right to the Hasmonean high priest Simon (142–135 B.C.). The Hasmonean coins are characterized by the nationalist and religious sentiment they reflect, a feeling shared by all the people whose desire was to reconstitute once more the glorious past. These convictions were justified by the accomplishments of their rulers, who expanded their borders almost to those of David's kingdom.

The motifs on the coins are inspired by the local flora (flowers, sheaves of wheat, etc.), an anchor representing new ventures in seafaring, cornucopias, and even more characteristically, the Temple's seven-branched candelabrum *(menorah)* on the coins of

Second century B.C. Hasmonean coin. An eight-horned star bearing a Hebrew inscription between the horns, spelling out the name of the Hasmonean king Jonathan, namely Alexander Jannaeus

Mattathias Antigonus (40–37 B.C.). The inscriptions on the coins are either in Hebrew alone, or else bilingual, in Hebrew and Greek. Another feature of the coins, characterizing the national spirit, is the use of archaic Hebrew script, dating to the days of the monarchy (the shape is shown in the inscription in Hezekiah's tunnel; see Part IV, C, 1: A Remarkable Hydraulic Engineering Feat), rather than the square characters current in Hasmonean times, as shown in our pictures. This insistence on the use of archaic letters is typical of the subsequent periods, right up to the time of Bar Kochba, who led a war of independence against Rome in A.D. 131–135 (see Part VI, A, 4: Bar Kochba's Rule of Jerusalem). An interesting point is that the coins which have only Hebrew on them bear the Hebrew name of the ruler, e.g. Jonathan (Alexander Jannaeus) or Yehuda (Aristobulus II), while the Greek inscriptions on the bilingual coins give the Greek name, Alexander, for example. The full Hebrew inscription on one side of the unilingual coins stresses the ruler's religious title, high priest, and near it was imprinted the name of the national institution, *Heber Hayehudīm*, as for instance, "Jonathan, the High Priest, and the Community of the Jews *(Heber Hayehudīm)*." The bilingual coins, on the other hand, stress his secular position — Jonathan *ha-Melech* (the King) in Hebrew, and Alexander Basileos (King Alexander) in Greek. A specifically new Hebrew title may be noted for John Hyrcanus II (son of Alexander Jannaeus): "Jonathan the High Priest and Head of the *Heber Hayehudīm*," which may suggest the new title, ethnarch (national ruler) granted to him in 47 B.C. by Julius Caesar as a vassal of the Roman Republic.

6. THE HASMONEAN KINGDOM

The fate of the Hasmonean Kingdom was decided by two interacting elements. The theocratic element in Jewish society was expressed in the title of high priest borne by the ruler. In this capacity, he was intimately connected with the Temple, the core of the religious and spiritual life of the nation. The secular element designated the ruler as king, and as time went by the Hasmonean rulers became kings, enjoying the great power and wealth characteristic of contemporary hellenistic rulers. It was the inevitable sequel to the creation of a strong kingdom which had fought many wars and expanded its borders, a kingdom which promoted a progressive economy and a style of life considerably influenced by the hellenistic civilization which had taken root in neighboring lands.

Considering the complex nature of Jewish culture, it was only natural that these developments contributed to several divergent religious trends among the pious elements in the country. Each of them played a vital role in the national life and its psyche. Josephus mentions three main sects or divisions: the Pharisees, the Sadducees, and the Essenes, who were already in existence in the days of the Hasmonean high priest Jonathan (*Antiquities* XIII:171). The *Sadducees*, originating in the priesthood, the landed aristocracy, the court officials, and the great merchants, held fast to tradition and the way of life sanctified by the circle close to the Temple. They were the pillars of a theocratic community, and strove to maintain their great influence in religious and political life. The pietist *Pharisees* had evolved from earlier Hassidean circles, and in the days of Judah the Maccabee they had been closer to the ordinary people among whom they lived. They were dedicated to a strict observance of the Law and to ritual purity, and it was they who applied themselves exceedingly to setting up the *halakhot*, the interpretation of the Law and its rules of behavior. The Hasmonean rulers strove alternately to gain the cooperation of one or the other section, thus creating strife and frequent confrontations between the king and his people. Alexander Jannaeus, for example, collaborated with the Sadducees in preference to the Pharisees, while his widow and successor, Shlomzion (Salome, 76–67 B.C.) restored the Pharisees to favor and assured them of a dominant position. The *Essenes*, a religious communalistic sect or brotherhood, shunned power and pomp and thus figured even less, or not at all, in royal politics. (The beliefs of the Pharisees, Sadducees and Essenes are summed up in the Glossary.) On the whole, the Hasmoneans failed to resolve the basic conflict between secular and hellenistic culture on the one hand, and biblical traditions, Mosaic regulations and the spiritual needs of the nation on the other.

7. ROME APPEARS

Internecine struggle was one of the main causes of the decline of the dynasty and its tragic end. The strife culminated in civil war just at the time that republican Rome was trying to gain a foothold in near eastern affairs. Through poor statesmanship and inability to settle internal differences in the face of an external threat, the last Hasmoneans virtually threw away their kingdom. The Roman general Pompey marched on Jerusalem to find it in the throes of a civil war between Aristobulus II and Hyrcanus II, the sons of Alexander Jannaeus. Hyrcanus surrendered the city and the Hasmonean palace to Pompey without a struggle, though Aristobulus continued to fight and took refuge in the Temple Mount which was a stronghold in its own right. Pompey stormed the Temple Mount and captured the Birah fortress at its northwestern end after a three-month siege in 63 B.C. The struggle ended in the subjugation of Jerusalem under Roman domination.

Jerusalem's capture by the Romans foreshadowed a tremendous change in the fortunes of the capital and of Judea. Alexander, son of Aristobulus, made an attempt to restore Hasmonean rule over Jerusalem, but this venture was thwarted by Gabinus, the Roman governor of Syria, who marched on Jerusalem in 57 B.C. By that time, Jerusalem

Detail of the Hasmonean city wall (second century B.C.) over which Herod built his Citadel in the following century

was no longer the independent capital city of the Jewish state, but perforce a vassal of Rome. When Hyrcanus II was reinstated by Pompey, he was given authority only over the Temple. Real power in Judea, under Roman suzerainty, was vested in Antipater the Idumaean, who was named financial administrator of Judea. He was Herod's father.

8. THE JUDAIZED IDUMAEANS

Antipater was a member of a distinguished Idumaean family. His rise to the ruling power in Jerusalem (as described by Josephus in *War* I:37–38) came through skillful maneuvering during the internecine struggles of the last Hasmonean princes. In post-exilic days, Edomites had moved northward from their towns in Mount Seir (Edom) towards southern Judah. They settled alongside of the Jewish natives in this area and in the course of time were assimilated. The district, whose centers were the cities of Maresha and Adorāim, became known as Idumaea, and its inhabitants Idumaeans. They were converted to Judaism in the days of the Hasmonean hegemony, when Idumaea was annexed to the Jewish kingdom. Though still labelled as Idumaeans because of their mixed background, to distinguish them from 'Jews' in the strict sense, they nevertheless were acknowledged as full co-religionists and played an important role in the Jewish community, especially with regard to economic and political matters. What was true of Idumaeans generally, applied in particular to Antipater and Herod. While the latter provoked a great deal of hostility and resentment on the part of pious Jews, there can be no question of his own devotion to the faith, as his life-long commitment to the reconstruction of the Temple Mount, including the holy Temple itself, and the other public buildings indicated.

F. HEROD'S PERIOD

Antipater's ascent to power in the days of Hyrcanus II was accompanied by a division between the political and religious sectors of government, under Roman supervision. Julius Caesar invested Hyrcanus with the title "High Priest and Ethnarch" or, in Jewish terms, "High Priest and Head of the Jewish Council." At the same time, he named Antipater *Epitrophos* (Procurator), which made him the effective ruler of Judea. Permission was granted to Hyrcanus to rebuild the walls of Jerusalem but the work was actually carried out by Antipater. This background helps to explain the rise to power of Antipater's two sons, Phasael and Herod, who were appointed *Tetrarchs* (district civil administrators) in the State of Judea following the murder of their father, the evil genius of the Hasmonean dynasty. But this did not yet end the struggle of the Hasmoneans to maintain their right to rule over Jerusalem and Judea. The invasion of the Parthians, Rome's enemies, into Syria in 40 B.C. enabled the Hasmonean, Antigonus, to reestablish his sovereignty over Jerusalem (40–37 B.C.). He remained in power for only a brief period, while Herod was busy securing effective Roman support for a counterattack. Anthony and Cleopatra saw in Herod a useful instrument against the Parthians, and the Roman Senate crowned him King of the Jews and Friend of Rome. With Roman help, Herod besieged Jerusalem. Josephus gives a dramatic account of the siege, then of his successful assault on the city, in which the walls north of the Temple were smashed with the use of ramming engines, and finally of the capture of the Upper City and the Temple *(Antiquities:* XIV:487). According to our historian, Herod and his Roman cohort stormed and captured the city on the Day of Atonement, and a frightful slaughter ensued. Herod then consolidated his power as an ally and vassal of Rome. Major political changes occurred when Herod, with the backing of Roman troops supplied by Anthony, defeated Antigonus and captured Jerusalem in 37 B.C. After his enthronement as the king of Judea, Herod, having decimated the aristocracy of Jerusalem, found it necessary to create a new establishment upon which he could depend.

Herod reigned as King of the Jews, an epithet by which he was tagged to distinguish him from a 'Jewish king', from 36–4 B.C. over a strong, substantial kingdom. His rule was marked by the tyranny and ruthlessness characteristic of the hellenistic states of the near east, a style not greatly improved by the Roman intrusion into that area. But it took this very ruthlessness, combining cunning and courage in equal parts, to hold power despite radical changes in external and internal circumstances throughout his long reign. Herod effected a thoroughgoing transformation of Judea; its metropolis, Jerusalem, expanded enormously and its population, drawn from the whole kingdom and from every part of the Jewish diaspora, from the near east and northern Africa, from southern Europe and the Mediterranean islands, grew at an astonishing rate.

Herod favored the hellenizing elements in Jerusalem society for administrative, military, and diplomatic purposes; indeed, many gentiles occupied key positions in the kingdom's hierarchy and undoubtedly helped to reshape in basic ways the character of the kingdom. Notwithstanding, he remained faithful to the Jewish tradition, insofar as it did not affect his position as king and the attitude of the Roman-hellenistic world towards him. He had to face constantly the challenge of serving the religious interests of the Jews, and was therefore very careful not to offend popular sensibilities by disregard of age-old customs and practices upheld by the orthodox Pharisees whom the populace respected. He observed Jewish ritual very closely. Some scholars believe that Herod's main achievement in building the Temple was motivated by his desire to gain divine approval and also in order to deny the argument put forth by the orthodox Pharisean rabbis that his kingdom would meet the same tragic end as that met by the Hasmonean dynasty because it was not descended from the House of David. At the same time, he was bound to safeguard his position as a faithful vassal of the Roman empire, and maintain his ties with the hellenistic world. His arbitrary acts were dictated by reasons of state. This ambivalence in Herod's divided loyalties met different responses among the people. The more orthodox Jews distrusted him, though they enjoyed the general prosperity of the time. The more cosmopolitan circles who were exposed to hellenistic cultural influences, as well as the wealthier classes, appeared to see both sides of the picture. On the whole, the people's attitude swung from enmity to tolerance depending on the flow of events, but traditional Jewish writings seemed to have remembered the negative attitude. Josephus as historian was more objective.

1. HEROD AND THE HIGH PRIESTHOOD

Herod was especially interested in strengthening his ties with patrician Jewish families in the hellenistic Diaspora, in particular in Alexandria and Babylonia. He was able to do so through the deliberate selection of successive high priests from such families, disregarding the tradition, by then well established, that the high priest should come from the Hasmonean line. It is not suprising, therefore, to learn that the House of Phiabi, which attained eminence in Jerusalem and claimed the high priest Joshua appointed by Herod, was apparently of Egyptian origin.

The same was true of the famed House of Boethus, whose priestly ancestor was believed to have come from Egypt (*Antiquities* XV:320). This powerful clan played an important part in shaping the character of the high priesthood during the Herodian era. The latter part of the period from the time of Herod's son, Archelaus, down to the destruction of the Temple witnessed the rivalry of the two great priestly houses — Hanan and Boethus. Though other priestly families strove for preeminence, these two were dominant, and in the long run the House of Hanan was the more successful, having achieved approval in Roman eyes. It is possible that Joseph Caiaphas, who collaborated with the Roman authority, was related to Hanan the First (i.e., son-in-law; cf. John 18:13–14).

2. SEPARATION OF POWERS UNDER HEROD

The official separation of secular and religious rule in Herod's time actually worked to the disadvantage of the high priests and radically weakened their authority. Not only did the king interfere in their activities, but their very appointment was subject to his approval. The *Heber Hayehudīm*, which had cooperated with the Hasmonean rulers, was transformed into a Sanhedrin, a judicial institution in the form of a supreme court, lacking any political prerogatives. Many changes had occurred in the nature and status of the sects. The Sadducees were more firmly entrenched than ever as the upper class, along with the priests and large landowners, all closely attached to the royal court and dependent on the king (see above: The Hasmonean Kingdom). The Pharisees, on the other hand, gradually took over the teaching function in the community from the priests and devoted themselves to the preservation of religious life and the adaptation of tradition to changing circumstances. While they wielded great influence over the common people, their influence over political affairs diminished. Meanwhile, Zealots and other enemies of the king's regime, recruited from Pharisaic circles and Essene groups, some of whom lived in Jerusalem, though the center of the sect was at Qumran in the Dead Sea region, had become more active in the course of the years.

3. HEROD THE BUILDER

In some respects, Herod may be regarded as the successor of the Hasmoneans, for example in his drive to consolidate and expand the Judean kingdom. While preserving its character and traditions — and they were truly preserved, no matter what Herod's intentions may have been — Herod also developed the economy and enhanced the prestige of Jerusalem, transforming it into a splendid metropolis, notable among the famous hellenistic cities of the Empire. At the same time, it was the religious center of the Jewish people of the Diaspora, its magnificent Temple Mount teeming with pilgrims from everywhere who went up to Jerusalem three times a year, on Passover, Shabuot (Pentecost) and Sukkot (Tabernacles), though many went less frequently.

Herod was a great builder like his ancient predecessor, Solomon, and he carried out monumental architectural projects throughout the land and even beyond its borders (to the extent permitted by the Roman governors). His main effort was centered in Jerusalem, however. His foremost endeavors were the building of his palace northwest of the Upper City, as described in great detail by Josephus (*War* V:176 ff.) and even more important, the rebuilding of the Temple on the original Mount Zion. This was Herod's own undertaking, described by Josephus and in the Mishna. The Talmudic sages declared: "He who has not seen Herod's Temple has never seen a stately structure in his life" (*Baba Bathra* 4:5). (See Part III, D: Herod's Temple, for the detailed design).

a. Herod's Palace

Herod's palace occupied an area six times as large as that occupied by regular city blocks in large hellenistic cities. Excavations of the site have given us a good idea of the palace's huge dimensions, but they do not help to recreate its true design. The palace and gardens sprawled over more than 4.5 acres which stretched through the Armenian Garden, from the present Citadel in the north to the Turkish city walls to the west and the south. The palace was built on an elevated podium and the vestiges

The base of the Tower of Phasael in Herod's Citadel (large ashlars, center) is built into the second century B.C. Hasmonean wall

excavated by Magen Broshi show that it was built over an area of 1000 × 430 feet (330 × 130 m.). The excavations unearthed five walls preserved to a height of 11.5 feet (3.5 m.). They probably belonged to the foundations of the palace and considerable portions of the podium. Nothing was found of the superstructure. Thirteen centuries later, the Crusaders erected over it the *Curia Regis*, the royal palace.

Josephus wrote that Herod's palace consisted of two main complexes, with towering structures and surrounded by parks and gardens (*War* V:176 ff.) This royal administrative complex was the active headquarters of government for Jerusalem and Judea throughout the Herodian era and later. It became the seat of authority of the Roman Procurators during the first century A.D., and this is indeed the site of Pontius Pilate's Praetorium referred to in the Gospels (though Christian medieval popular tradition places it at the head of the Via Dolorosa at the eastern end of the city). Josephus is not less eloquent in describing the three towers of the city wall which guarded the palace's northern side, which was the most vulnerable (*War* V:161). The towers were named for Herod's brother Phasael, his friend Hippicus, and his wife Mariamne, the Hasmonean princess. Nothing of these structures has survived except the base of the main tower, Phasael (popularly called the Tower of David). It is a 66 foot square, approximately 66 feet high, the same dimensions as those given by Josephus and as shown in our illustrations. Herod's building followed Roman-hellenistic architectural standards in general, though a blend of hellenistic-oriental elements is most apparent in decoration motifs. There the resemblance to hellenistic art ended. Moreover, contemporary Jewish art eschewed any pagan motifs in architecture, or in home or tomb decorations, as is evident from frescoes, panels and mosaics. (See details of Herodian building undertaking and the overall picture of the city in Part V, C, 2).

b. Expansion of the Walls

There is no doubt that Herod reinforced the Hasmonean wall which surrounded the Upper and Lower City (see above: Architectural Achievements of the Hasmonean kings), that is to say, the First Wall of Josephus, at the northwestern corner of which stood the palace and the three towers. Excavations in the present-day Citadel prove that the Phasael tower was built over the line of the original Hasmonean wall at the northwestern angle, which then turned east towards the Western Wall of the Temple Mount, north of the causeway which led from the Upper City to the Temple Mount (the Wilson Arch).

It is also known that Herod added another system of fortifications to it, described by Josephus as the Second Wall, intended to shield the urban residential quarter lying to the north of this part of the First Wall. The northern residential quarter included the marketplaces and bazaars in the upper reaches of the Tyropoeon Vale. This wall around it stretched from the towers situated north of the Palace in a northerly direction toward today's Damascus Gate, where vestiges of a Herodian tower-gate have been found. After contouring the vast urban quarter, it ended at the Antonia Tower, a new citadel built on the spot of the previous Birah. Described by Josephus (*War* V:238 ff.) as a very strong and magnificent structure commanding the Temple area, the Antonia Tower stood probably on the rock scarp on which the Arab Omariya school now stands (at the head of the traditional Via Dolorosa, a site called the First Station of the Cross). There is scant information about this wall on which fourteen towers were built, according to Josephus.

4. HEROD'S SUCCESSORS AND THE HERODIAN PERIOD

The years following Herod's death in 4 B.C. were marked by internal dissension, a legacy of bitterness from the reign of Herod, as explained above (Herod's Period). These resentments had developed in Jerusalem, in particular among the middle and working classes, over Herod's oppressive policies, the heavy burden of taxation and, above all, Herod's hostile attitude towards the Pharisees, champions of the Law. Herod's son, Archelaus, could not overcome the rebellious tendencies. These came to a climax during his visit to Rome, where he had gone to secure the sanction of Emperor Augustus for his kingship.

Bloody riots broke out on Shabuot (Pentecost) between the cohorts of Sabinus, the Roman commander governing Jerusalem, and the populace, resulting in the desecration of the Temple and the burning of the magnificent Southern and Western Porticos of the Temple Mount (see Part III, E, 2, a: The Royal Portico), which Herod had erected. The rebellion was quelled only when Varus, Roman governor of Syria, arrived in Jerusalem with fresh troops. He rescued Sabinus, who was under siege in the Royal Palace where he had taken refuge; in the aftermath, the Romans crucified about two thousand Jews. Archelaus finally returned from Rome, not as the king but simply as the titular head or Ethnarch. Even this reduced role seemed too much for him, as he was unable to consolidate his positon. In A.D. 6, his appointment was cancelled and Judea was reorganized as an administrative district within the Province of Syria. At its head was a Roman Procurator or Prefect appointed by the Emperor.

a. The Procurators' Regime (A.D. 6–41)

Very little is known about the first Procurators. Their seat of power was Caesarea, but their military and fiscal authority was centered in Jerusalem, which remained the Jewish capital. Roman administration was firm in principle, often harsh in practice, and friction with the local population and swarms of pilgrims frequently developed as a result of Roman insensitivity to Jewish religious scruples and obligations.

Pontius Pilate was Procurator from A.D. 26 to 36. According to the testimony of Josephus, he offended the Jews by bringing into Jerusalem the *signae* (insignia) of the Legion, i.e. military banners bearing the Imperial eagles, and by taking funds from the Temple treasury to build the 'Arub aqueduct bringing water from the Hebron region. In the Gospel narrative of Jesus' arrest, trial, and crucifixion in Jerusalem, Pilate is characterized as a cruel and autocratic governor. The Alexandrian Jewish philosopher Philo likewise describes him as a corrupt governor who put many innocent people to death. The tensions between ruler and ruled reached the breaking point four years later, when the Emperor Caligula ordered his statue placed in the Temple. Jerusalem was spared a bitter massacre only by the death of the emperor in A.D. 41.

What does the evidence of archeology tell us about the official title of Pontius Pilate? Instead of describing him as *Procurator*, the Latin inscription found in the amphitheater of Caesarea refers to him as *Prefect*:

[Po]ntius Pilatus
[praef]ectus Iuda[ea]e

A Latin inscription found in the amphitheatre of Caesarea describes Pontius Pilate as 'Prefect'

Right: The excavation of the foundations of the Third Wall proved conclusively that they had been erected by King Agrippa I. The building was interrupted, then resumed in A.D. 66. View looking west

Left: Its position parallel to the northern walls of the Old City

This was the title of the Roman governors up to time of Claudius. They were known later as Procurators, and historians apparently applied the later title to those who preceded them.

The existing political difficulties did not hinder Jerusalem's expansion or affect adversely the prestige of the Temple as the vital center of Jewry. The Temple continued to attract multitudes of pilgrims and to serve as a dynamic focus of nationalist, religious, and social movements. The appearance of Jesus and his disciples in Jerusalem and at the Temple illustrates the central role of the city and the Temple at that time.

b. The Glorious Reign of Agrippa

Jerusalem's development continued through the comparatively short but significant reign of Agrippa I (A.D. 37–44), grandson of Herod and Mariamne. He ruled over the entire Jewish area of Palestine only during the last three years of his reign. He was an outstanding spokesman of compromise, like his grandfather had been, though without Herod's glaring faults. He succeeded in winning the favors of Caligula, and of Claudius after him. First appointed as the ruler of the Roman province north of Palestine, he ruled also over the entire Jewish area of Palestine only during the last years of his reign. Many of the people may have been less intransigeant than in Herod's time, but Agrippa proved more popular. In any case, the Pharisee leaders appreciated his strict conformity with the tenets of Jewish law and they must have shut their eyes to many of his acts, such as minting coins bearing his own image, which Herod never dared to do. On a cultural level, his short reign represents a further link in the toleration of hellenistic ways by the Jews. Any literature which typifies this trend has largely perished, but monuments of the Herodian period after the death of its initiator are extant and attest to it. In a few short years he was able to carry out important projects in the city. He laid great stress on Jerusalem's economic welfare, and is probably responsible for the development of its trading centers: the upper and the lower markets in the Tyropoeon Vale. This is evidenced by the weights we uncovered near the western and southern walls of the Temple Mount, which dated from the fifth year of his reign (A.D. 41) and are inscribed with his name and the title of king (*Basileus*, in Greek). In the sixth year of his reign, he struck coins intended for use by the Jewish population, using the hallowed canopy as the symbol of his rule. The coins intended for the foreign sections of his kingdom bear the Emperor's head and figure. This is the only image of a king ever to appear on a Judean coin.

c. The Third Wall

Agrippa's reign is also associated with the reinforcement of the city walls, particularly those sections which protected the city to the south and east (in the Lower City). His greatest achievement, however, was the Third Wall, described by Josephus (*War* V:148 ff.). It encircled the New City lying to the north of Jerusalem on its western, northern, and eastern sides, comprising, at that time, the spacious quarter known as Beth Zeta (Bezetha). There is good reason to believe that the Third Wall, which started, according to Josephus, at the Hippicus Tower built by Herod in his Citadel, reached the

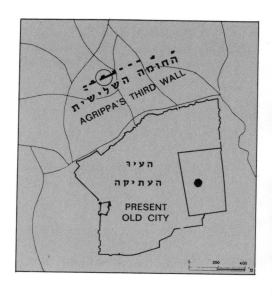

Psephinus Tower at its northern extension (in modern Jerusalem's Russian Compound) and from there turned east as far as a spot facing the Mausoleum of Queen Helen, the so-called Tombs of the Kings in East Jerusalem (see Part V, E: The Mausoleum of Queen Helen). It continued around the New City on the north and east, and then descended into the Kidron valley. The ambitious plan of the Third Wall could not be completed, according to Josephus. The work was interrupted owing, apparently, to Roman misgivings and possibly by order of Emperor Claudius himself. In any case, a last attempt was made to complete it after the death of Agrippa I during the great rebellion (A.D. 66–70), right up to the eve of the Roman capture of Jerusalem.

Remains of the wall were identified by E.L. Sukenik and L.A. Mayer in 1925–1927 and 1940, confirming Edward Robinson's nineteenth century survey. More sections have come to light in recent years. To date, a total of some 4,125 feet (1,200 meters) of the wall have been traced. The identification of this line of the Third Wall has been questioned and even opposed by a few scholars. Father L.H. Vincent tried to identify it with what he termed "Bar Kochba's improvised protective wall" thrown up in A.D. 135. On the basis of new excavations in 1961–1967, Kathleen Kenyon suggested that the wall constituted the circumvallio (siege wall) erected by the Roman legions to face the walls of Jerusalem in A.D. 69–70. However, there has been further investigation. In the fall of 1972, excavations were resumed under the direction of Sarah ben-Aryeh on behalf of the Department of Antiquities of the Israel Government. They uncovered the substructures of the wall and, in their midst, the remains of a tower which bulged north-wards (the more vulnerable exposure, unprotected by natural ravines) by some 30 feet (9 meters) over a length of about 148 feet (45 meters), between the Nablus Road and the Road of the Engineering Corps. Various features — the width of the wall (14 feet; 4.3 meters), the northern orientation of the tower and, more significantly, shards of the

Above right: The 'burnt house' of the priest Kathros discovered in the Upper City

Below: A heap of objects found *in situ* in the house included a stone table, a high-footed stone vase, a stone weight marked *dbr Kathros*

Herodian period found in the fill in the area south of the wall's substructure — point to the identification of this structure with Agrippa's Third Wall as described by Josephus. In view of its thickness and tremendous size, its stones cut in the Herodian style (i.e. their flat margin around the four edges and the slightly raised flat boss), its ninety towers, each one about 198 feet (60 meters) distant from the next and set in a line 13,860 feet (4,200 meters) long and its masonry stones robbed from other structures, testifying to poor planning, it could be attributed only to the fact that though it was started in the days of Agrippa, it was finished hurriedly at the time of the great rebellion.

d. Agrippa II

The death of Agrippa I in A.D. 44 proved a severe shock to Jerusalem and to Judea. After Agrippa's death, Claudius decided that his son, Agrippa II, was too young to reign and he re-instated the procuratorial administration, which lasted until the beginning of the great rebellion in A.D. 66. The Procurators' power was seriously restricted, however, owing to the high position of Agrippa II, who was eventually granted a smaller kingdom in Galilee and northern Transjordan which were occupied by mixed populations. He was later re-instated in Jerusalem, where his main headquarters were in the renovated Hasmonean Palace in the Upper City. This location proved to be a source of friction between him and his sister Berenice on the one hand, and the city notables on the other, for Agrippa and his sister were in the habit of watching the performance of certain holy rites in the Temple courtyard from the roof of their palace, thus offending religious sensibilities as the rites were the exclusive province of the priestly caste. In fact, the priests erected a partition on the west side of the Temple area in order to prevent onlookers from observing the ritual (*Antiquities* XX:189).

The king was keenly involved in the city's improvements and is known to have employed large numbers of construction workers to pave city streets with white slabs (*Antiquities* XX:129). We have become familiar with this paving in the course of our excavations, and can definitely attribute the impressive wide pavements uncovered west and south of the Temple Mount to Agrippa II (see Part V, C, 1, d: Archeological Links of the Central Thoroughfare).

5. THE OLIGARCHY OF THE HIGH PRIESTS

The high priests' standing in public life had risen considerably through the era of the Procurators because they also represented the highest administrative authority over an important and prosperous kingdom. They remained, however, dependent on Agrippa II who had the power, for a time, to appoint and dismiss the high priest. In the thirty years which preceded the war with Rome, there had been twenty-eight high priests, stemming mainly from four families: Boethus (which included the Cantherus family), Hanan (Annas), Phiabi, and Kimchit (Kathros). As was natural in those days, the priestly oligarchy held most of the important positions in the land, including direct responsibility for the ritual as well as the administration and fiscal affairs in the Temple.

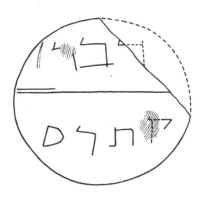

This situation is echoed with bitterness in the Talmud, *Pesachim* 57:71.

> Woe is me because of the House of Boethus; woe is me because of their staves.
> Woe is me because of the House of Hanan; woe is me because of their incantations.
> Woe is me because of the House of Kathros; woe is me because of their pens.
> Woe is me because of the House of Ishmael, the son of Phiabi; woe is me because of their fists.
> For they are the High Priests, and their sons are treasurers, and their sons-in-law are trustees, and their servants beat the people with staves.

a. Discovery of the House of Kathros

Professor N. Avigad's excavations on Misgav-Ladach Street in the Jewish Quarter (formerly the Upper City) uncovered remains of this period, consisting chiefly of a patrician house 592 square feet (55 square meters) in area, dating from the Herodian period. It had been destroyed during the sack of Jerusalem by the Roman legionaries. The two-story dwelling had been carefully planned. It consisted of a hall, four rooms, a kitchen, and a *mikveh* (ritual bath) on the ground floor; nothing, however, remained of the floor above it. An interesting collection of artifacts was found there, including pottery,

Stone relief, dating to Hasmonean times, of a cornucopia with hanging ribbons. A pomegranate is depicted between the two horns

stoneware, glass, a clay inkwell and stone tables. The household furnishings and other artifacts bespoke the wealth and noble status of the family which lived there. It was therefore not surprising though gratifying to find in this house a stone weight marked *Dbr Kthrs* (belonging to bar Kathros), the name of one of the high priests of that time, a direct reference to the priestly House of Kathros referred to in the passage quoted above. A pathetic human touch was the discovery of a young woman's forearm leaning against the kitchen wall. She had failed to escape from the burning house before it collapsed over her (see Part I, G, 3: The Patrician Life-style).

b. Contemporary Art Designs, Decorations and Mosaics

The many finds in this dwelling are of priceless value for the study of art patterns, decorative designs and styles of workmanship exhibited by the master artisans of Jerusalem; the same applies to sections of frescoes still visible in the wall plaster with their wealth of geometric and floral designs. One of them depicts a seven-branched menorah (candelabrum), probably a representation of the menorah in the Temple. Similar geometric and floral designs were discovered by Magen Broshi in his excavation at the Saint Saviour Church area on Mount Zion. The latter, however, included figures of birds. It should be noted, in this connection, that neither the contemporary mosaics uncovered in Avigad's excavations in the Jewish Quarter nor the remains of art work discovered in the excavations near the Temple walls have any representations of animal figures or particularly the human form, in strict conformity with the ancient Jewish taboo forbidding this form of art (cf. the Decalogue, see Exodus 20:4).

c. The City of Holiness and Religious Teaching; Its Internal Government

In the years between the reign of Agrippa I (A.D. 41–44) and the start of the rebellion against Rome (A.D. 66) Jerusalem had reached an apogee of growth and flourished as never before. Following an orderly plan, the city had been rebuilt and enlarged gradually since Herod's time. Many public undertakings had been accomplished by the local authorities, Herod's successors, and even Roman procurators. The community had managed to preserve its autonomy in internal affairs through the agency of the high priesthood and the City Council *(Bouleh)*, which was recruited from the civic leaders. In addition, the Sanhedrin, made up of Pharisee and Sadducee masters of the Law, regulated judicial and religious matters by drawing up directive rules (*Halakhot* or rabbinic law) from an interpretation of the commandments of the Torah (Law). At the top of this pyramid was Agrippa II (A.D. 48–70), whose prestige stood unchallenged because of his close ties with imperial Rome.

Dedicatory stone from a first century A.D. synagogue in the Ophel. The Greek inscription reads: "Theodotus son of Vettenos who was priest and Archisynagogos, son of Archisynagogos, and grandson of Archisynagogos, built this synagogue for reading the Law and teaching the commandments, also the hospice, chambers and water installations for the service of visiting guests from abroad. This synagogue was founded by his ancestors and the elders and Simonides"

The City of Holiness absorbed an ever-increasing stream of Jewish immigrants and converts of high standing, who came to settle or to acquire burial sites in the numerous cemeteries encircling the city. The proliferation of synagogues was phenomenal; Talmudic sources mention, with obvious exaggeration, the presence of as many as 480 synagogues, each with a school for scholarly study of the Law, and many with a hospice for pilgrims.

d. Synagogues

Synagogues had developed naturally throughout the Jewish Diaspora in the Hasmonean and Herodian periods. They were required also throughout Palestine in the days of the Second Temple for daily worship, public assembly and for study. They were of the type in which Jesus was accustomed to speak to the people (Matthew 4:23, etc.). The synagogues discovered in the country date to the centuries after the destruction of the Temple, but two synagogues built before that time have been discovered, one by Yigael Yadin at Masada, and the other in the winter-palace built by Herod at Herodion, east of Bethlehem.

The ruins of a synagogue were uncovered by R. Weill in a group of structures at the southern end of the Ophel. Among the remains was found a smoothly squared stone, inscribed in Greek, recording that Theodotos, the son of Vattenos, son and grandson of a priest and archisynagogos (head of the synagogue) had completed (or rehabilitated) the synagogue for the reading of the Law and the teaching of the commandments, and built an inn with rooms and a water supply for housing needy travelers. The family which initiated this project may have originated in Rome and then come to settle in Jerusalem. The synagogue was apparently built in A.D. 65.

Literary sources and numerous inscriptions left behind in Jerusalem and its tombs testify to the great variety of the groups for whom the Holy City was their ultimate destination. The book of Acts (2:5 ff.) reflects this diversity in its vivid description of the Jews resident in Jerusalem, "devout men from every nation under heaven," who gathered at Mount Zion and heard with amazement "each of us in his own native language," although all those speaking were Galileans.

Another illustration of this process of integration of patrician families from the Diaspora is found on a complex of family tombs on Mount Scopus in northeastern Jerusalem (see Part V, E, 4: The Family Tombs on Mount Scopus).

G. THE WAR OF THE JEWS

1. THE GATHERING STORM

During this period, the people of Jerusalem were undergoing a series of crises, of increasing severity, involving religious, social, and political divisions and conflicts. They lived under the rule of a series of Procurators who were basically corrupt and incompetent, with persistent leanings toward cruelty and violence all too characteristic of Roman provincial officials, combined with a callous if not calculated contempt for Jews and the things which they held most sacred. Also part of the machinery of government and the establishment was a local oligarchy consisting of the high priesthood, its retainers, and civil administrators drawn from or bound to the wealthy classes, who were dependent upon the Procurators.

Messianic movements proliferated, ranging from passive apocalyptic to active political, mostly at odds with each other, and united only by their total opposition to the establishment. Thus proliferated the different Zealot parties, composed of militant resistance fighters, among the masses in Jerusalem and Judea. Clashes broke out continuously among these parties, but in the end the pendulum swung toward widespread rebellion and open war.

Insurrection broke out in the days of the last Procurator, Gessius Florus, who marched on Jerusalem from his headquarters in Caesarea in A.D. 66. He plundered the Temple treasury to begin with, then his soldiers overran the Upper Market, causing many deaths. The people resisted the Romans' attempt to capture the Temple area and as a result a fire broke out in the Royal Porticos on the Temple Mount. Florus' authority was rejected by the rebels and the efforts of Agrippa II to restore order and stability failed dismally. The formal sign that the whole population of Jerusalem had renounced their allegiance to Rome was the cessation of one of the Temple sacrifices in honor of the emperor, in this case Nero who had succeeded Claudius. A sacrificial ceremony in honor of the head of state in Rome had apparently been instituted on the Temple Mount, possibly since Jerusalem's capture by Pompey in 63 B.C. (or since Herod's time, according to some scholars). It symbolized Judea's submission to the overlord, but its fulfillment was a thorn in Jewish flesh.

In the first phase of the war, the Zealots took over the Lower City. They attacked the Upper City where the wealthy classes lived, burning the palaces of the high priest Ananias and Agrippa II. They also destroyed the city archives, and the council house facing the causeway opposite the Western Wall of the Temple Mount (see Part V, C, 3, d; D, 1. The Xystos; The Wilson Arch). The later phase of the open war between A.D. 66 and 70 involved a succession of dramatic clashes with the enemy, punctuated by internecine strife between the Jewish parties. Such was the nature of the desperate and ultimately doomed struggle of a divided people fighting for independence.

The Zealot uprising, backed by the people of Jerusalem, brought the governor of Syria, Cestius Gallus, to the gates of Jerusalem, destroying one Jewish settlement after

Coins of the First Revolt against Rome (A.D. 66–70)

another in his advance. Upon encountering determined resistance in Jerusalem, he withdrew and suffered a severe reverse in the pass of Beth-Horon in November of 66. The leaders of Jerusalem proceeded to form a national government of resistance, thus turning the insurrection into full-scale war.

2. TESTIMONY OF THE COINS

An expression of the spirit of national self-determination was the minting of several series of Jewish coins, many of which have come to light, throughout the years of the war. In the first year, silver coins of the Jewish Revolt were struck with the legend "Šeqel (shekel) of Israel" (or half or quarter-šeqel) on the obverse, and "Jerusalem the Holy" on the reverse, as well as bronze coins of various small denominations. In the second year of the war (A.D. 67) the legend on the reverse of the coins was changed to "Freedom of Zion," surrounded by a vine branch with leaf and tendrils; in the fourth year, the legend became "For the Redemption of Zion." The language and script of the coinage are archaic Hebrew, following the policy adopted by the Hasmonean kings on their coins, and evoking the glories of the kingdom of David and Solomon and the First Temple. The emblems inspired by liturgy or Temple rites were adopted, as shown in our pictures of contemporary coins. Such were the goblet of the Sabbath repasts and three flowers on the shekel, or the amphora of the Feast of Tabernacles, baskets of the first fruits, branches and citron trees on bronze coins, or palms and vine leaves on the Second Year coins. Thus the nation proclaimed its independence to itself and to the world during the years of the uprising in A.D. 67–70, when the Romans were repulsed and busy reorganizing for the final attack. The Holy City was free, meanwhile, so the Temple dues could now be paid in Jewish coinage, while Imperial coins depreciated.

3. THE DESTRUCTION OF THE TEMPLE

The turning point in the revolt came with the defeat of the Jewish field armies by the Roman commander and future emperor, Vespasian, who methodically subdued Galilee and the outlying parts of Judea. In Jerusalem, there were clashes between Jewish

A silver coin of Emperor Vespasian, father of Titus, found on the plaza facing the Southern Wall of the Temple Mount

groups which sapped the strength, energy and resources of the resistance movement. Extremist Zealots finally gained ascendancy, first a group led by John of Gischala and later another led by Simon bar-Giora. John of Gischala established himself in the Temple area and reinforced it with four towers, thus securing a position which dominated the upper ridge of the Ophel. Simon bar-Giora controlled the Herodian palace to the west, the Upper City and other quarters. In A.D. 69 Vespasian was proclaimed emperor and returned to Rome. He left his son Titus to continue the war, now in its last stages, and to lay siege to Jerusalem in the spring of the year 70.

Titus commanded an army of four legions plus auxiliaries, eighty thousand men in all. He also had at his disposal the best siege equipment of the period: great *ballistas* which propelled stones and iron darts, siege towers, and battering rams. He built a wide circumvallatio (siege-wall) around the city to isolate it from help and supplies. Then he threw up earth ramparts against the walls in preparation for a direct assault. His forces made the initial breach in the Third Wall; then they broke through the Second Wall and finally, in July, they stormed the Antonia Citadel and entered the Temple Mount platform and the outer courts. The fate of the city was already decided but the fighting continued with terrible bloodshed around the Inner Courts until the collapse of bitter resistance around the sanctuary itself.

Titus seems to have deliberated at length as to whether to preserve the Temple or destroy it. According to Josephus, he decided against destroying it, but a Roman source

This is how Roman battering rams were operated to break down the walls of Jerusalem

Roman war engines, resembling those used by Titus in the siege of Jerusalem. *Ballista* shooting heavy arrows. The siege towers, pulled close to the besieged walls, were manned by archers and (top) by the soldiers operating the battering rams (bottom). The attackers approaching the walls were protected in huts on wheels covered with hides to deflect the arrows or boiling oil poured down from the walls

Left: When the city fell (A.D. 70), Titus carried off great booty and thousands of prisoners. He was given a "Triumphal" reception on his return to Rome; the details of the procession are recorded on the Arch of Titus erected for the occasion and still standing

Right: The seven-branched candelabrum or menorah noticeable in the procession

asserts that he was in favor of doing so. According to Josephus, the matter was taken out of his hands by a Roman legionary who threw a burning brand into the sanctuary, setting it afire.

With the burning of the Temple, the organized religious, social and political life of the Jewish people was demolished and their dream of national independence shattered. The ninth of Ab (in the Jewish calendar), date of the destruction of both the First and Second Temples as accepted by Jewish tradition, was forever to be seared in the Jewish psyche as a symbol of supreme tragedy.

After the attack on the Temple, the Romans quickly captured the Lower City, but the Upper City held out for another month. Five months after the beginning of the siege, the massive towers of Herod's Palace and Citadel, the final stronghold of the Zealot defenders, were stormed and taken. The whole city with its fortifications, buildings, and market places was destroyed by September of the year 70. There was wholesale slaughter of the population, with thousands of survivors of the war being crucified in front of the wall as a gruesome reminder and grim warning to any who might challenge the authority of Rome. Other thousands were deported to the slave markets of the empire. Though Josephus' exaggerated figures must be examined critically, his record of a million and one hundred thousand dead and ninety-seven thousand prisoners may be taken as an indication of the magnitude of the disaster that befell the nation. The population of Jerusalem, including a large number of pilgrims trapped in the city, had been decimated and the whole city was a shambles.

Among the few structures left was the northern tower (Phasael) of the Citadel, which Titus had left intact as a monument to show how well fortified the city had been (*War* VII:505). The lower layers of the walls of the Temple Mount also survived at various heights, but this was not by design. Rather, they were so massive and so solidly built that they proved almost indestructible — thereby providing one of the major finds of the present excavations. Josephus writes an epitaph for Jerusalem and its tragic demise: "But neither its long history, nor its vast wealth, nor its people dispersed through the whole world, nor the unparalleled renown of its worship, sufficed to avert the ruin. So ended the siege of Jerusalem" (War X:10).

The leaders of the rebellion were captured. John of Gischala was sentenced to imprisonment for life, while Simon bar-Giora was led, a prisoner, in the triumphal procession of Titus and put to death at its close. The capture of Jerusalem was memorialized on Titus' Triumphal Arch in Rome. On it are depicted the sacred objects from the Temple, including the seven-branched candelabrum *(menorah)*, being carried in procession to symbolize the triumph of pagan Rome over Jerusalem the Holy.

Two specific incidents described by Josephus in reference to the rebellion are of particular archeological interest in determining the location of the Xystos (see Part V, C, 3, d: The Xystos). One of them relates to the causeway which led from one side of the Tyropoeon Vale to the Temple Gate over the Wilson Arch (see above, E, 1: The Hasmoneans). This causeway, in the fourth year of the war, served to separate the two rival commanders, John of Gischala and Simon bar-Giora. Each of them erected a tower at

his end of the passage, "John over the gates above the Xystos (on the side of the Temple Mount) and Simon on the Xystos side..." When the Roman general, Titus, wished to address the Jews who had shut themselves up in the Temple fortress, he took up a position at the western end "near the gates of Xystos, and called on them to surrender" (*War* VI:191, 337; VI:324 etc.).

The other incident relates to Simon bar-Giora's attempt to escape during the last days of the siege. He led a group, including experienced diggers, down to one of the secret subterranean passages under the Temple Mount. Under his direction, they started to excavate a tunnel through fallen debris which would lead out to freedom. The attempt failed, however. Dressed in a white tunic over which floated an ample purple robe, he emerged suddenly, like a phantom, from beneath the earth, amid the ruins of the Temple area. At this point, he was captured by the Romans. Each of these two events points to a specific locality which can be further pinpointed by reference to Josephus' account, and they can both be traced on our map 3 (p. 207).

H. REBUILDING ATTEMPTS

A number of attempts had been made to restore the Temple after A.D. 70. The first attempt in A.D. 132-135 has been described in Part I, B: The Romans Ignored the Temple Mount.

וראיתם ושש לבכם
ועצמותם כדשא

וראיתם ושש לבכם
ועצמותם כדשא

One of the most sensational discoveries made while uncovering the Western Wall, was the Hebrew inscription citing an inspired passage from Isaiah 66: 14. It epitomized a hopeful attempt to restore the Temple in the days of Emperor Julian the Apostate in the third century A.D.

1. A SECOND ATTEMPT

In A.D. 362–363, the emperor Julian, called "the Apostate," sought to break up the alliance between the empire and the Christian church, and to restore pagan worship. In order to alienate the Church he also decided to allow the Jews to resettle in Jerusalem and to restore the Temple in the most Christianized city of the Holy Land. This decision evoked tremendous enthusiasm among Diaspora Jewry. Work on the Temple actually began, but when Julian died in 363 it had to be abandoned.

The Isaiah Inscription in the Western Wall

Hope had been crushed once more, and an inscription which we found in the course of uncovering the Western Wall seems to be the only mute relic left of this fourth century project. Carved in one of the huge stones, it reads, "You shall see, and your heart shall rejoice; your bones shall flourish like the grass" (Isaiah 66:14). This passage is quoted from the brilliant vision of the prophet beginning with the words "As one whom his mother comforts, so I will comfort you; you shall be comforted in Jerusalem, and you shall see, and your heart..." (Isaiah 66:13–14). The carved verse stands as the written evidence of the people's devotion to the holy place through centuries of hope and disappointment.

2. A THIRD REBUILDING ATTEMPT

In the early seventh century, near the end of Byzantine rule, the emperors of Byzantium had alienated the majority of the people of Palestine. Many Jews still living in the country, especially in Galilee and southen Judea, were driven to despair by imperial attempts to convert them. This explains the relative ease with which the Persians, allies of the Jews, conquered the Holy Land in A.D. 614. For a time, local administration was handed over to the Jews in Jerusalem and hopes of restoring the Temple ran high. But as

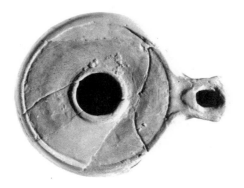

Oil lamps, Herodian period

the Jews were in a minority, the Persians changed their attitude and restored Jerusalem to Christian control. Eventually, Emperor Heraclius reconquered Palestine in A.D. 629 and restored Byzantine rule. Nevertheless the incident seems to have left its mark on the Temple Mount precincts: a late Byzantine building uncovered near the southwestern corner of the Temple Mount showed evidence of Jewish habitation: drawings of menorahs (seven-branched candelabra) were found in the lintel and the entrance room of the building. (See Part VI, B, 2: Roman and Byzantine Structures near the Temple Mount.)

3. THE EVERLASTING HOPE OF THE CITY'S REDEMPTION AND RECONSTRUCTION

As far back as Herodian times, a number of groups of diehards, regarding themselves as the 'true defenders of the faith of Israel' (such as the Hassideans in Maccabean days) held fast to the belief that the Temple would fall but be rebuilt by the will of the God of Israel. This provides the obvious explanation of Jesus' utterance regarding the downfall of Jerusalem and its eventual reconstruction through other than a human agency. Later Christian theologians have placed a different meaning on this expression of deep concern for the Holy City. Let us look for a moment at some ancient records:

a. The longing for the redemption of Jerusalem after it fell under Roman domination is manifest in many ancient writings we know such as Luke 2:38 who speaks of "all who were looking for the redemption of Jerusalem." The concept finds popular expression in the coins of the Jewish rebellion and war with Rome which proclaim: "The Redemption of Jerusalem." One of the hymns which came to light in the Dead Sea Scrolls declares:

"Your hopes, O Zion, are great indeed

For your expectation of redemption and peace will come true..."

b. The only ancient source which affirms that the 'New Jerusalem' will descend from God out of heaven is found in the New Testament book of Revelation (21) which dates to the days of Emperor Domitian (A.D. 81–96). This concept assumed an even deeper meaning in the theology of the Middle Ages.

c. Prior to Jerusalem's collapse, people firmly believed that it would never be destroyed. Others thought that the city would fall, but that the Temple would be saved.

d. The flight of the early Judeo-Christians from the city before the war with Rome was prompted by the fear of its doom.

e. The view expressed in Luke's prophecy over Jerusalem (Chapter 21) was shared by many circles. The Temple was destroyed once more. This was followed by long subjection to Rome as well as the dispersal of Israel. But the people kept hoping for a return to Zion, the rebuilding of Jerusalem and the Temple.

PART III

THE TEMPLE MOUNT AND THE TEMPLE

A. THE TEMPLE MOUNT

Located at the highest point (2,437 feet above sea level) of the northern end of Mount Zion, the Temple Mount of Jerusalem is separated from the Upper City (the Western hill) by the Vale called Tyropoeon by Josephus, and from the Mount of Olives on the east by the Kidron valley. The Ophel hill of ancient Jerusalem, site of the Lower City, the City of David, is actually only the southern and lower slope of the same mountain.

Information about the Temple Mount is sparse for the period preceding David, i.e. prior to about 1000 B.C. It certainly lay outside the confines of the fortified hill of ancient Jerusalem, but was under the control of the rulers of the Citadel of Zion since David's time. Moreover, an ancient tradition, associated with the story of Abraham's near-sacrifice of Isaac (Genesis 22), links the site with one of the mountains in the Land of Moriah where the Patriarch Abraham erected an altar, naming it *Yahweh-yir'eh*: "the Lord will see; as it is said to this day, 'on the mount of the Lord he will be seen.'" (Genesis 22:14) — a symbolic allusion to Jerusalem. The site seems to have been held in reverence since very ancient times.

According to tradition, King David erected an altar to the God of Israel on Mount Moriah (II Chronicles 3:1) on the threshing floor which he had purchased from Araunah (Ornan) the Jebusite, apparently the former ruler of the Jebusite Citadel of Zion. Threshing floors situated on prominent and exposed areas in the proximity of cities often served as centers of ritual and public assembly in ancient times. The hilltop, in any case, was hallowed by divine command; the Prophet Nathan and other seers of the royal court regarded it as holy ground, appropriate to serve as the national center of the Jewish people. It is for this reason that Mount Zion and Mount Moriah came to be known by other names, such as the Temple Mount, the Mountain of the Lord, the Holy Mountain. It continues as the focus of faith, hope and devotion for all future generations.

View of the so-called Solomon Stables or underground vaulted halls situated beneath the southeastern angle of the Temple esplanade. The vast structure supports the southeastern surface of the esplanade. The halls were used as the storehouses of the Temple. The bases of the arches are Herodian and belong, in fact, to the time of Herod's erection of the platform. The upper part of the arches were rebuilt in the Crusader period, when the halls were used as stables

Below: Archways of the Solomon Stables

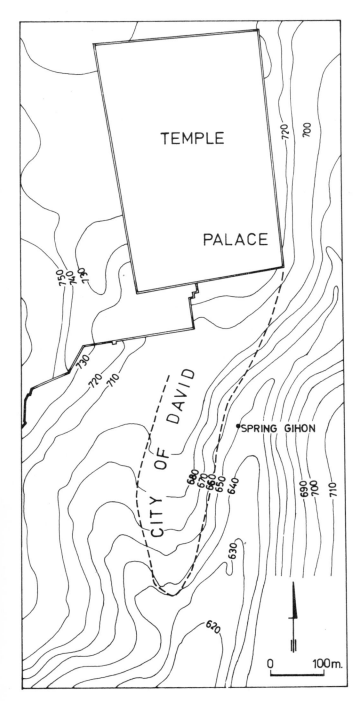

Conjectural plan of the site of the First Temple of Solomon in relation to the City of David prior to the city's expansion during his reign. The continuous black line is the present wall of the Temple Mount (the Haram es-Sherif) and Old City, and is included for orientation (see Map 1, p. 56)

This inscribed shard found in the Israelite temple at Arad, dating to the period of the Judean Monarchy, mentions "bet YHWH", the typical biblical designation for a temple

B. THE FIRST TEMPLE

The Temple built by King Solomon on the hill of Moriah, where the Dome of the Rock now stands, was the main structure among the magnificent buildings he erected within the royal enclosure or acropolis of the House of David. It adjoined but was separate from the City of David, which lay south of it and was inhabited by the general population. With the completion of the Temple and the royal palace, Jerusalem became both royal domain and royal shrine, capital of the people and the Land of Israel and the "City of God, the Holy Sanctuary of Israel," exalted and hallowed by ancient tradition.

The book of Chronicles maintains that David had, in fact, made plans for the construction of the Temple, apparently during his co-regency with his son Solomon (in approximately the years 967–965 B.C.). The actual building began during the fourth year of Solomon's reign, after he had consolidated his position and formed close ties with Hiram, the Phoenician king of Tyre, who supplied him with skilled builders and masons as well as the required building materials, chiefly squared cedar wood of Lebanon. These heavy beams were tied into rafts and floated along the Mediterranean shores from the coast of Lebanon to the mouth of the Yarkon River (in present-day Tel-Aviv), and then carried overland to Jerusalem on ox-carts.

The work was completed seven years later, in the eleventh year of Solomon's reign. Then Solomon took the Holy Ark from the Tabernacle set up in the City of David, where it had been placed by his father, and brought it to the *Debir*, or Holy of Holies, of the Temple, "an exalted house, a place for thee to dwell in for ever" (I Kings 8:13). The care of the Temple was entrusted to the Davidic dynasty "for ever."

We have two descriptions of the First Temple: an earlier one in I Kings 6–7 and another, of later authorship, in II Chronicles 3–9. In addition, various biblical passages provide additional details about particular events, including repairs and renovation work which took place in its precincts for a period of nearly four centuries right up to the time of its destruction by the Babylonian king Nebuchadnezzar in 586 B.C. (see Part II, B, 8: In the Shadow of Babylon).

1. SITE OF THE ALTAR OF SACRIFICES AND FOUNDATION ROCK

The great altar of burnt sacrifices was erected east of the Temple's entrance. It was ten cubits high (approximately 6.5 feet) and was built in stepped tiers. The highest tier or *har'el* (Mountain of God) was topped by horns at the four corners. Fragments of such an altar, dating to the period of the Judean monarchy, were recently discovered in the excavations of Beersheba.

The popular notion, still supported by some, that the Altar of Sacrifices was located on the rock over which the Islamic Dome was later erected, is negated by topographical considerations. The area west of the rock could not have been sufficient to accommodate

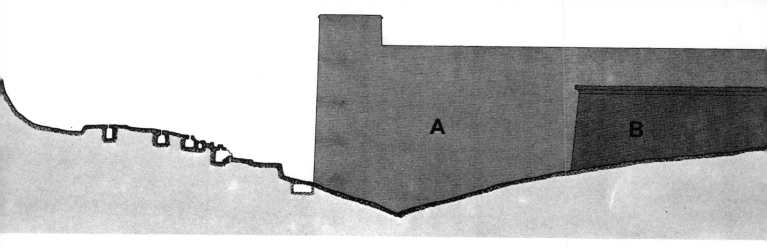

the Temple structure since the westernmost edge falls away too steeply to have served as a base for the Debir. Hence, the rock itself must have served as the platform of the Debir (see below: The Plan of the Temple).

In order to determine the architectural plan and construction of the Temple and the precise nature of its decorations and ritual furnishings described or alluded to in the Bible, comparative archeological material must be sought elsewhere.

2. ANALOGIES WITH OTHER TEMPLES

A number of plans and sundry details relating to the construction of a royal acropolis in the country and in adjoining lands have been found. Similar acropolises dating from the tenth-eighth centuries B.C. have been unearthed in the excavations of other capital cities in Syria and northwestern Mesopotamia. They followed an architectural pattern then common in Syria and Phoenicia, as seen in the cities of Sam'al (Zinçirli) in the kingdom of Yaudi in northwestern Syria, Karkemish on the Euphrates, and Hamath (modern Hama) in central Syria. One characteristic of all these cities was the separation of the royal capital (the acropolis) from the walled city which accomodated the citizens (see p. 56).

A similar temple was discovered at Tel Tu'einat on the Syrian coast. The ancient name of the city was Kunulua and it was the capital of the neo-Hittite kingdom of Khattin in northern Syria in the first quarter of the first millennium B.C. The temple is of particular interest because of its resemblance to the larger Jerusalem Temple; it was oblong and divided into three component parts; the vestibule, the sanctuary, and the Holy of Holies. Another and much earlier prototype which may serve as a basis for comparison is the Late Bronze Temple (sixteenth-thirteenth centuries B.C.) found at Hazor in Galilee.

The excavated acropolis of Tell Tayanat (Kunuluwa) in northern Syria is similar in plan to Solomon's acropolis. Behind the central ceremonial palace of Tayanat (marked b) is a small royal shrine (a) strikingly similar in plan to Solomon's tripartite sanctuary (1, 2, 3), which he built north of his palace

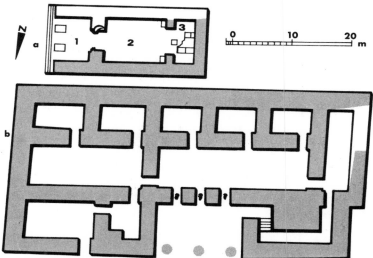

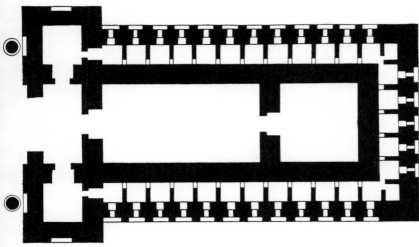

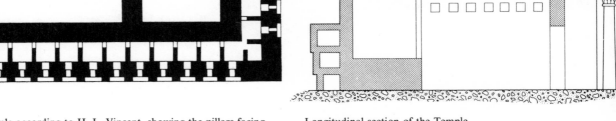

Plan of Solomon's Temple according to H. L. Vincent, showing the pillars facing the entrance *(Ulam)* and the three divisions of the Temple: the *Ulam, Hechal* and *Debir*. The outer chambers *(yaṣia)* flank three sides of the sanctuary

Longitudinal section of the Temple

3. THE PLAN OF THE TEMPLE

The distinguishing feature of the Jerusalem Temple was its east-to-west orientation and its division into three parts, one leading into another. The first section was the *Ulam* (vestibule) which faced eastward towards the rising sun. The second was the main sanctuary, the *Hechal* (pronounced *hekhal*), and the third was the *Debir* (Holy of Holies). The Hechal and the Debir formed a separate unit divided from the Ulam by a partition containing two olive wood doors. Steps led up from the Hechal to the opening of the Debir. The small inner dimensions, 60 cubits (approximately 96 feet) in length and 20 cubits (approximately 32 feet) in width, are explained by the fact that the Temple was not intended to be an assembly hall for crowds of people, but a sanctuary, the resting place of the Holy Ark, symbol of the Covenant between the people and its God, and the "seat of the divine presence" of the Lord of Israel. None but the high priest could enter the Holy of Holies.

The curtain *(parokhet hamasakh)* which divided off the Hechal from the Debir is well known from descriptions of the sanctuary in the Bible. According to II Chronicles 3:14 "...he made the veil of blue and purple and crimson fabrics and fine linen, and worked cherubim in it." According to I Kings 6:31, however, olive wood doors divided the Hechal from the Debir.

It should be noted that the roof of the Temple was not supported by pillars set in the center of the room, as was the practice in palaces of the period, and that its width was the maximum structurally possible. This arrangement allowed for the greatest possible unbroken expanse in the halls. The Temple was larger than most Canaanite temples and undoubtedly taller as well (50 cubits high = 82 feet). The large courts had a practical function since they served as the place of assembly.

The method of construction was the standard one in Palestine and neighboring countries in that period: a layer of timber was intercalated between each three rows of trimmed stone. These long beams of cedar were used to brace and strengthen the walls and also to panel the interior of the building.

100

4 THE TEMPLE FURNISHINGS

What Solomon's Temple may have lacked in size was more than compensated in beauty and splendor. He constructed it of large rectangular stones and precious cedar and cypress woods, and decorated it with handsome ivory carvings. The ritual furnishings and objects were equally elegant. All were patterned after contemporary models derived from the Phoenicians, who also provided much of the skilled labor for the enterprise. Great care was lavished on the two large sphinxlike *cherubim* (mythological winged figures) standing in the Debir and facing the Hechal. Their outspread wings touched one another to shelter the Holy Ark below and form the throne of the invisible deity above. The cherub motif was also represented in the cedarwood paneling of the walls and doors. A stone fragment of such a cherub was found in Jerusalem. Figures of winged creatures are known from the art and religious symbolism of the ancient near east. Cherubim flank the throne of Hiram, king of Byblos, and are well known in various decorations in Phoenicia and other countries. They also appear on incense altars from Megiddo and Ta'anach in ancient Israel.

The ancient cherubim in the Temple were made of gold-plated wood. The Hechal was furnished with ritual objects of great beauty, including two golden menorahs flanking the entrance to the Debir, as well as a golden table and an incense altar of cedarwood plated with gold. A three-story *yaṣi'ah* (pronounced Yatziā), a complex of superimposed chambers built along the full length of three sides of the sanctuary (except the facade), surrounded the sanctuary, leaving open the Ulam. The Yaṣi'ah served as a treasury and storehouse for the Temple; c.f. I Kings 6:5.

The Temple stood within an inner court surrounded by a thick wall. In the court and facing the entrance to the vestibule stood the great Altar of Sacrifices, built of untrimmed stone; it served as the focus of the daily ritual. In the courtyard was the enormous "sea" of bronze, a bowl of huge dimensions, its brim "made like the brim of a cup; like the flower of a lily" (I Kings 7:26). It was held up by four groups of sculptured bulls, three bulls in each group. It is not known whether this grouping bears any relation to the twelve tribes. However the figure twelve recurs many times in biblical tradition and is of a prestigious nature, though it is a specifically Jewish symbol. The sea of bronze could hold about 1,700 cubic feet of water and must have weighed thirty tons. The Bible also mentions the wheeled pedestals or bases supporting bronze lavers used to wash the sacrificial victims. Cups, braziers, and other implements were used by the priests in the ritual. In the later years of the Monarchy, a pillar near which kings were crowned stood in the courtyard (II Kings 11:14).

Two massive free-standing columns called *Yakhin* and *Boaz* flanked the outer entrance to the Ulam. These columns were elaborately decorated and crowned with bronze capitals. Similar columns have been discovered in Israel, and Greek sources refer to Phoenician temples as containing such columns; Herodotus II:44, discussing the temple of Heracles-Melkart in Tyre, describes two columns, one of gold and the other of precious stone. It is possible that Yakhin and Boaz represented the link between the royal house

Phoenician carvings of winged sphinxes suggest the form of the huge *cherubim* which hovered over the Ark in the Holy of Holies of Solomon's Temple. Above: Sphinx decorating a Canaanite king's throne on ivory inlay from Megiddo. These sphinxes are a clear indication of Phoenician (Canaanite) influence on early Israelite art. Solomon was also guided and helped by Phoenician craftsmen in the execution of his building plans; Below left: Israelite engraving of a cherub in an ancient royal quarry

Below right: Fourteenth century B.C. tripod stand from Ugarit (Phoenicia) similar to the ten bronze mobile pedestals of Solomon's Temple which supported a bronze laver used to wash the sacrificial victims

and the Temple. Some scholars believe that the names suggest the Temple was essentially a royal chapel *(miqdāš melek)*, a familiar feature of Canaanite and Mideastern civilizations (cf. Amos 7:13). This would mean that it had been placed under the guardianship of the house of David, as it had been built upon the plot of land David had purchased from Araunah the Jebusite. In accordance with this interpretation, the names Yakhin and Boaz would be the initial words of laudatory pronouncements or benedictions and other prayers in behalf of the royal family: e.g. *yākīn YHWH 'et-kissē' Dāwīd lᵉʿōlam wāʿed*, "The Lord will establish the throne of David forever and ever"; or: *beʿoz YHWH...* "By the power of Yahweh..." Other scholars believe that the name derives from the distant ancestor of David, mentioned in the book of Ruth. These proposals are hypothetical, however, and we may never know the precise significance of the names on the free-standing pillars in front of the Temple. By the time of the Second Temple, the House of David had lost its earlier status, and the Temple was regarded as the proper domain of the high priests and their associates.

Several gates led from the inner courtyard to the outer court. One of these gates, the Gate of the Courtiers, lay to the south and guarded the path that led from the palace complex to the courts of the Temple.

In subsequent centuries, much work was done on the Temple, including reconstructions, renovations, and repairs. Generally speaking, the Bible does not provide detailed descriptions of specific alteration, but does refer to repair work from time to time and to other changes resulting from foreign invasion (stripping the rich decorations to pay tribute) or religious reforms (removing objects regarded as defiling or pagan in nature). Religious reforms receive special attention in the accounts of the deeds of Joash and particularly Josiah. II Chronicles 34 reflects the great reform of Josiah who centralized national worship in "the place which the Lord had chosen," the Temple of Jerusalem, as ordained in the scroll of the Law. This scroll, which apparently contained substantial parts of the book of Deuteronomy according to a common assumption, was discovered in the Temple when repairs were in progress in 622 B.C.

5. EZEKIEL'S PLAN OF THE TEMPLE

Reverence for the holy site of the Temple never wavered in the years following its destruction in 586 B.C. by Nebuchadnezzar of Babylon (see Part II, B, 8: In the Shadow of Babylon). One example of this hope and longing is the Temple Plan envisioned by Ezekiel, who had been exiled from Jerusalem in the days of King Jehoiachin (597 B.C.). He lived at Tel-Abib, near Nippur, on the Khebar River in Babylon. It is a comprehensive blueprint of what Ezekiel imagined would be the new Temple in Jerusalem and the reconstructed city in the heart of an idealized Land of Israel. Ezekiel's vision was a strange mixture of the fanciful and the objective, but doubtless it reflected in some way the real Temple which the prophet had known in the last years of its existence. Ezekiel's Temple Plan had considerable impact on later generations and particularly on the priesthood of the Second Temple.

C. THE SECOND TEMPLE

When Babylon was conquered by Cyrus, king of Persia, in 538 B.C., the dream of returning to Zion was realized. The proclamation was sent throughout his kingdom: "Thus says Cyrus, king of Persia: 'The Lord, the God of Heaven, has given me all the kingdoms of the earth, and he has charged me to build him a house at Jerusalem which is in Judah. Whoever is among you of all his people, may his God be with him, and let him go up to Jerusalem, which is in Judah, and rebuild the house of the Lord, the God of Israel'" (Ezra 1:3; II Chronicles 36:23).

The royal edict included a specific authorization to rebuild the Temple on Mount Zion. We have very little data about this Temple, its architecture and furnishings, or the courts around it and the altar. Evidently the new structure was rebuilt on the original site, but it was not comparable in beauty or splendor to its predecessor. The exiles, newly arrived from Babylon, were in no position to restore their Temple as it had been. Those very aged ones who had seen the First Temple in all its grandeur and had worshiped there (Ezra 3:12) thought how small were the dedication ceremonies in comparison with those of Solomon's Temple. Nonetheless, it symbolized the Jewish presence in the Persian province of Judah and served as a focus of worship for Jews in all the lands of the dispersion. Moreover, the contemporary prophet, Haggai, predicted that a great future lay in store for the Second Temple: "The latter splendor of this house shall be greater than the former, says the Lord of Hosts" (Haggai 2:9).

1. WHAT DID THE SECOND TEMPLE LOOK LIKE?

A little information about the temple built by Zerubbabel (see Part II, C, 1, a: A Modest Second Temple and Beginnings of the Second Commonwealth) may be gleaned from casual remarks in the Bible. More can be learned about its later stages from hellenistic records (see Part V, B, 1: Simon's Works). Around 200 B.C. the high priest Simon was given assistance by the Seleucid king, Antiochus III, to repair the Temple and more particularly the regal Porticos which surrounded it. It is now possible to link together several significant facts relevant to this time. Like the First Temple, the Second Temple was built of large untrimmed ashlars and cedarwood beams. The general plan and layout of the second was similar to the original, though there were significant changes. Among other things, the *Debir*, the inner sanctum or Holy of Holies, was left empty as the Ark had been lost (probably through the Babylonian destruction) and was not replaced. On the other hand, the *Hechal*, the holy chamber or nave, was furnished with a table for "Bread of the Holy Presence" (shewbread), as well as the traditional menorah (candelabrum) and the incense altar. In the inner and outer courtyards and below them there were rooms used by the priests as well as storerooms for donations in agricultural products and sacred objects. Nehemiah 13:4–9 tells that Eliashib, the high priest, had appropriated one of these rooms for his relative and close friend Tobiah, the Jewish governor of Ammon, east of Jordan. The great altar of sacrifices for burnt offerings had been erected at the same spot as its predecessor, but no mention is made, in this period, of the two columns called Yachin and Boaz which had stood in the inner court at the entrance to the *Ulam* (vestibule). Their absence from the Second Temple may reflect a deliberate dissociation of Temple and king in the post-exilic period, when Judah was not an independent nation but a province. In any case, whereas the First Temple had been linked with the Royal Palace, forming the royal acropolis, no administrative structures were erected at the southern end of the Temple area in the rebuilding.

2. DEFENSE PROJECTS

As noted earlier (Part II, D, 1: The Letter of Aristeas), the *Birah* fortress was constructed at the northwestern corner of the Temple area to guard the sanctuary, especially to the north where the city and the Temple were most vulnerable. There was a resident commander of the fortress, Hananiah, in the time of Nehemiah (7:2). In later years (third century B.C.) when Jerusalem was governed by the Ptolemaic officials from Egypt, the fortifications of the Temple are also mentioned. The *Letter of Aristeas* cited above mentions three walls of the Temple, meaning probably the walls of the city and the Temple, first repaired by Nehemiah, to which another wall had been added to protect the Temple Mount. The same source describes these walls as being seventy cubits high (approximately 110 feet).

It must not be supposed, however, that the Second Temple was a poor or ramshackle structure. The building was solid and substantial and the work was carefully executed. The sanctuary was eminently suitable for worship (Ezra 6:4, 8), even if it did not match the splendor of Solomon's edifice. The Second Temple was greatly improved in later years and at the end of the fourth century B.C. Hecateus of Abdera, cited by Josephus in *Against Apion* (I:22), testified that it was a large building encircled by a wall; a century or more later, the *Letter of Aristeas* stresses the splendor of the sanctuary. Herod, toward the end the first century B.C., decided to rebuild the entire Temple. His motives were both religious and political: He was devoted to the faith and wished to enhance the glory of the central sanctuary; at the same time he carried out all his great building enterprises in the grand imperial manner of the day. In addition, he regarded himself as the chosen leader of his people, an authentic king of the Jewish nation, for whom he carried out his gigantic building program in the style and manner of imperial Rome. His private life and autocratic methods alienated his subjects and earned him their permanent hatred and hostility. Posterity overlooked his great achievements and diplomatic and political successes, stressing rather the negative side of his character and policies (see Part II, F: Herod's Period).

D. HEROD'S TEMPLE

1. THE NATURE OF THE WORSHIP ON THE TEMPLE MOUNT

In order to appreciate the real grandeur of the various structures which once graced the Temple Mount, one of the greatest sanctuaries of antiquity, one must grasp the relevance of its size and complexity to the multitudinous functions it fulfilled, and to realize how the Temple's components were used by the multitude of worshipers. The Mishna and Talmud provide us with minute details which help to reconstruct the type and nature of the services performed in different parts of the sanctuary, some of them actually observed by eye-witnesses.

This information helps us to relate the objects of our exploration with the meaning they held for the Jews in Judea and in the Diaspora, and, in turn, to connect the meaning of a number of physical links which have come to light, with the customs with which they were associated.

a. The Chief Functions of the Temple

The Temple was, above all, the heart of Jerusalem and the source of spiritual life for the Jewish people. It was the seat of wisdom and learning. Scholars and wise men were invited to expound the Law and its interpretation there, while laymen, male and female (peasants, laborers, artisans, tradesmen, wealthy people and the nobility) were encouraged to inquire. This vision of the Temple emphasized its intellectual and spiritual role in society, and these activities accompanied the traditional functions of the Temple.

The most ancient function was to maintain and perform the sacrificial rituals: to prepare communal and individual burnt offerings and other sacrifices, burn incense, and hold worship services with singing and music. Secondly, it was the duty of the priests to give guidance to the people who came to them, and to answer the many questions of ethics and sacrificial rites (described below), of the way to pray and the way to live. Thirdly, there were the duties and activities of the scribes, levites, and rabbis who taught and worked close to the holy precincts. These activities included sessions of the Great Sanhedrin of seventy-one members and of the two smaller divisions of this large body, all of whom supervised the sacrificial rites. The Temple also served as an important center for diffusing and regulating religious observances and jurisdiction, and for the study and direction of political and social affairs affecting the people of Israel and the Diaspora to whom Jerusalem was the religious capital, a famed center of faith and learning.

b. Zones of Holiness within the Temple

The Mishna defined a precise gradation in sanctity of the different parts of the Temple Mount from the center outwards in relation to the city of Jerusalem: The Temple enclosure, the outer and inner courts, the ritual objects, all varied in the degree of purity and holiness they possessed, according to Jewish belief. Mishna *Kelim* 1:809 relates that the worshiper senses an aura of holiness from the moment of entry within the walls of the city. This becomes more potent as he ascends the Temple Mount itself and increases progressively the more deeply he penetrates into the sanctified area, from the Ḥel rampart through the Women's Court, then the Court of Israel, then the Court of the Priests (all of which surrounded the Temple proper) on into the Ulam and the Hechal, finally reaching its nadir in the Debir, the Holy of Holies.

c. The Morning Service

Twenty-four divisions of priests and levites were posted by night to watch over the Temple area and were regularly inspected by the overseer of the watch posted in the tower of the Place of Abtinas (see below). All the silent night, a flicker of light came through its gate. The whispering hot embers of the constant fire on the Altar of Holocausts were barely audible as a young priest turned them over with a long fork and fed the fire. The voice of a levite rang through the night: "Out of the depths, I cry to thee, O Lord! Lord, hear my voice! Let thy ears be attentive to the voice of my supplications!" (Psalm 130:1).

The ritual began before the break of dawn. The priests in charge of the keys who slept in the Chamber of the Hearth (see below) arose and proceeded to the Chamber of Ritual Immersion by way of an underground passage lit with clay lamps placed in niches of the wall (see below). Following their purification, they donned their priestly garments — linen shirts, trousers, tunics, and turbans — and passed in two groups through the portals to the "Chamber of Hewn Stone" (Lishkat Hagazit) where they stood in a circle around their elder. Lots were drawn to determine which of the priests would remove the fat ashes from the altar, place them in appointed places for disposal, and prepare the fresh heaps of firewood for the morning sacrifice. They then returned to the Lishkat Hagazit where lots were drawn again for further duties, including the immolation of the sacrificial lamb, the preparation of lights and candelabra within the Temple halls, the meal offering, wine oblations and other prescribed tasks. The honor of attending to all these sacred duties was sought by hundreds of priests, so tasks had to be apportioned by means of the casting of lots.

The elder then bade a priest go up to one of the towers surrounding the inner courts, and asked him: "Did the light of dawn in the east spread as far as Hebron [to the south]?" When he was answered in the affirmative, he ordered a ewe-lamb to be brought up from the pen of ewe-lambs in the Chamber of the Hearth. Though the animal had been carefully examined for four consecutive days — as it had to be perfect and unblemished — it was inspected again by torchlight. It was then immolated, cut up and drawn on the marble slaughterhouse tables situated north of the altar; certain meat sections were washed in the washing chambers and the other sections readied for the altar. The priests proceeded once more to the Lishkat Hagazit to pronounce the first three verses of the benediction, "Shema Israel" (Hear O Israel, Judaism's confession of faith proclaiming the absolute unity of God as prescribed in Deuteronomy 6:4). Lots were drawn twice more, once to decide who would carry the censers and spread incense over the altar, and once to choose who would place the sections of the sacrificial lamb, first over the lower gradients of the short ascent leading up to the high altar, and eventually on the altar itself.

As a priest hurled a *magrefa* (a gong-like musical instrument) towards the middle of the court between the altar and portal of the Temple, the tremendous clatter alerted all priests and levites in the area to attend morning song.

(1) *The Stage Now Set for the Morning Communal Sacrifice:* The lay worshipers assembled in the Court of Israel (see below: The Court of Israel) and near the entrance to the inner court. The ninety-three officiating priests stood in a group south of the altar carrying censers, torches, fire-pans, tongs, and other paraphernalia, and blessed the worshipers in the ineffable name of Yahweh. Libations of wine were poured on the altar; offerings made of fine flour were prepared for the meal oblation and pancakes for the high priest. As the officiating priest bent to pour the libation, the deputy high priest raised a standard and signaled ben-Arza, the leader of the levitic band, to strike the cymbals, and the priests to blow the silver trumpets. The levites intoned the prescribed daily Psalm and portions of the Law (Torah). As they finished each verse, they stopped and the priests repeated the blowing of trumpets. The worshipers bowed in prayer (Mishna, *Tamid* 7:13).

This ceremonial lasted several hours and was impressive and interesting to the people. While the ministering priests attended to the sacrifices on the altar, other priests blew the trumpets as the choir of levites sang to the accompaniment of the band of instruments. (Mishna, *Tamid*: Chapters 1–7 and corresponding Talmudic references.)

(2) *Individual Sacrifices:* After the morning service, the priests were kept busy for the rest of the forenoon sacrificing individual guilt or sin offerings (expiation, propitiatory, or thanksgiving offerings) brought by the people; the offering might be a lamb, or a turtledove or young pigeons brought by a poor man. The priests listened with compassion to all the tales of woe in order to sacrifice the offerings of the simple men and women in conformance with the proper rite. The women did not go beyond the limits of the Women's Court (see below: The Women's Court), while the lepers and other sick stopped at the Nikanor Gate leading to the Court of Israel, as their offerings were immolated, skinned or feathered, and sacrificed on the altar. Throughout the day, scores of people, rich and poor, brought their sacrificial offerings and were attended by hundreds of priests. Many more people came to the Women's Court to cast their silver shekel Temple dues into the stone horns.

(3) *The Humble Women's Sacrifice:* At this point we may note an interesting point of contact between the literary sources and archeological investigation. In the course of excavations along the southern street (see below, Section F, 4, f: The Road Along the Southern Wall), we found a polished stone fragment bearing the Hebrew inscription *Qorban* (Sacrifice) and two incised representations of birds, upside-down. This find suggests that the inscription and representation refer to the offering by a woman after childbirth stipulated in Leviticus 12:8. There are old traditions regarding the brace of pigeons in their little wicker baskets, intended as sacrificial birds for the ritual on the Temple Mount (*Kritot* 2:7 et al).

Poor women were allowed to bring a sacrificial offering of a pair of birds. These

Silver shekel dating to the last days of the Second Temple. The inscription over the chalice reads "Shekel of Israel" and "Third Year" (of the War) in initials

humble women brought their offerings to the Women's Court. It is related that they often travelled for many weary days on their way to Jerusalem, where they stayed in the inns while awaiting their turn to bring their offerings. One could often hear them cry out at the outrageous prices asked by the dealers for the *kinnim* or brace of pigeons or fowl in a wicker basket. A Talmudic source relates that their price once rose to as much as a golden dinar for a "basket" *(ken)* and that the crisis was only resolved through the intervention of the beloved Rabbi Simon ben-Gamaliel. As a result the price was reduced overnight to a quarter of a silver dinar. Petahia, a kindly priest responsible for these sacrifices, collected the birds from the women at the Nikanor Gate, together with each woman's prayer and wish, then slew the birds and tore off their feathers before offering them on the altar.

d. *Other Sacrifice Rituals*

In the afternoon, the second communal sacrificial rite of the day was performed. The morning and afternoon prayers were recited at the time corresponding to these communal burnt offerings. An additional *mussaf* prayer was recited on Sabbaths and on festivals, corresponding to the additional sacrifice of the day; special sacrifices were offered for the first of every month. When sacrifice at the Temple ceased after A.D. 70, prayer was regarded by Jews as a substitute until the wished-for rebuilding of the Temple would take place. The concomitant renewal of the sacrifical service was petitioned for in all the prayers.

The animal offerings as described were divided, according to Josephus, into two classes: (1) The highest class of sacrifices (burnt-offerings, sin offerings, guilt offerings, congregational peace offerings) for the people in general, and (2) sacrifices of a minor grade (individual peace offerings, first-born offerings, animal tithes, the paschal lamb). The higher category of offerings was immolated to the north of the altar and was eaten by the priests inside the enclosures of the court, except for the burnt-offering which was entirely consumed by fire. The high point of the sacrificial worship was the set of rituals involved in the Day of Atonement services, including the ceremony of the scapegoat and the red heifer (see Section F, 5, a below: The Red Heifer and Scapegoat Exits). The above sums up public sacrifice offered within the Temple precincts. The paschal lambs destined for the Passover sacrifice were immolated near the great altar, but were then returned to their owners to be roasted and eaten outside the Temple in any pure place, meaning within Jerusalem. As tens of thousands partook in the latter private rite, the occasion turned into a mass celebration in the holy city.

e. The Scapegoat Rite and the Ritual of Purification on the Day of Atonement

The origin and nature of the scapegoat rite are summed up in Leviticus 16:3–28. Yom Kippur (the day of Atonement) was solemnized as a day of ritual purification, expiation, and penance on which every man must confess his sins and abstain from any kind of work or food or any sensual pleasure. Its outstanding feature was the elaborate Temple ceremonial (described in the Talmud tractate *Yoma*), including two special rites: the particular sacrificial rite by the high priest clad, not in his customary golden vestments, but in white linen symbolic of purity and humility; and the symbolic expulsion of the scapegoat.

(1) *The Sacrificial Rite:* The high priest took two goats as a sin-offering and a ram as a burnt offering for the community. Lots were cast for the two goats "before the Lord" (Leviticus 16:78), one lot marked "for the Lord" and one marked "for Azazel". Purification and expiation were made by a sin offering of a ram, then the first goat, and by sprinkling or dabbing the blood of the immolated victims on the altar of incense, on other appurtenances located within the sanctuary and on the inner part of the curtain in the inner sanctuary. In pre-exilic times the blood was dabbed on the area above or facing the *kapporet*, the sculptured lid of the Ark. On that day only was the high priest allowed to enter the inner sanctuary, and only in this rite was the sacrificial blood applied there. The atoning agent was the blood of the victim which signified the essence of life.

The priest then laid his hand on the goat singled for despatch to the wilderness of Judea, and confessed the sins of Israel. The goat, thus symbolically laden with the national guilt, was driven into the desert, the domain of mythical Azazel, an evil genius. The description of the ritual in *Yoma* sheds light on the process of communal purification and protection against the intrusion of impurity into the inner sanctuary as understood by those who participated in the awesome ceremony. In post-exilic days the people as a whole participated in this purification rite. Thus the expiation of the priest was interpreted as applying with equal force to the people. When the high priest appeared at the conclusion of the service, he was greeted with rejoicing by the people, confident that sin had been forgiven.

(2) *The Scapegoat*: The expulsion of the guilt-laden goat from the community was of central symbolic importance. It reflects one basic aspect of prophylactic purification, the elimination of the sins in which all persons are entangled. The goat carried away these sins, and in effect consigned them to their source, *Azazel*, defined by some as a wild desert area outside human habitation, the domain of evil forces, and, in the Greek (Septuagint) translation of the Bible, as the actual designation of the scapegoat. The final act, hurling the goat from a precipice overlooking the wilderness, prevented any possible return of the sins and recontamination of the Israelite community.

(3) *The Mystique of Purification by Blood*: The other principal feature was the use of the blood of the sin offering to purify the inner sanctuary. It was a prophylactic device intended to protect the center of the sanctuary, where the invisible deity was mysteriously present. At the conclusion of the ritual of purufication, the blood of the offering there would prevent the intrusion of impurity. The blood, which had been sprinkled over the

horns of the altar of incense within the sanctuary (in contradistinction to sacrificial blood used on the great Altar of Holocausts) thus guarded the inner sanctum against the evil forces that bring impurity.

The dread of impurity — originating from outside — seems to have found expression in the employment of time-honored magical measures of a propitiatory and prophylactic nature. These were used not only in the priestly ritual, but also in the medical procedures of ancient physicians to appease the evil one or to offset the effects of his attacks on their patients. Thus, a close analysis of the rites of purification on Yom Kippur reveals new factors in the role played by sacrifice in the complete Temple ritual (as described briefly above).

Though such ritual and medical practices derive from the mystique of blood of remote ancient near-eastern origin, they were passed on to Israel through common popular tradition, and they thus affected the priestly rites. There is an element of inconsistency or contradiction in the preservation of such procedures, since the Bible denies the practice of magic and affirms that it is helpless and meaningless against the power and majesty of Yahweh. But in accordance with popular pagan practice and as a survival of pre-Mosaic faith, the dread of impurity evoked superstitions and called also for measures of prophylaxis which persisted in the functions of the official priestly cult as long as the Temple stood.

These are but some of the wondrous manifestations of Jewish life during the centuries which preceded the destruction of the Temple. They were an integral part of the total devotion to ancestral beliefs and customs, and it was apparent in many ways, for example a rigorous abstinence from any representation of the human figure, the minute observance of the sacrificial ritual, and the rules of *halakhah* (oral law) including the rites of purification.

f. Physical Links with the Past

The tremendous activity at the Temple Mount made necessary vast installations above and below the expansive pavements of the courts, in order to maintain the permanent woodfire, to wash down the blood and water around the altar, to dispose and care for the skins and to preserve sanitary precautions and purity; to serve the people and to regulate the comings and goings of the priests and levites, their entry and exit, their purification rites within the Temple area as well as the purification rites of the lay Israelites outside the thresholds of the Temple area. A number of traces of these installations have been discovered in the course of our excavations, as described in Section F, 4, d, below: The Ritual Baths between the Stairways); the rest may still be buried beneath the vast pavements of the Haram es-Sherif (see Part VI, C: The Early Moslem Period).

2. THE CONSTRUCTION OF HEROD'S TEMPLE

Herod's Temple surpassed in architectural splendor and majesty anything ever seen on the Temple Mount. The popular saying, quoted in Tractate *Sukkah* 51:2, exulted: "No

one has seen a truly beautiful building unless he has seen the Temple." Indeed Herod devoted a great deal of attention, time and effort to redesigning, renovating, and redecorating the Second Temple. This great enterprise required vast quantities of building materials, including the huge hand-chiselled smooth stone rectangles so distinctive in their size and workmanship that they are called "Herodian," as well as a great number of skilled masons and stone cutters. According to Josephus (see Part I, A, 3: Josephus), ten thousand of these artisans, including a thousand priests, were put to work, and not fewer than a thousand wagons were manufactured to bring stone from the quarries. Josephus underlines the fact that the Temple was built *at the top of the mountain* (*Antiquities* VIII:430).

The exact date of the renovation of the Temple is not known since Josephus provides conflicting reports of the events. In *War* I:401 he states that the work was begun in the fifteenth year of Herod's reign (23 B.C.), but according to *Antiquities* XV:389, it was in the eighteenth year (20 B.C.), which may be more likely. The plan as a whole was not completed in his lifetime, but the Temple proper was, its reconstruction taking a year and a half. The Southern, or Royal Portico (also called *Stoa Basileos*) was finished as well, over a period of eight years (*Antiquities* XV:420). In the Gospel of John 2:20 it is reported: "It took forty-six years to build this Temple." That would extend the period of building to about A.D. 26. John's statement is supported by Talmudic references (*Sanhedrin* 41:2; *Aboda-Zara* 8:2) which state that the seat of the Sanhedrin was transferred from the *Lishkat Hagazit*, "Chamber of Hewn Stone" (probably situated at the northwest angle of the upper podium within the inner courts), to the place called the Ḥanuyot in the Temple precincts (most likely in the Royal Portico) forty years before the destruction of the Lishkat Hagazit, i.e. about A.D. 30. This is very probably the time when the monumental Ḥanuyot colonnade was completed (see below).

Josephus further reports (*Antiquities* XX:219) that the work on the Temple Mount continued even as late as the administration of the Roman Procurator Albinus (A.D. 62–64) in the last years before the outbreak of the War with Rome. The vast multi-columned Royal Portico had been damaged during the riots and repressions that took place in the days of the Procurator Florus (A.D. 64–66; *War* II:33). Repairs and alterations in the Portico were under way in this final stage, and the work was interrupted only at the beginning of the Great Revolt.

Reconstruction model of the southwestern angle of the Western Wall and the
stairway leading up to the gate over the Robinson Arch (left) and the Southern
Wall (right). A stepped street skirting the wall, as well as a wide stairway lead up to the
Double and Triple Hulda Gates. The top of the Royal Portico is seen above

3. WHAT WERE THE INNER COURTS OF THE SANCTUARY LIKE?

a. Sources of Information

A wealth of information about the Inner Courts of the Sanctuary is available from various ancient sources. The many separate accounts, however, cannot be fitted together to form a homogeneous and integrated picture, and in fact some of the material is contradictory. Detailed descriptions of the Temple, its courts and various structures, as well as precise particulars about the ritual performed in the sanctuary, are preserved in the Mishna — mainly in the tractates *Middot* and *Tamid* — and in Josephus' writings, in particular *War* V:184–247, and *Antiquities* XV:391–425. In addition, sundry details are scattered throughout the Talmud, the Midrash (Homilies) and other sources. It would be relevant to compare Josephus' orientation with that of the Mishna and the Talmud. Josephus' works were intended for Greek-reading Gentiles, while the descriptions in the Mishna and Talmud stemmed from the faithful bearers of hallowed tradition, who entertained the hope of an eventual restoration of the Temple in all its former glory.

The inner confines of the Temple Mount have never been properly examined, owing to the understandable opposition of the Moslem authorities in control of the site. However, limited information has been secured about the vast network of underground substructures, the vaulted halls under the southeastern corner of the Temple platform known as *Solomon's Stables*. There is material, as well, concerning the water reservoirs and cisterns throughout the underground area (see Diag. 4). In addition, a small number of inscriptions have been found, among them the two in Hebrew described below which contain the Hebrew word *bayit* (house), which may best be rendered "place" (e.g. "Place of Trumpeting") denoting chambers in the Temple Mount buildings which fulfilled specific functions either in the administration or in the ritual routine.

b. The Inner Core of the Temple

The focus of our study of the inner courts is the rock face, called *Es-Sakhra* in Arabic, which lies under the Dome of the Rock at the summit of Mount Moriah. This rock is identified in Hebrew as *eben hāštīyā* (Foundation Stone), which the Mishna attests "stood three fingers higher than the ground" (*Yoma* 5:2). As indicated, it has been identified as the site of the Holy of Holies (i.e. the *Debir*) in both the Temple of Solomon and its successor (see above). A passage in the Bible describing the inner courts of the Temple may be traced to an earlier tradition: "It had a wall around it, five hundred cubits long (875 feet) and five hundred cubits wide, to make a separation between the holy and the common" (Ezekiel 42:20). This is echoed by the Mishnaic passage in *Middot* 2:1: "The Temple enclosure was five hundred by five hundred cubits." It formed a square which encompassed the Temple's structures and its Inner Courts, and was bounded by the *Soreg* or balustrade.

(1) *The Balustrade:* The *Soreg* (Balustrade) was a low latticed stone wall about five feet (1.5 meters) high, marking the border of the inner sanctuary. At regular intervals were placed elegant stelas, carved stone slabs bearing inscriptions in Greek and Latin

prohibiting Gentiles from entering the sacred internal courts (*hieron* in Greek). Josephus refers to the *Soreg* several times (*War* V:193–200; *Antiquities* XV:417 etc.), stressing the fact that it warned against trespassing on holy ground on pain of death. This interdiction is confirmed by two Greek inscriptions which have come to light. One was discovered by Charles Clermont-Ganneau in 1870; the other, a fragment, was found in the vicinity of the Lion's Gate in 1935. Their contents are the same: "No foreigner is allowed within the balustrade surrounding the sanctuary and the court encompassed. Whoever is caught will be personally responsible for his ensuing death." Measures against foreign intrusion into the sacred courts have a long history. Some are itemized in the list of rights which King Antiochus III granted the Jews about 200 B.C. (*Antiquities* XII:138–144). Philo, the Alexandrian Jewish philosopher, mentions having seen this inscription when he visited the Temple Mount. Paul was accused of violating the sanctity of the Holy Place by bringing a Greek into the Temple (Acts 21:17–29).

(2) *The Temple Proper: Debir, Hechal and Ulam:* The Temple itself as it was reconstructed by Herod retained the tripartite division and basic measurements prescribed from the time of the Solomonic edifice. It included, as previously described, the *Debir* (Holy of Holies), the *Hechal* (Sanctuary) and the *Ulam* (Hall or Vestibule). The *Debir* was the holiest place: "none entered there except the high priest on the Day of Atonement" (Mishna, *Kelim* 1:9). It was a dark, windowless thirty-three foot cube with a flat roof. Except for two curtains stretching north to south which separated the Sanctuary from the Holy of Holies, it was empty, for according to tradition, the Ark had disappeard after the end of the Monarchy.

According to one tradition, two curtains *(parokhet)* divided the Hechal from the Debir, one fastened to the northern wall and the other to the southern at a distance of one cubit (18 inches or 0.5 m.; *Middot* 4:5). Another tradition (*Middot* 5:1) mentions one curtain only. Josephus maintains, as did Aristeas, that the curtain of the Debir was *katapetasma*, meaning that it opened from below and not on the side.

The *Hechal* was connected to the Debir by a ramp, or possibly some steps, and was the center of the priestly ritual. Its walls were decorated with gold plating, and its furniture consisted of the golden menorah or seven-branched candelabrum, the gold plated table of the shewbread, the golden altar, and other precious vessels. The menorah and table for shewbread are depicted in the reliefs carved on the Arch of Titus in Rome. The menorah is depicted on the arch as having a pedestal, but this seems to be an artistic liberty as the original apparently did not have one. There were two pairs of gold plated

114

doors at the entrance to the Hechal. When these were open, the curtain remained to cover it. The Hechal and the Debir were bounded on three sides (north, west, and south) by the *Yaṣi'ah* (pronounced Yatziā) which was three stories high and contained thirty-eight chambers interconnected by passages. They were used by the priestly attendants for the varied services connected with the ritual observances, as well as for the storage of the vessels and treasures of the Temple.

The *Ulam* formed the front of the edifice, and stretched across the width of the building (seventy cubits; 122.5 feet) with a room at the north and another at the south, enlarging the frontage to one hundred cubits (175 feet), according to Herod's plan: "And the Hechal, namely the Sanctuary, was one hundred by one hundred... and its height forty cubits (70 feet); Mishna, *Middot* 4:6. It may have been Herod's intention to heighten the facade to one hundred cubits. A statement attributed to him is pertinent at this point: "Our fathers, indeed, when they returned from Babylon, built this temple to God Almighty; yet does it want sixty cubits of its largeness in altitude; for so much did that first Temple which Solomon built, exceed this temple... but since I am now, by God's will, your governor... I will do my endeavor to correct that imperfection which has arisen from the necessity of our affairs" (i.e. that of our forefathers and their vicissitudes; *Antiquities* XV:385). According to Josephus, the people were astonished at Herod's good intentions but worried that he might not have the means to complete the work and would ultimately leave the Temple in ruins. This stems from a dim fear that Herod's dynasty could not last forever (according to preconceived Jewish traditions) as it did not stem from the House of David (see Part II, F: Herod's Period).

The *Ulam*, which was "narrow behind and broad in front, is shaped like a lion," states the Mishna (*Middot* 4:7). This fits Isaiah's call: "Ariel, Ariel, the city where David encamped" (29:1), for "Ariel" which means "Lion of God" may represent a mythical lion and at the same time be a symbolic name for the Temple and Jerusalem. Other items mentioned in the different sources include the golden chandelier over the entrance to the portal which led from the Ulam to the Hechal. This was a gift from the convert, Queen Helen of Adiabene (see Part V, E, 5: The Mausoleum of Queen Helen), according to the Mishna (*Yoma* 3:10), as was the decoration of interlaced golden vines and leaves at the entrance to the Ulam where two tables stood, one of gold and the other of marble. The facade was of vast dimensions, twenty cubits wide (35 feet) and forty cubits high (70 feet), and this presented an unforgettable spectacle in depth, looking in. From the Court of Israel where the throngs of worshipers would gather, it was possible to see right through it to the interior of the entrance hall. This main columned portal of the Temple was provided not with doors but with curtains embroidered with star patterns (*War* V:212; Mishna, *Shekalim* 8:4–5). Over the pilasters which framed the columns of the portal, Herod had affixed the golden eagle which infuriated the people and led to riots (*War* I:648): "and young men set about to work... let themselves down from the top of the temple with thick ropes, and this at midday..." The magnificent facade was described in varying terms by different sources. It is represented on a coin dating to the time of Bar Kochba (A.D. 135). It is also depicted as resting on four great columns and a flat

115

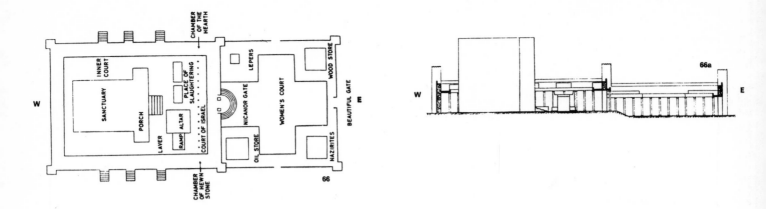

architrave. It is probably this same facade which appears on a mosaic depiction in the third century A.D. Dura Europos Synagogue. A portal stood between columns, flanked by doors and surmounted by a shell. The entrance hall was reached by a flight of twelve curved steps, thus further enhancing the height of the edifice over the Inner Courts. It is this portrayal of the Hechal, seen from the Court of Israel through the Ulam, that was handed down through the ages.

(3) *The Altar of Holocausts*: The great austere stone Altar of Holocausts stood in the Court of the Priests (*Azarat ha-Cohanīm*) in the inner courts, some 39 feet from the facade of the Ulam and slightly to the east of it (Mishna, *Middot* 5). On its southern side, a ramp without steps, the *Kebeš*, ascended to the top. Both the altar and ramp were constructed of untrimmed stones, untouched by iron "because iron is made to shorten man's life, whereas the altar was erected in order to lengthen man's years" (*Middot* 3:4). Various bits and pieces of information have been preserved on the nature of the altar and the *Kebeš*, leading to the supposition of some scholars that the altar had three tiers and was a small-scale model of the many-storied tower or *ziggurat* of the Babylonian sanctuaries. Other scholars have gone even further and conceived of it in the form of the altar which King Ahaz had seen in Damascus (II Kings 16:10 ff.).

(4) *The Consecrated Court of the Priests*: The wider part of the Inner Courts (see diagram), measuring 313 × 227 feet, surrounded the Temple building; under normal conditions they were accessible only to the priests. Among other installations in the Court of Priests, the most notable were the bronze laver and bowl, and the sacrificial Place of Slaughtering (*Bēt-Hamitbāḥayim*). The laver and bowl stood west of the *kebeš*, and were similar to those which had occupied the same site in the days of the First Temple. The Place of Slaughtering, a structure provided with marble tables, posts and hooks to hold the slain animals, stood north of the altar.

c. The Court of Israel

East of the sacred Court of the Priests and on a lower level was the Court of Israel, a long narrow strip measuring 135 × 11 cubits (222 × 19 feet). It was filled to overflowing with pilgrims during the holidays, and the worshipers would "stand and prostrate themselves in turns" (*Yoma* 21:1). The Passover sacrifice had to be performed in three shifts in order to accommodate the crowded participants in this narrow court.

The Court of Israel was reached by passing westward through the Women's Court (see below) and ascending a flight of fifteen curved steps ending at the exquisite Nikanor Gate. It had doors on each side which were made of beautifully wrought copper and plated with copper, not gold, as were the other gates. This was the entrance to consecrated ground beyond which women might not pass.

116

Left: Layout of the inner Temple courts standing on the upper podium of the esplanade. Oriented east to west, the various sections are identified with the nature of the ritual. The main entrance faced east while the sanctuary and Holy of Holies stood to the west. The Place of Abtinas stood near the Chamber of Hewn Stone.

Right: Longitudinal plan of the inner courts

d. The Chambers, Appointed Places and Gates of the Inner Courts

The Inner Courts were surrounded by a wall with gates along its length. Between the gates were "chambers" and "places," each of which fulfilled a specific function in the schedule of rites (see below, Section F, 3: The Place of Trumpeting). It is still difficult to identify these structures or even the gates mentioned in the sources. There were apparently seven major gates, one of them to the east (Nikanor Gate) and three each in the north and south walls, each door measuring twenty cubits (33 feet) in height and ten cubits (16.5 feet) in width. All the gates were provided with bevelling off the wall and with doors, and all were surfaced with gold except the Nikanor Gate as explained above. An elaborately designed flight of steps led to them from the Outer Courts.

(1) *The Chamber of the Hearth:* Noteworthy among the inner structures adjacent to the Sanctuary building was the Chamber of the Hearth *(Bēt Hamokēd)* near the north-western wall of the Inner Courts, where priests of the watch spent the night (see above, Section D, 1, c: The Morning Service). It was a sizeable building covered by a dome and it offered protection from the elements; it was warm enough in winter, cool enough in summer. Broad stone slabs were set within the circumference of the building and these served as beds for the priests of the watch.

(2) *Place of Abtinas and other Chambers:* Another interesting chamber or hall was the "Place of Abtinas" *(Bēt Abtinas;* see diagram) built into the southern wall of the inner courts about 38 feet over the "Water Gate." It was used for the preparation of incense *(Shekalim* 4:1) and its upper chambers housed the priests in attendance at the Temple *(Tamid* 1:1). Another link with the ancient Water Gate may well be the anchor-shaped underground reservoir situated at the southeastern corner of the raised platform upon which stand the Dome of the Rock and the Rock (Sakhra) itself. Close to the "Place of Abtinas" were the "Chamber of the High Priest" and the "Chamber of Hewn Stone" *(Lishkat Hagazit)* to the south, which served as the seat of the Sanhedrin court up to about A.D. 30, forty years before the destruction of the Temple.

Diag. 4 indicates the location of the ancient underground reservoirs situated below the Haram es-Sherif enclosure (see p. 129).

e. The Court of Women

The Court of Women was situated east of the inner consecrated courts, as stated, and on a lower level. It was remarkable in size, consisting of a square, 135 × 135 cubits (222 feet); it had four gates, one in each of its walls (one was the imposing Nikanor Gate which led to the Court of Israel). There were four "chambers" or "places" in the corners, each with a little court of its own, with its own specific function. At the entrance to the enclosure was a place assigned to one of the minor Sanhedrin courts — the "Court of the Three" *(Sanhedrin* 11:3).

Receptacles for the Temple dues in the form of horns were placed in the Court of Women for the collection of silver shekels which were contributed to maintain the services and build up the treasury of the Temple. Surrounded by galleries, this court also served for gayer occasions such as the rejoicing on the last day of Succoth, the *Simchat Bet-*

Presumed layout of the Temple Mount according to L. H. Vincent. 1–8: Chambers around the Inner Courts, within the Ḥel rampart; 9: the Ḥel; A: The Sanctuary; B: Altar; C: Court of Priests; D: Court of Israel; E, 10: Nikanor Gate and stairs; F–G: Women's Court; H: Halls or reservoirs; I¹: Upper exit of a ramp which led to the Temple esplanade from K, the Kiphonos (Barclay) Gate; I²: Upper exit from the Double (Hulda) Gate; I³: Upper exit from the Triple (Hulda) Gate; J: Gate over the Robinson Arch; L: Gate over the Wilson Arch and end of causeway; M: Fourth (Warren) western gate; N: Presumed other gate; O: Tadi Gate. The thick black dots on the outskirts indicate the Portico colonnades; the entrance ramps ran under them. The Soreg or outer balustrade is indicated by the outer rectangle in the center of the esplanade. The thinly dotted line indicates the restored podium (in the center of the esplanade) over which the Arabs built their sanctuary, arcades, etc. P: Susa Gate (east)

Hashoeva. This celebration has been interpreted exclusively as a water libation festival, but it was in fact a feast of lights which were arranged to light up all of Jerusalem. Candelabra and torches were lit in the Court of Women as priests and worshipers mingled together and danced all night long in joyous celebration. In the morning water was drawn from the Pool of Siloam and libations were poured over the altar on the occasion of the morning holocaust (i.e. burnt offerings).

The steps leading up from the court to the Nikanor Gate are reported as the location where the levites stood singing and playing their instruments. But they were more notorious as the place where women suspected of adultery were tested. According to ancient law (Numbers 5:18–28) such a woman was given the "water of bitterness" to drink — a potion mixed with cereal offering, over which was pronounced a traditional curse. If she were guilty, "the water that brings the curse shall enter into her... and the woman shall become an execration among her people..." In addition, the judges could wear down the woman's opposition to admit guilt by making her go up and down the steps to the gate (Mishna, *Sotah* 8). An echo of such a scene is found in John 7:53 – 8:11, where the Pharisees brought up a woman condemned to be stoned for adultery. When the Pharisees asked Jesus for his opinion of the law and the sentence, they heard his astounding reply, "Let him who is without sin cast the first stone."

f. The Ḥel Rampart

The entire enclosure of the Inner Courts and the Court of Women was protected by a massive retaining wall and served effectively as a fort during the many wars in which the Temple Mount was involved. Its height, according to Josephus, was forty cubits (66 feet). Around it ran the bulwark or rampart, 14 cubits (23 feet) wide. A flight of steps led down from it to the outer courts, the Courts of the Gentiles. Beyond the steps stood the *Soreg* (balustrade) bearing the warning of death to strangers.

The wide platform stretching across the outer courts was used for mass gatherings. At the same time it was provided with many chambers and storerooms for the Temple. In them were stored oil, wine, and grain; apparently, the underground halls situated under the southeastern corner of the platform, named by the Crusaders "Solomon's Stables," were used for the same purpose. They were formed by rows of vaults resting on dozens of piers.

E. FUNCTIONS OF THE OUTER COURTS OF THE TEMPLE MOUNT

The insights gained through our investigation of the Temple Mount have thrown new light on data gleaned from ancient sources on the one hand, and established archeological links between the new discoveries and the ancient buried structures on the other. They have also helped in reassessing ancient ceremonial and observances on and around the the Temple Mount. These aspects will be dealt with in the following sections.

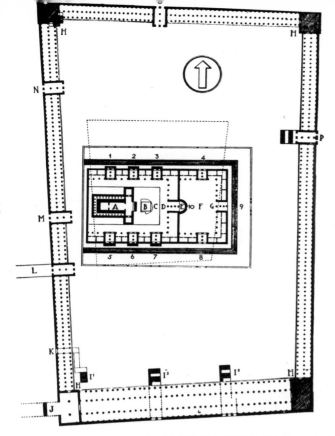

1. DISCOVERY BEARS OUT CONTEMPORARY ANCIENT WRITINGS

Archeology has often confirmed the descriptions of constructions in the Temple Mount area, found in Josephus and the Talmud, notably the Tractate *Middot*, and many of the details have been clarified. Problems that Herod's architects and master builders encountered because of the master plan of the Temple Mount and its adjoining areas have been revealed. Archeology has also brought to light changes effected during the decades preceding the destruction of the Second Temple.

Since 1968 we have been excavating the wide area south and southwest of the Temple Mount and its precincts. Our findings bear out strikingly the revolutionary topographical changes wrought on the Temple Mount in keeping with Herod's vast architectural plans. He doubled the area of the Temple courts by filling in both the Tyropoeon valley bordering it to the west and the upper slope of the Kidron valley to the east, as well as a small vale to the north. In order to fill in the slope of the Tyropoeon valley, he had to change its direction and divert it westward. He leveled the whole upper area to form a vast platform and edged it with tremendous retaining walls whose foundations lay on bedrock. The whole formed an irregular trapezoid which has been preserved to the present day. In essence it is the enclosure surrounding the Temple area, now the Islamic sanctuary called the *Haram es-Sherif*.

a. Comparative Dimensions

The Haram's dimensions are approximately 930 feet (280 meters) on the south side, 1620 feet (485 meters) on the west side (the Western Wall), 1050 feet (315 meters) on the north side, and 1550 feet (470 meters) on the east side. The enclosed surface measures approximately 172,000 square yards or about 40 acres, one-sixth of the total area of the

Old City within the walls. The present measurements do not conform, however, to those cited by Josephus; his total circumference is given as 6 stadia or 3,660 feet (1110 meters) as compared with today's measurements of 5,150 feet (1,550 meters), nor do they bear any relationship to those reported in the Mishna (*Middot* 2:1) which give the Temple Mount an area of 500 by 500 cubits or 77,700 square yards (approximately 16 acres), in accordance with an ancient tradition based on Ezekiel's Temple blueprint (45:2). This more limited area apparently refers to the *Soreg* or sacred enclosure and the differences noted are not due to a slip in calculating or measuring (see below).

When we compare the Jerusalem shrine with other eastern sanctuaries of the Graeco-Roman world, we find that the area of the *temenos*, the complex of the Temple structures surrounded by its walls, exceeded by far other famous sanctuaries. The *temenos* of Jerusalem was three and a half times as large as that of *Jupiter Heliopolitanus* at Baalbek (Lebanon) which incorporated the temple of Astarte-Venus as well. It is also worth noting that the *Forum Romanum* erected by Emperor Trajan was only half as large as the area of the Temple Mount.

120

The wall surrounding the Tomb of the Patriarchs at Hebron (Cave of Machpela shrine), dating from Herod's time has preserved the outer pillars (center) which decorated the upper half of the wall. The same architectural feature characterized the external surface of the Herodian walls of the Temple Mount

b. The Typical Herodian Masonry

The most remarkable feature of the area is the surviving complex of supporting walls which enclosed the Temple Mount. The product of precise planning and meticulous construction, the massive Herodian masonry fit together perfectly without the use of mortar or any other cementing materials. All the edges and surfaces of the huge light-grey ashlars were chiselled with fine precision and bordered in what is regarded as typical of Herodian building style. Those in the upper and visible layers have a large flat margin around the four edges, often in contrast to the blocks of the lower foundation layers, which were cut with narrower margins around the edges of the slightly raised, flat boss in the center of the stones. The height of most of the ashlars is 3.3–4 feet, but one of the continuous layers in the Southern Wall, the "master course," is made up of ashlars 6.2 feet high. Another characteristic of the walls is a slight downward (and outward) inclination by means of a slow grading of their layers. The ashlars are remarkable for their length; some of them, including several at the southwestern corner and even more in the Western Wall itself, measure 36.7 feet. Other outstanding features included pilasters (rectangular pillars set into the wall and topped with capitals). They decorated the upper exterior side of the Western and Southwestern Walls, and rose to the level of the Temple Mount inner platform. They closely resembled the outer walls which Herod built around the shrine at the Cave of Machphela in Hebron, the traditional burial site of the Hebrew Patriarchs and one of the holiest places in Jewish tradition. Its walls, which stand to this day, form an impressive rectangle measuring 194 × 112 feet. All the stones are the same height, and some are as long as 23 feet.

c. An Engineering Puzzle

The question remains: How could Herod's engineers raise tremendous stones weighing fifty to one hundred tons or more to a height of 30–40 feet (9–12 m.) and position these stones to fit so precisely into the walls or over standing colonnades? The author could find no answer in the engineering treatise written by Vitruvius. However, by courtesy of Dr. Luigi d'Amore of the National Museum of Naples, a photograph was obtained of a fresco found in the excavations of Stabia, one of the three cities buried under the ashes of Mount Vesuvius. It depicts the work yard of a Roman builder of the time, with various items of large equipment.

If the blurred lines of the fresco reproduced here are any indication, the very large object on the left, resting on wheels, seems to be the lower part of a balanced apparatus, connected to a lever with a boom and used to raise columns. It is still not known how stones were raised to the walls. They may have been pulled up along removable inclined ramps.

d. Evidence of the Fallen Fragments

Numerous fragments of such pilasters and their capitals, as well as pieces from two stone sundials, together with fragments of other architectural elements including friezes, panels, cornices, as illustrated, some of which fell from the top of the wall and some

121

Plan of excavations along the southwestern and southern walls (Herodian period): 1. Stairway leading to the gate of the Royal Portico. 2. The Robinson Arch resting on vast piers over the Tyropoeon street. 3. The main paved street of Jerusalem (west of the Western Wall). 4. The Aqueduct. 5. The Western Wall of the Temple area. 6. The Southern Wall. 7. The street skirting the Southern Wall and the communicating underground chambers. 8. The paved plaza. 9. The western Hulda Gata. 10. The Eastern Hulda Gate. 9.a. 10.a. 11.a.: Ascending ramps leading to the wide esplanade (outer courts of the Temple area). 11. The Kiponos Gate (Barclay Gate). 12. The street leading to the Upper City. 13. Tombs of the period of the Judean kings (right) and cistern (left). 14. Traces of the top of an eastern staircase leading to the "Solomon Stables" from the street at the upper Kidron Valley

The blurred lines of the Roman fresco of an engineer's yard at Stabia (southern Italy) seem to indicate a balanced apparatus possibly used to raise columns

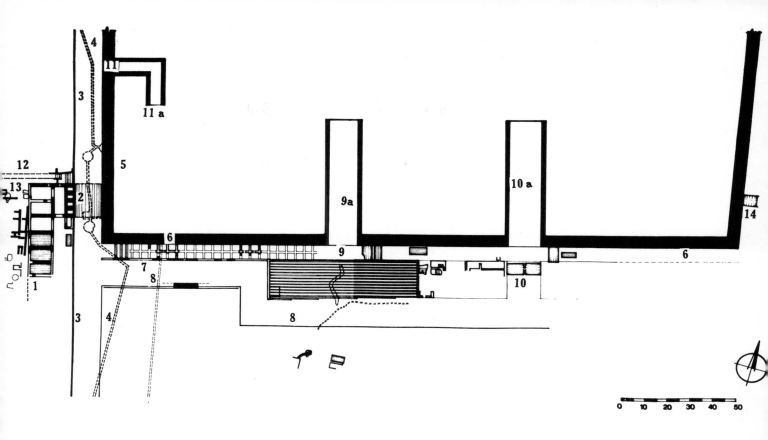

The quarrying of stone blocks was effected by the insertion of wet wooden wedges through narrow trenches hacked through the rock; as the wedges swelled, they ended by sundering the rock. The stones were subsequently sawn and hammered to size with chisels

Decorated fragments of upper sections discovered in the debris excavated around the southwestern angle of the Temple Mount

from the Royal Portico, were found in abundance among the debris which had accumulated along the area facing the whole length of the Southern Wall and close to the Western Wall. These fragments bear typical Herodian decorations comprising the rich variety of geometric as well as floral patterns characteristic of the artistic repertoire of the period. Similar patterns figure prominently in the decoration of the facades of the sumptuous mausoleums, monumental tombs, and ossuaries and sarcophagi of this period in Jerusalem (see Part V, E: The Necropolis of Jerusalem).

Despite Herod's other affinities to the Roman manner, the decorative style of Herodian architecture bears no relationship to the Imperial Roman style. The Herodian style is paralleled in many parts of the ancient Middle East. Its origins lie in the specific oriental-hellenistic art of decoration which represents a fusion of classic hellenistic features with oriental variety, together blending into the cosmopolitan culture which characterized the oriental peoples associated with the Graeco-Roman world, as exemplified by the sanctuaries of Baalbek in Lebanon, the Nabatean desert city of Petra, or Palmyra in the eastern Syrian desert.

2. THE PORTICOS

The outer Porticos (*Stoa* in Greek) surrounding the Temple Mount platform were formed by two rows of columns. Each portico was thirty cubits (49 feet) wide, except for the Southern Royal Portico, described below. They lent great splendor and majesty to the lofty Mount and served also — the Royal Portico in particular — as the gathering place for great assemblies.

a. The Royal Portico

A considerable amount of information about the Royal Portico (*Stoa Basileos* in Greek) which Herod built all along the southern end of the Temple courts is to be found in Josephus' *Antiquities* XV:430: "And this portico was more deserving of mention than any under the sun," the historian proudly declares. Our excavations have uncovered important data which help to explain the planning, design, and character of the Southern or Royal Portico.

The center of this Portico was in the shape of a basilica, consisting of a central nave

124

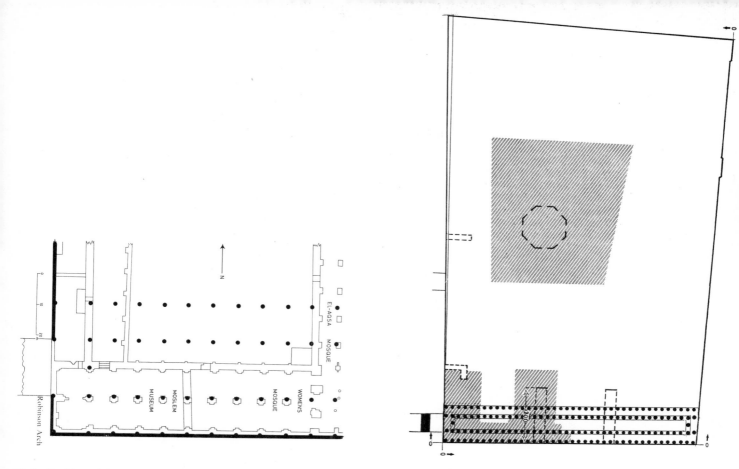

Right: Position of the Royal Portico (south) and ramps under it. The shaded areas indicate the later Moslem superstructures. Left: Plan of the south-western corner, with partial plan of the Royal Portico superimposed schematically

and two aisles. It was oriented towards the spot now marked by the Robinson Arch situated on the Western Wall, which is the site of the ancient double gate that led to the basilica. According to Josephus' detailed description, there were one hundred and sixty-two monolithic columns in four rows erected on the site, each 27 feet (8.2 meters) high and 4.6 feet (1.4 meters) in diameter, each topped by a capital in the Greek "Corinthian" style distinguished by its bell-shape and rows of acanthus leaves. Several fragments of these columns and their capitals were found in the accumulated debris or embedded in other walls and structures, having been reused by later builders as late as Islamic times. Among the latter may be mentioned two monolithic columns standing in the inner vestibule of the Western (Double) Hulda Gate, directly under the floor on which stands the 'Aqṣa Mosque (see below: The Western Hulda Gate). Owing to their massive size, large numbers of them were apparently used in laying the foundations or building the walls of later Byzantine or Islamic structures. This may account in part for the compar-atively small number of columns which turned up in the debris at the foot of the walls.

We are still seeking the answer to several problems concerning the Royal Portico and its dimensions; they also bear on the renovations and reconstructions which were carried out during the Herodian period and right up to the destruction of the Temple. In the main, the evidence bears out Josephus' description of the Temple complex as illustrated in our reconstruction model. The large number of decorative architectural fragments found among the debris illustrates details of the elaborate structures built by Herod and his successors.

b. *The Ḥanuyot of the Temple Mount*

The Southern Royal Portico may be identified with the *Ḥanuyot* mentioned in Talmudic sources. According to the Mishna, "the Sanhedrin had been expelled forty years before the destruction of the Temple (from the Chamber of Hewn Stone, on consecrated ground) and took its seat at the Ḥanuyot" (*Sanhedrin* 41:2; *Aboda Zara* 8:2). This would have occurred about A.D. 30, in the days of Pontius Pilate.

c. *Jesus at the Ḥanuyot*

At the time the Sanhedrin moved to a section of the Ḥanuyot, the head of the Sanhedrin, Rabban Gamaliel (known as Paul's teacher) taught there as well. These Porticos served several functions concurrently from about A.D. 30 on, when certain public activities were transferred there and reorganized on a more efficient basis than in former years. Their most prestigious function would be serving as the new seat of the Sanhedrin. The reorganization also allowed money changers and other dealers in ritual objects to operate in other sections of the Ḥanuyot (shops, in Hebrew). This relaxed attitude was not considered unusual in ancient oriental usage (the same is true of the casualness characterizing ancient Greek public places). Moreover, the Ḥanuyot must have been differentiated in the public eye from the truly sacred areas beyond the Soreg (see above, Section, D, 3, b: The Balustrade). Nevertheless, it is possible that these modernizing trends irritated some of the more puritanical people who saw the change as an unbecoming intrusion of business into the procedures and areas of worship, even though many others regarded the Ḥanuyot as only a semi-sacred area.

Jesus, like other puritanical Jews, might have taken the attitude that the spirit of worship and reverence was undermined by the intrusion of such dealings. It will be remembered that the prophets of the Old Testament and the ascetic Nazirites of later days seem to have reacted similarly to activities in and around the sanctuary in the days of the First Temple. James, the brother of Jesus, was known to have been a Nazirite, and he may well have spent his days in devout seclusion and prayer in the same precincts.

There is no serious problem with regard to chronology, since the date of the crucifixion accepted by many scholars is March-April 30 A.D. (chiefly on the basis of Johannine chronology), though some scholars set it a year earlier or one to three years later. It may also be observed that the figure of forty years preceding A.D. 70 mentioned above may simply be a round figure, the popular 'generation' estimate often found in the Bible.

3. ARCHEOLOGICAL LINKS WITH STRUCTURES UNDER THE HARAM ES-SHERIF

As the Islamic structures (see Part VI, C: The Early Moslem Period) were built on top of previously existing Jewish structures which had not undergone total or possibly great destruction, it is reasonable to determine whether or not archeological links may

An underground corridor lying below the level of the Single Gate (which once led to the Solomon Stables). It emerges 112 feet (33.6 m.) west of the southeastern angle of the wall. It is 69 feet (21 m.) long, 3 feet (1 m.) wide and 11.5 feet (3.45 m.) high. It is constructed of blocks of Herodian style, closely bonded together. The corridor ends at its northern extremity before a doorway leading to a hall situated below the Solomon Stables

be established between certain underground structures in that area and any remains of the older structures of the Jewish Temple Mount associated with its religious and other activities (see above, Section D, 3: What Were the Inner Courts of the Sanctuary Like?).

a. The Underground Passage under the Single Gate

Mention should be made, first of all, of an interesting link in the form of an underground passage or corridor which we discovered at the eastern side of the Temple area, below the level of the so-called Solomon Stables. The entrance to the passages is 112 feet (34 meters) west of the southern corner of the area. It is 69 feet (21 meters) long, three feet (one meter) wide, and 11.5 feet (3.5 meters) high (see illustration).

The southern entrance to this passage lay under one of the vaulted rooms supporting the sloping narrow street which started at the Eastern (Triple) Hulda Gate (see below, Section F, 4, c), and descended to the Kidron valley. The passage was certainly built

127

Excavation of the area along the Western Wall under the Robinson Arch (center). Below is the lower pier of the arch, with four chambers which faced the Tyropoeon street pavement to the east, and were probably used as shops. The huge arch rose above the piers and came to rest at the Robinson Arch. A winding stairway led to this arch, and through it to the entrance of the southern Royal Portico. At the right is a section of the Crusader's wall of the city (twelfth century A.D.). Details of the structures are described in the pictures below (see Part III, F)

The rock-hewn subterranean conduit unearthed below the Triple Hulda Gate leads deep within the underground of the Southern Wall, where it merges apparently with an abandoned reservoir marked 10 in Diagram 4 below

together with the massive southern supporting wall of the Temple Mount and is constructed of stones carved in Herodian style. They are closely bonded into a uniform construction with emphasis laid on its solidity. The end of the underground passage at its northern extremity is a doorway which probably leads to a hall lying below the so-called Solomon Stables.

It is commonly assumed that the 'Solomon Stables' above them were also used as storerooms for objects held in trust by the administrators of the Temple area.

b. The Chamber of Ritual Immersion

On the northwest corner of the inner courts was the descent to the Chamber of Ritual Immersion (*Bēt Hatvila;* see above, Section D, 1, c: The Morning Service). The approach to it, according to the Talmud (*Middot* 1:6), was through a winding stairway going into an underground passage or *Messiba* illuminated by oil lamps placed in niches on both sides. It led beneath the northern Tadi Gate to a purification bath outside the city.

It is very likely that the long (198 feet) and narrow underground cistern presently situated under the platform of the Haram es-Sherif is connected with this ancient installation (No. 1 in diagram 4). There is a gallery proceeding in a northerly direction

Interior of the aqueduct of the Herodian period beneath the Tyropoeon street which skirted the Western Wall (looking north). The aqueduct lies 190 feet (5.5 m.) below the street. Its sides are rock-hewn and the vaulting is constructed out of chiselled stone blocks. It served to gather the rainwaters flowing into it from other channels (see Part III, F, 1, d)

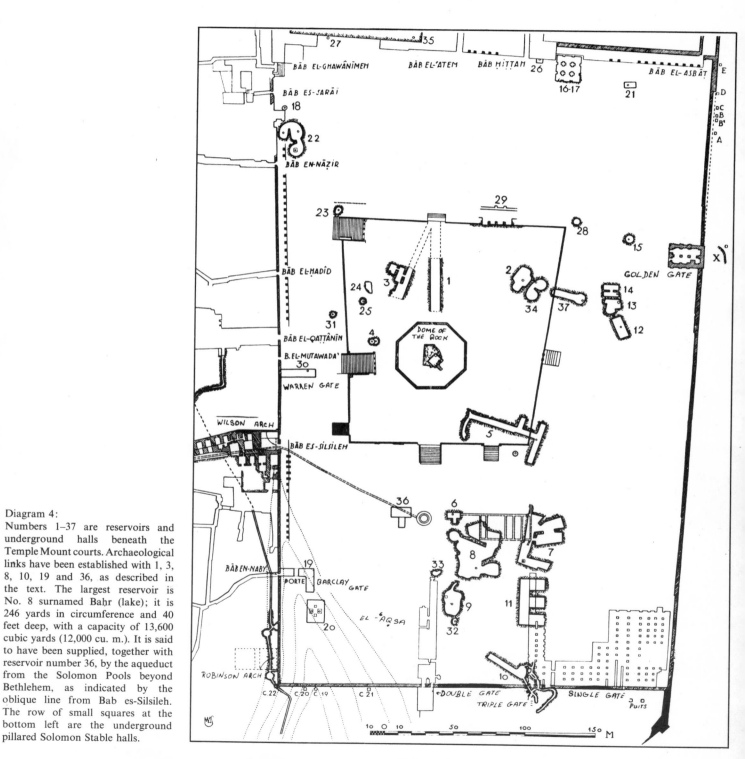

Diagram 4:
Numbers 1–37 are reservoirs and underground halls beneath the Temple Mount courts. Archaeological links have been established with 1, 3, 8, 10, 19 and 36, as described in the text. The largest reservoir is No. 8 surnamed Baḥr (lake); it is 246 yards in circumference and 40 feet deep, with a capacity of 13,600 cubic yards (12,000 cu. m.). It is said to have been supplied, together with reservoir number 36, by the aqueduct from the Solomon Pools beyond Bethlehem, as indicated by the oblique line from Bab es-Silsileh. The row of small squares at the bottom left are the underground pillared Solomon Stable halls.

129

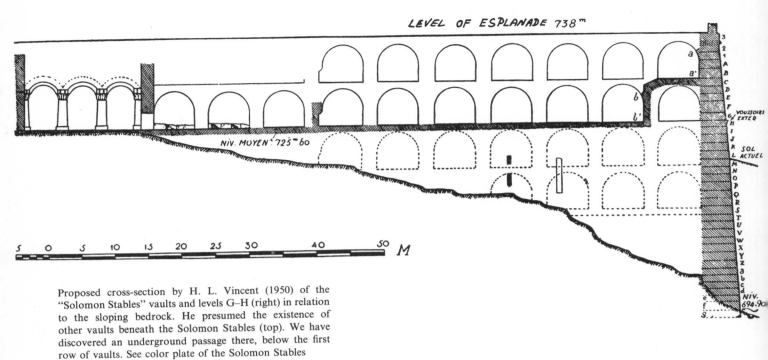

LEVEL OF ESPLANADE 738ᵐ

NIV. MOYEN 725ᵐ60

S O 5 10 15 20 25 30 40 50 M

VOUSSOIRS EXTER

SOL ACTUEL

NIV. 694.90

Proposed cross-section by H. L. Vincent (1950) of the "Solomon Stables" vaults and levels G–H (right) in relation to the sloping bedrock. He presumed the existence of other vaults beneath the Solomon Stables (top). We have discovered an underground passage there, below the first row of vaults. See color plate of the Solomon Stables

from the northern side of the Dome of the Rock; it is all that remains of a still longer structure which led to the northern *mikveh*.

The chamber of immersion itself may be identified with the underground cistern (No. 3 in diagram 4) which lies to the west of the gallery, formed of a cluster of four or five rooms. Here we have two other important archeological links between important parts of the Herodian Temple and cisterns which are located under the Haram es-Sherif platform. Several attempts have been made to identify other underground chambers with structures mentioned in ancient Jewish sources, but their verification must await further research and analysis of the data.

Head of one of the water reservoirs located under the Haram es-Sherif esplanade

The public segment of the Western Wall has become since 1967 the largest open air center of Jewish worship, as well as a site for mass gatherings on festivals and other occasions. This scene shows *hora* dancing, the men on one side and the women on the other side of the fence, as ordained by orthodox custom. The arch in the background is the entrance to the Wilson Arch area

F. THE OUTER WALLS AND GATES OF THE TEMPLE MOUNT

1. THE WESTERN WALL SECTION FORMERLY CALLED THE WAILING WALL

For close to two millennia, Jewish worshipers and pilgrims have gathered at the foot of one part of the Western Wall of the Temple Mount, a section known also as the 'Wailing Wall.' It was regarded as sacred in popular belief as far back as Talmudic times, and regular services were held there in later centuries. Until 1967, only five lower courses dating from Herodian times were visible, each over three feet high. The courses above these five, constructed of far smaller stones, are more recent. After 1967, two more, deeper, courses were exposed, and the immense esplanade facing the wall was transformed into Jewry's open air center of worship, pilgrimage and celebration. There are nineteen Herodian courses still underground, ascending from bedrock lying sixty-nine feet (21 meters) deep. These courses have been uncovered in part or in whole further south along the Western Wall.

131

The section of the exposed wall in question extends along some 188 feet (57 meters), from the Moslem structure called the *Mahkameh*, built over the Wilson Arch, to a dilapidated stairway giving access to the buried Barclay's Gate (see below).

This whole neighborhood, as will be described in Part V, formed part of the public section of the Lower City of Herodian Jerusalem; the Upper City was a residential section. Important links with the latter and other sections are now coming to light.

a. The New Significance of the Robinson Arch

The Robinson Arch is one of the most spectacular of the surviving remains of the Herodian period. The visible lowest stones of the arch where they curve outwards, jut slightly from the Western Wall and are part of a huge arch which stood about forty feet from the southwestern corner of the Temple platform. Four layers of large blocks have remained in the arch, which originally came to rest on a tremendous pier built parallel to the Western Wall and at a distance of about forty-two feet from it. The arch itself was fifty-one feet wide and spanned a paved road running along the foot of the Western Wall.

Scholars generally believed this arch was only the first of a series of arches resting on piers which formed a causeway spanning the width of the Tyropoeon Vale. This causeway was supposed to have connected the Temple Mount with the Upper City, even though there was no mention of any causeway in the ancient sources. The hypothesis has now been disproved completely as a result of our excavations. They have demonstrated the existence of a line of equidistant arches grading downward in height as one proceeds in a southerly direction, until they reached the pavement below. It is clear that the arches formed part of a monumental stairway system which led from the paved road toward the double gate that stood over the Robinson Arch in the Western Wall of the Royal Portico, as illustrated in our reconstruction model. A fragment of the doorpost of this gate has been found, as well as a large number of the steps leading to it which have fallen down. Some of the steps are still attached to the original threshold which occupies its ancient site to this day.

Top of the Robinson Arch (upper background). Its lower end rested on vast piers built in the Tyropoeon Valley and both ends were joined by a stairway as illustrated in the resconstruction model

b. What Were the Gates of the Western Wall?

Josephus mentions four gates in his description of the Western Wall (*Antiquities* XV:410). He says the southernmost gate leads down "by means of many steps" to the Tyropoeon Vale, and it is possible to reach the Upper City from there. The "many steps" must refer to the monumental stairway just described. Ascending north of the great pier (see previous section) from the paved road in a westerly direction, it winds over a series of vaulted structures, built of small well-edged masonry stones which lead to the Upper City or the Western hill. The whole arrangement is entirely in harmony with the plan of the area in Herodian times.

Where were the other three gates described by Josephus? One of them, now called the *Barclay's Gate* after the British architect who discovered it in mid-nineteenth century A.D., is most likely the gate mentioned in the Mishna, *Middot* 1:3 as the *Kiphonos* (Coponius) Gate: "There are five gates to the Temple: the two Hulda Gates in the south which serve for entry and exit, the Kiphonos Gate in the west which served for entry and exit..." It is believed that the Kiphonos Gate is named for the Roman Procurator Coponius (A.D. 6–9) who may have contributed towards its reconstruction and adornment. The gate is still in a fair state of preservation, though hidden and overlaid by various obstructions. Its tremendous single-stone sill, twenty-five feet long and over

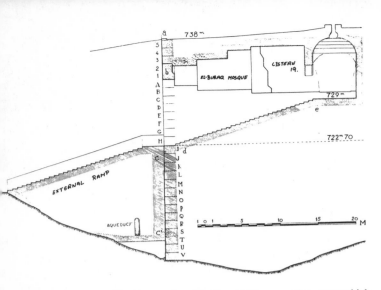

Plan drawn by H. L. Vincent showing the possible ascending ramp which led from the Herodian paved street skirting the Western Wall, and the southwestern angle of the wall. The ramp then rose underground at the 729 m. mark to the court esplanade. Since Islamic days, a mosque and reservoir have blocked this passage

Reconstruction model of the southwestern corner of the wall, the parapet and the stairway nearby leading to the Robinson Arch. The latter spanned the pavement skirting the Western Wall

seven feet high (7.5 × 2.1 meters), rests on the master course of the Western Wall, that is, at the level of the thresholds of several of its gates. The gateway (opening) is 28.7 feet (8.75 meters) high, but the threshold is missing. The Kiphonos Gate can still be seen, part of it from the outside and southern end of the Western Wall section popularly called the Wailing Wall, south of the area now reserved for women's worship. The buried gateway abuts, inside, on an abandoned mosque called *El Buraq*; a late Moslem legend has it that this is where the Prophet Mohammed tethered his miraculous mount before ascending to heaven (see Part VI, C: The Early Moslem Period).

Inside the gate, there was once a vestibule which is now blocked by a wall. Behind the wall a passage leads through one or two ancient cisterns with vaulted roofs which are situated under the Haram platform. Before they were converted into reservoirs, they were stone hallways and formed an underground ramp leading in a southerly direction from the Kiphonos Gate to the upper courts of the Temple area. The ramp and remains are illustrated in our diagram. The interior of the Kiphonos (Barclay) Gate, now blocked, represents another archeological link with the remains of the Temple courts.

J.T. Barclay lived in Jerusalem in 1855–57. He had been sent there with a Turkish architect to effect some repairs in the Dome of the Rock, and was the first to point out the existence of the ancient gate, since named after him.

A third gate in the Western Wall stood over the eastern side of the causeway (the Wilson Arch) which linked the Upper City to the Western Portico of the Temple Mount (see Part V, C, 3, d: The Xystos). The fourth gate, whose name is also not mentioned in the ancient records, is the so-called 'Warren Gate' (see map 3) named after its discoverer. It is situated north of the Wilson Arch, but little information is available about it and it is not possible to survey or excavate the site.

The existence of the four gates of the Western Wall, as described by Josephus, have been confirmed and the gates themselves identified correctly through archeological investigation. Two of them led to the Porticos: the Royal Portico beginning at the gate now identified with the Robinson Arch, and the Western Portico over the Wilson Arch. The other two (the Barclay and Warren Gates) led from the paved street which bordered the Western Wall, into underground passages below the Western Portico, and from there upward, through ramps, to the courts of the Temple.

134

Pavement of the Tyropoeon street, the main street which skirted the Western Wall of the Temple Mount area and crossed the city from north to south. A continuation of this street was discovered by F. J. Bliss and A. C. Dickie in 1898 half a mile to the south in the Lower City. The street, bordered by a curb to help rainwater flow downhill, is forty-one feet wide and is supported on three rows of solid chambers beneath as it lay on sloping ground. The pavement runs along the level of the eighteenth course of the Western Wall counting from bedrock

The aqueduct of the Herodian period which ran beneath the pavement of the Tyropoeon street. It gathered rainwater flowing into it from other channels

c. The Paved Road along the Western Wall

In the course of excavating the area around the Robinson Arch, several stretches of the paved road leading along the Western Wall were uncovered. As already noted, it passed between the wall and the pier of the Robinson Arch and continued southwards, finally reaching a point west of the Siloam Pool. The discovery of the last stretch of this important street was made by F.J. Bliss and A.C. Dickie. This was Jerusalem's main street in the Herodian period, and led to the southern gate of the city, which opened into the Valley of Hinnom (see map 3). A branch of this road led east to the Siloam Pool (see Part V, C, 1, b: Continuation of the Tyropoeon Street in the City of David). The road, in all likelihood, had been paved throughout its length with great hewn slabs about three feet long, towards the end of the Second Temple period. It was Agrippa II, according to Josephus (*Antiquities* XX:547), who had ordered the streets of Jerusalem to be paved with white stone and at least one of his motives, was to provide the citizenry with work.

d. The Underground Drainage Tunnel

Further study exposed a north-to-south underground channel which had been dug in the bedrock below the paved street and covered by built-in low vaults. This catchment system collected rain water which was brought there by means of other channels leading down from the west and the east, and which were identified in the course of our excavations. The underground channel actually sloped downward in a shallow gradient in the direction of the pools situated south of the City of David. It is possible that the water was used to irrigate the gardens and vegetables patches near the city limits. The channel was first discovered by Charles Warren a hundred years ago. It was only partly excavated and examined. We could trace its course across the Tyropoeon valley where it ran under the causeway leading to the Wilson Arch (see Part V, D, 1: The Wilson Arch; and diagram).

2. THE HERODIAN FINDS LEFT BY PILGRIMS

The great hoard of pottery and stone artifacts of the Herodian period included many which had apparently been brought there by people entering the Temple area. Of equal or greater importance are the thousands of coins, most of them of copper, some of silver and a precious few of gold. They range in date from Hasmonean (Maccabean) times, up to the destruction of the Temple, tracing the succession of rulers and the changes in government during that momentous period. In addition to providing a capsule history through their brief inscriptions and representations, they are of special value in fixing an exact chronological framework for the strata and loci of the Temple area.

It is of interest to note that there was a smaller proportion of coins of foreign origin dating from Herodian times, compared with the large number of coins struck in Jerusalem, probably because these foreign coins had been exchanged for Jewish currency in Jerusalem, for payment of Temple taxes and sacrifices.

3. THE PLACE OF TRUMPETING

Another important discovery relating to Josephus' description of the Temple area was a trimmed stone block found near the southwestern corner. It was the source of extraordinary interest, chiefly because of a monumental Hebrew inscription which was carved at the edge of a niche. The block had undoubtedly fallen from the tower of the southwestern parapet at the corner of the wall, and as a result its left edge had broken off, destroying the concluding letters of the inscription. The inscription reads as follows: "*LBYT HTQY'H LHK...*" It may be vocalized: "*L'BET HATQI'A LEHAKH(RIZ)*" — the first two words meaning "To the Place of Trumpeting" and the third, "lehakhrīz" meaning to proclaim or herald. The inscription can be interpreted in the light of certain details provided by Josephus in *War* IV:502. It stood at the edge of the outer Temple court chambers. On the eve of the Sabbath one of the Priests would ascend this tower and sound a trumpet to signal the advent of the holy day, and at sundown the process was repeated to announce its conclusion. It is evident therefore that the niche in which the priest stood, at the pinnacle, had to be located very close to the southwestern corner of the wall; furthermore, it would have been entirely logical to call it the Place of Trumpeting. It will be observed that this strategic point overlooked most of the city's quarters, as well as its streets, residences and bazaars. The literal meaning of the Hebrew word 'BYT' is 'house' but it is used to designate a variety of places or structures, large or small. The word which occurs in this inscription also appears on a carved fragment of stone found near the Eastern Hulda Gate (the term is still legible on the upper line). In Talmudic literature it is used in reference to a certain category of Temple court chambers. It was at this site of the rampart, the southwestern corner parapet, that the Zealot leader John of Gischala erected one of the four towers attributed to him.

138

Above: Typical collection of pottery dating to the 8th century B.C. (Judean monarchy) discovered in more ancient layers excavated near the walls

Center: Oil lamps of the Herodian period

Below, right: Painted ware of the Herodian period

Below, left: This revealing inscription uncovered below the northwestern parapet of the wall, reads: "To the Place of Trumpeting... to herald." A priest stood in a niche on the angle of the upper parapet and proclaimed to the town the advent and end of the Sabbath

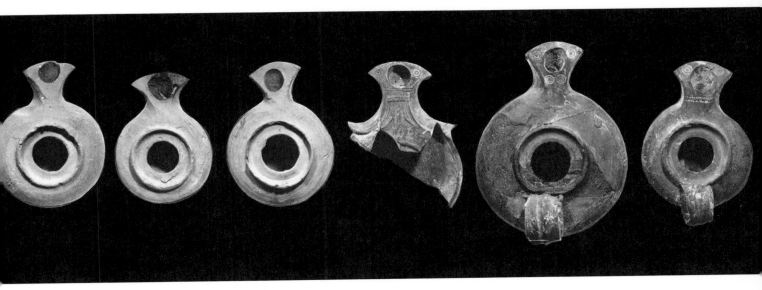

The ascending paved street, constructed of large stone slabs, along the foot of the Southern Wall, near the southwestern corner. It led to the Hulda Gates. The squared blocks at the bottom had toppled from the top of the wall and lay on the paved street since A.D. 70

4. THE MONUMENTAL SOUTHERN GATES

Our examination of the area south of the Southern Wall of the Temple revealed a complicated arrangement of buildings and passages which reflects the same master plan already encountered in the area facing the Western Wall. As stated previously, the road which bordered the Western Wall turned east and ascended, by means of steps, to the Western Hulda Gate (now called the Double Gate). It proceeded to the Eastern Hulda Gate (the Triple Gate) and then sloped gradually to the angle of the Ophel lying at the southeastern corner of the Temple Mount walls (see Part IV). South of this street and at a lower level was a wide paved plaza. It undoubtedly served as a general meeting place for the large crowds of pilgrims before they entered the gates of the Temple Mount. Two continuous rows of small rooms had been built below the street, one at the western and one at the eastern edge. They were covered with vaults over which the heavy paving stones of the street had been set. The small chambers must have served as storerooms, and were provided with connecting passages. The differences in height between the street and the plaza made it possible to build doors and windows into the wall which bordered the street at the side of the plaza.

Below, right: The outer Herodian vestibule of the Double Hulda Gate has been walled up since Crusader times at the point where the small white square porthole appears. The doorway in the center leads to the inner Herodian vestibule and wide underground slowly-ascending passage, which today runs under the whole length of the 'Aqsa Mosque and leads to the upper platform of the Temple Mount. Two monolithic columns (below, center) stand there and support the cupolas of the vestibule which lies under the floor of the mosque. They are similar in dimension to those of Herod's Royal Portico, or approximately 5.9 feet (1.8 m.) in diameter. The white marble of the columns shows through the unsightly concrete armature in which they were encased after the 1927 earthquake. These columns serve also as underpinnings of the southern floor of the 'Aqsa mosque

Above right: Detail of the doorway leading to the inner vestibule, showing the vaulted roof of the outer Herodian vestibule (above)

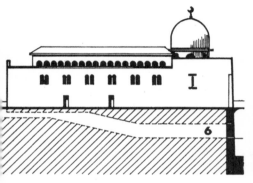

The ancient underground passage under the 'Aqsa mosque, leading from the Double Gate to the esplanade

Below, left: A gallery leading from the Double (Hulda) Gate to the so-called Solomon Stables (ancient storehouses) was discovered during repairs of El-'Aqsa mosque foundations. This exposed the inner face of the southern supporting wall of the Temple Mount and the gallery which skirts this wall

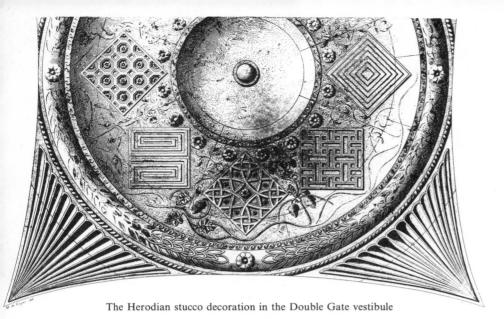

The Herodian stucco decoration in the Double Gate vestibule

Below, left: The wide Herodian stairway which led from the Ophel to the Double Hulda Gate (since walled up by the structures meeting at an angle)

Right: Detail of the Herodian stucco decoration

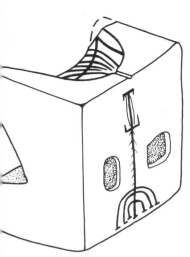

A small stone sundial or *gnomon* of the Herodian period. The twelve hours are marked in furrows which radiate from the master groove

Fragment of a marble slab uncovered south of the Western Wall, inscribed in archaic Hebrew characters (unlike the square alphabet used in Herodian times), but dating, nevertheless, to the last years of the Second Temple. National pride and a sense of historic continuity favored the archaic custom

a. The Western (Double) Hulda Gate

The underground passages beneath the Royal Portico on the south, described above, led from the Hulda Gates (*Middot* 1:3) to the outer courts of the Temple Mount. The inside passage from the inner side of the immured Western Hulda Gate has been preserved in its ancient form almost throughout its length, despite renovations made in the area in the course of the centuries. The Western Hulda Gate had apparently been blocked in Crusader times. Seen from its outside or southern end, part of the immured section of the gate and lintel are hidden by later structures. The gate is forty-three feet (12.8 meters) wide, with a thick pier in the center dividing it into two entrances. The gate led to a square vestibule built of massive Herodian blocks in the center of which stands a thick monolithic column (4.6 feet in diameter) supporting four arches and flat cupolas which rest in the corner with pendentives (i.e. spherical triangles formed by the intersection of arches). The cupolas still retain traces of beautiful acanthus decorations in Herodian style. Another monolithic column of similar girth stands nearby and has been buttressed recently by heavy concrete reinforcements to protect the floor above it, on which stands the apse of the 'Aqṣa Mosque (see E, 2, a above: The Royal Portico).

b. The Monumental Stairway to the Hulda Gates

In the course of our excavations in the area facing the Western Hulda Gate, we uncovered a gigantic stairway which led from the Lower City (Ophel) to the gates. It is two hundred and fifteen feet wide; the foundation steps were cut into the natural bedrock on the slopes of the Temple Mount. The stairs were constructed of wide, trimmed and smoothed stone paving blocks, fitted together snugly. The stairway comprised thirty steps set alternately in wide and narrow rows. It ascended twenty-two feet to the upper road, also paved with large stones, immediately facing the Hulda Gates. South of it and below lay the wide plaza.

c. The Eastern (Triple) Hulda Gate

A fragment of the western jamb has survived at the Eastern Hulda Gate, as well as a section of the paved street facing its sill. This was a very large gate, about fifty feet wide,

A panoramic view of the mid section of the southern wall and the *Ophel* beneath, showing the wide stairway (left) which worshipers ascended to reach the gates of the Mountain of the Lord. Tops of cisterns and ritual baths are visible in the upper background as well as the road which skirted the southern wall (see Part III, F, 1, 2–4 ff) and gates. The structures in the foreground were erected by the early Moslem conquerors (Part VI, C) ▶

Above: The Eastern (Triple) Hulda Gate of the Southern Wall before excavation. The gate is about fifty feet (15 m.) wide and its inner vestibule is divided by rectangular pillars engaged in the wall

Below: The excavated paving of the street (middle ground) which skirted the Southern Wall and led from the intersection of the southwestern angle to the Kidron valley. Below is the strong arch which supported the wide stairway leading from the lower plaza to the gates

Another underground passage was found below the Southern Wall, emerging under the Single Gate and the 'Solomon Stables'. It is constructed of heavy Herodian blocks and ends 69 feet further in, before a doorway leading to a hall situated under the Solomon Stables (Part III, E, 3, a). Notice the niche in the wall intended to hold a clay lamp

Above: The backbone of the supporting arch is dug in the bedrock (see corresponding picture on p. 144)

Below: Section of the southern wall east of the Triple Hulda Gate and left, below, a remnant of the underground cells which ran below the street that skirted the wall

apparently with a broad portal at the center and two smaller ones at each side. South of the street pavement which faced the gate, the remains of a deep vault were discovered. The vault extended across the full width of the street. Its lower part had been cut into the bedrock. It had obviously supported a stairway which led from the lower plaza to the paved street facing the gate. The steps of the stairway had been torn away long ago, but some of them lay among the debris along with the fragments of decorated stones which formed an integral part of the gate's design.

d. The Ritual Baths between the Stairways

During the excavations of the wide stairway there appeared simultaneously a number of ritual baths (in Hebrew, *mikveh*), pools and plastered cisterns, hewn out of bedrock. These poorly preserved structures lay directly to the east of the monumental stairway leading to the Western Hulda Gate. They were destroyed and only the bottom parts of the cold-water baths lay exposed. Further east there was probably another stairway leading to the Eastern Hulda Gate, and the *mikvehs* thus lay between the two stairways. What we had actually come upon were the historic "Stairways of the Temple Mount" often mentioned in Talmudic literature. One relevant passage speaks of Gamaliel and the Elders who stood at the top of the stairs of the Temple Mount (*Tosefta, Sanhedrin* 2:2), while a parallel reference states: "...on top of the stairway to the Temple Mount." The Gamaliel referred to was Rabban Gamaliel the Elder, known also from the New Testament as Paul's teacher (Acts 5:34–39). The Elders were the members of the Sanhedrin. In the episode referred to, Rabbi Gamaliel and the members of the Sanhedrin are standing at the top of the stairway, over the upper pavement facing the Hulda Gates and overlooking the ascending stairway. Another story in the Talmud (*Berakhot* 58:1) refers to Ben-Zoma who "observed the crowds marching up the stairway which led to the Temple Mount and said: 'Blessed... art thou... who art wise in all secrets, and blessed... art thou... who hast created all these people to serve me.'" He rejoiced at the sight of such a vast crowd of Jews who had come to worship God in accordance with the requirements of their Law.

Our expedition has restored the wide stairway leading to the Western Hulda Gates to their original condition, thus enabling visitors to visualize the press of the multitudes in ancient times, as they converged in song and prayer on the approach to the Temple Mount.

e. The Monumental Inscription Fragments near the Eastern Hulda Gates

Interest was aroused by the discovery of an inscribed stone fragment among other architectural pieces in front of the Hulda Gates. By a strange coincidence, the French explorer, F. de Saulcy, had found a stone slab fragment inscribed in Hebrew near the Eastern (Triple) Gate over a hundred years ago. It now appears that the two fragments belong together as complementary pieces of a monumental inscription. The inscription is incomplete and difficult to interpret, but the initial letters in the first line can be completed to form the word *ZKNYM* (Z°QENĪM) or 'elders' and this may well refer to

146

From left to right: This inscribed stone slab fragment uncovered in front of the Hulda Gate (top) could not convey any meaning but for the chance discovery of another fragment found over a hundred years ago (center), by the archeologist, F. de Saulcy. It complements the first fragment, to form a monumental inscription (right). This refers, apparently, to the *z'kenim* or Elders of the Sanhedrin. The monumental inscription was bordered by a protruding stone frame

the Elders of the Sanhedrin. A Mishnaic reference from *Sanhedrin* 11:2 indicates that there were three tribunals in the Temple Mount area: "One was situated at the entrance to the Temple Mount, one at the entrance to the Outer Court, and one in the Chamber of Hewn Stone" *(Lishkāt Ha-gazīt)*. The inscription found near the Eastern Hulda Gate may have referred to the seat of the first tribunal mentioned, which was located at one of the entrances to the Temple Mount.

f. The Road along the Southern Wall

Near the southwestern corner of the Temple Mount walls, a street branches off from the excavated main road. It is twenty-one feet wide and paved. Ascending as a graded incline along the Southern Wall, it passes the two southern gates (the Hulda Gates) and proceeds beyond them to the southeastern corner of the Temple Mount walls. At the western end of this paved road and close to the corner, great heaps of debris had accumulated. The lowest level of the debris rose about 6.5 feet (2 meters) against the wall and contained many architectural stone fragments, shards, and coins of the Herodian period and especially of the first century A.D., the latest dating to the fourth year of the war with Rome (A.D. 69).

5. THE GATES OF THE EASTERN AND NORTHERN WALLS

So far we have little information concerning the gates of the Temple Mount set in the Eastern and Northern Walls. One historic gate of the Eastern Wall was known as the *Shushān Habirah* (Susa the Capital) Gate. When the high priest sacrificed the red heifer and burned it, he would go out through this gate to the Mount of Unction (Mount of Olives), as described in the Talmud *(Middot* 1:3). The site of the gate is still undetermined, but it cannot be identical with the present nearby Golden Gate (also called *Gate of Mercy* by Moslems and Jews), as is believed, because the latter belongs to a later period, the Byzantine or the Ommayad. It is situated 1023 feet (310 meters) from the southeastern angle of the walls. When Charles Warren excavated there in 1867–69, he discovered thirty or forty feet of debris just outside the gate; eighty-five yards farther north he discovered 100–125 feet of debris. There are also some twenty feet of debris between the surface and the rock at the Lion's Gate to the north.

The southeastern angle of the retaining walls overlooking the Kidron valley. The top of the Single Gate (left) marks the end of the more ancient Herodian stone courses. The higher courses date to later Moslem and Christian times. The low wall at the right is of Byzantine origin and contoured the lower city (fifth century A.D.)

The top (right) is known as the "pinnacle of the Temple" (Mark 11:11; Luke 4:9)

Huge columns of the Royal Portico which had tumbled over the Herodian stairway (see p. 124 and 142)

Inner vestibule of the Golden Gate (Gate of Mercy), dating to the Byzantine period (fourth-fifth centuries A.D.) The columns were taken from the debris of the Temple porticos

Below, right: The emergent Herodian tower at the northeastern angle of the Temple area, an outstanding relic of the Herodian supporting wall north of the Temple.

Another interesting feature of the eastern wall close to the southeastern angle high above the Kidron valley is the remnant of an arch at the upper part of the wall. Situated opposite the Robinson Arch, but on the eastern side of the Temple courts, it also supported a stairway which ascended from an eastern road skirting the Eastern Wall. The top of the stairway opened onto a gate which led to the vaulted halls known as the "Solomon Stables" (see above, E, 3, f).

a. The Red Heifer and Scapegoat Exits

There are problems as well in the attempt to identify the two pathways descending from the eastern side of the Temple courts. One of them, named the *kebeš-parah* (pathway of the Red Heifer) ran down from the Eastern Gate to the Kidron valley and then rose from there to the Mount of Olives. The second, the *kebeš-śeʿir* or scapegoat path, which led in the direction of the Judean wilderness, is mentioned in connection with the ritual on the eve of Yom Kippur, the Day of Atonement (*Shekalim* 4:2; *Parah* 3:6). No trace of these pathways was found.

An ancient rite was performed occasionally at the Temple by a priest, in conformity with the passage in Numbers 19 which prescribed that a red heifer without any blemish should be slain outside the town (or at the Mount of Olives in later days) and burned with cedarwood, hyssop and a scarlet string. The ashes were gathered and mixed with water to remove an impurity created by contact with the dead. It must be noted, however, that this purification rite of the red heifer was performed only five times throughout the whole period of the Second Temple, though the reason for their rarity is unknown. It is not likely that a permanent pathway had been constructed for these occasional rites; a temporary pathway was doubtless prepared for each occasion, and in the nature of the case, no evidence of it has survived.

The "Scapegoat" rite was observed annually and is described above: D, 1, e.

b. The Tadi Gate

We are equally in the dark regarding the location of the Northern Gate called *Tadi* which is described in the Mishna as "serving no purpose." This probably means that the

151

gate had no special role in relation to the Temple Mount rituals as it was understood in ancient times, and as may be gathered from the designation of the other gates (see above: What Were the Gates of the Western Wall?). Nevertheless, one of the classic references in the tractate alludes to a winding underground passage below the *ḥel*, the massive protective wall which surrounded the higher inner sacred courts of the Temple. Oil lamps were placed in niches in the walls on both sides of the passage, which issued from under the Tadi Gate and continued out of the city (Mishna, *Tamid* 1:1). There actually is a long underground hollow structure at that spot, under the Islamic sanctuary platform; it is now used as a cistern. It faces in the direction of the old gates of the Northern Wall, but exploration here is now prohibited by the Moslem religious authorities (see reservoirs No. 1 and 3 in diagram 4).

Another underground passage apparently of the same type has recently been discovered below the southern end of the Temple Mount. This passage also contains niches in the walls on both sides. It leads to an ancient underground and abandoned cistern under the 'Aqṣa mosque. In ancient times it emerged under the Double Hulda Gates (see below). We have uncovered the continuation of this passage leading south of the Double Gate.

CONCLUSION

In his description of the firing of the Temple by Titus, Josephus makes the following pathetic observation: "Deeply as one must mourn for the most marvelous edifice which we have seen or heard of, whether we consider its structures, its magnitude, the richness of its every detail, or the reputation of its Holy Places..." (*War* VI:261).

Jews have kept faith with the Temple Mount throughout the ages, bewailing the destruction of the Temple and nourishing the hope of building it anew and reviving its ancient glory. It is for this reason that Jewish scholars, beginning with those quoted in the Mishna and Talmud and referred to above, have continuously analyzed every detail pertaining to the Temple and its measurements, and all the ancillary data which has been preserved in the memory of the nation. The Temple was also a source of wonder among non-Jews, not only because of its magnificence, but also for its imageless worship unique in antiquity. It played a significant role in early Christianity, which originated during the generation before its destruction. We have already alluded (Part I) to the developments which led the Moslems to build their sacred sanctuary on the site of the Temple, that is to say on the great Rock (Sakhra), though they were inspired by different motives (see also Part VI, C).

PART IV

REMNANTS IN THE CITY OF DAVID

A. THE EARLIEST SETTLEMENT

Historical and archeological investigations have established beyond question the location and extent of early pre-Israelite Jerusalem on the southeastern ridge to the north of which rises the Temple Mount. This long and narrow ridge is the historic "hill of Jerusalem," the term found, e.g., in Isaiah 10:32. In the days of the Second Temple it was known as the Lower City to distinguish it from the Upper City which occupied the higher and larger Western hill. The latter adjoined the Tyropoeon valley (Josephus' term) and was thickly populated.

In tracing the history of occupation of the hill of Jerusalem and identifying the different groups resident there throughout the centuries, it is necessary to gather and assemble all available data, literary and historical as well as topographical and archeological. The principal literary source is the Bible, which contains numerous references and allusions to the city, its quarters and other features. The books of Samuel, Kings, Chronicles, and earlier prophets, among others, deal with the period of the First Temple. Nehemiah offers a detailed account of the restoration of the walls and gates in the early days of the Second Temple.

Next to the Bible, despite certain lapses, the most valuable source for detailed information about the city and the Temple area, especially in the last days of the Second Temple, is Josephus Flavius.

1. EXACT LOCATION OF EARLY JERUSALEM

On the basis of all known evidence, scholars are agreed that Jerusalem, from the time it was founded early in the third millennium B.C., until the capture of the Jebusite city by David in the early tenth century B.C., was confined to the area of the southeastern ridge. Under David's rule, the city began to expand northward. It grew even larger when Solomon erected the Temple and his own palace on Mount Zion and extended the city walls to encompass the Royal Citadel (see map 1). Furthermore, there are good reasons to believe that there were suburban settlements and cultivated farms beyond the western ridge during the same period (see below). The most significant western expansion took place during the latter phase of the Judean Kingdom, when the new quarters, the

View of the southeastern ridge over which lie the Ophel and the City of David, core of earliest Jerusalem, overlooking the Kidron valley (bottom). The crest of the ridge runs from right to left (under the Turkish wall of the Old City). The ruins of the wall and tower in the middle ground are Hasmonean (second century B.C.), and the rough ancient construction below the terraces (bottom) are Jebusite and early Israelite, the oldest known remnants of the City of David. The underground Gihon spring is located below them to the left. This whole area was protected by a city wall in biblical times. As the city expanded after Solomon's time, the new quarters, the *Mishneh* and *Machtesh,* arose over and below the Western hill, seen behind the Turkish walls

Mishneh and *Makhtesh*, were developed and incorporated into the enlarged capital, as evidenced by a large wall, a segment of which was uncovered by N. Avigad in the present Jewish Quarter of the Old City (see below C, 2).

2. THE GIHON SPRING, BASIS OF THE EARLY SETTLEMENT

The major reason for the location of the early settlement on the southeastern ridge was the presence of the perennial spring, Gihon (derived from gīah = to gush) on the lower part of the steep slope at the eastern side of the ridge (see map 1). We have described in Part II, A, 4, a: Ancient Fortifications and the Warren Shaft, the mode of access to this main source of water, and its elaborate underground system of installations. The inhabitants of Jerusalem had always exercised great ingenuity in protecting it, as it was vital for survival. But it was vulnerable, so at the time of Senacherib's invasion (701 B.C.), Hezekiah, the king of Judah, decided to improve the system by digging a tunnel which brought the waters of Gihon over a distance of 1692 feet (see below, C, 1: A Remarkable Hydraulic Engineering Feat) to the Siloam Pool. As a result of this achievement, the Gihon was closed off and the title 'spring' was transferred to the tunnel's outlet, which was then called the Siloam Spring. The name 'Siloam' is the Greek derivation from the Hebrew Šiloaḥ. The Arabs call the spring and adjacent village Silwān, apparently derived from the Greek name. It has been remarked that the oldest core of historical Jerusalem has preserved through four millennia comparatively more ancient names than other parts of Jerusalem. Among them are Siloam, Kidron, Gihon.

3. 'ĒN-ROGEL, THE MEETING GROUND OF ABRAHAM AND MELCHIZEDEK

Jerusalem possessed another source of water outside the city walls, a spring called 'Ēn-Rogel which is mentioned in the boundary lists of the tribal areas of Judah and Benjamin (Joshua 15:7). It is apparently the same as the "Jackal's Well" (Nehemiah 2:13). It seems likely that the meeting between Abraham and the priest-king, Melchizedek, at the "King's Valley" (Genesis 14:17) took place near 'Ēn-Rogel, outside the southern gate of the city. The ancient memory of the site finds strange echoes in biblical and post-biblical sources associating it with Melchizedek, Jerusalem's ancestor: Melchizedek, pre-Israelite king of Shalem, i.e. Jerusalem (Psalm 76:2) was "priest of El-Elyon (God Most High), creator of heaven and earth" who blessed Abraham by his God, in his own city, promised him victory, and received from him a tenth of the spoils (Genesis 14:18–20). In ancient Israelite tradition "El-Elyon, creator of heaven and earth" was a title specifying the central attributes of the supreme God. The identification of El-Elyon or its equivalent with Yahweh is made explicit in several passages, e.g. in Genesis 14:22. The figure of Melchizedek occupied a prominent place in traditions related to Jerusalem and it appears

156

that the kinship to Melchizedek claimed by subsequent rulers of Jerusalem was attributed, along with the rights of possession, to the House of David: "You are a priest for ever after the order of Melchizedek" (Psalm 110:4).

Josephus mentions an interesting legend to the effect that Jerusalem was originally built by a Canaanite chieftain called Melchizedek or 'Righteous King,' for such he was. On that account he was the first priest of God, and first built a temple there and called the city Jerusalem; which was formerly called Šalem (*Antiquities* I:40). The figure of Melchizedek, always somewhat mysterious, became even more awesome and portentous with the passing of the centuries, and ultimately a cosmic entity as in the accounts of Philo, the Jewish Alexandrian philosopher (20 B.C.–A.D. 40) and in the Epistle to the Hebrews, 7:1, ff. A fragmentary document from Qumran Cave XI, about 2,000 years old, identifies him as the eschatalogical high priest who will preside over the faithful during the messianic age.

The modern name of 'Ēn-Rogel is Bir-'Ayyūb (Job's Well), situated somewhat southeast of the apex formed by the junction of the two valleys, the Kidron and the Hinnom. Bir-'Ayyūb draws its water from an underground aquifer, though according to the general view it orginally had been a spring.

The well at 'Ēn-Rogel has two parts: the lower is built of huge rough-hewn blocks, which resemble those of the city wall, and has an average depth of thirty feet (9.5 meters). The upper part of the well rises about forty feet (12 meters) above the lower; it is built out of smaller stones and is covered by a domed room. The water issued from a cave at the bottom and welled up through the top part during the winter. A hundred years ago, Warren discovered this underground cave to which access was gained by a flight of stairs. The spring is quiescent in the summer, and the water remains underground. It must be drawn or pumped up from the well to irrigate the orchards of Siloam, which are descended from the biblical King's Gardens.

According to Father L.H. Vincent the lower construction may date from the early days of the Judahite Monarchy (tenth-eighth centuries B.C.) or to the time of the Assyrian siege of Jerusalem, when all the springs outside the walls were blocked off, according to II Chronicles 32:4. In those days, as in Nehemiah's time, the valley floor was over 33 feet (10 m.) lower than its present level, and rested on bedrock.

It appears that the lower part of the spring had been covered by debris as a result of the severe earthquake in the days of King Uzziah (Amos 1:1; Zechariah 14:5; and Josephus' *Antiquities* IX:263). According to Josephus, the earthquake caused the collapse of the ridge lying west of 'Ēn-Rogel. Its boulders were shaken loose, rolled a considerable distance and came to a stop at the ridge on the east, thereby blocking the roads and the access to the King's Gardens (II Kings 25:4 et al) which lay in the vicinity. The people of Jerusalem wanted to prevent its silting up with sediment from the Kidron valley, or its pollution by the seepage of contaminated water from the upper levels which drained into the valley. Hence, the mouth of the spring was reshaped into a well, and provision made for drawing the water from it. At a later date, according to J. Braslavi, the people added a super-structure forty feet high on top of the earlier well. A part of the latter is still visible at ground level on the east side, as shown in our picture. The well was in continuous use in the days of the Second Temple. Its present dilapidated appearance is due to much later haphazard additions intended for pumping the water, and to provide a cover at the top.

4. MEMORABLE BIBLICAL EPISODES RELATED TO THE SPRINGS

The special importance of these water sources for the people of Jerusalem is reflected in two episodes from the time of the United Kingdom: (1) Toward the end of David's reign, the supporters of Prince Adonijah, an elder son and claimant to the throne, assembled at the 'Zohelet Stone' (possibly an ancient ritual site) near 'Ēn-Rogel to anoint him king. On this solemn occasion they offered sacrifices (I Kings 1:9). (2) In response to this challenge to his authority, David sent his loyal followers with his younger son, Solomon, to the Gihon, there to anoint him king (I Kings 1:45). Apparently the two water sources were regarded as sacred high places, especially appropriate for such important rites.

We have just observed that Melchizedek's imposing figure occupied a special place in ancient Hebrew traditions in specific relation to Jerusalem, and that is why a special claim of kinship, though not determined by descent, existed with the founders of the House of David. This may be compared with an 'adoptive' link with Jerusalem's ancestor, Melchizedek, bequething upon David the right of kingship over Jerusalem, which he claimed as his royal domain in the 'City of David.' This emerges from a reassessment of the inner meaning of the story in the opening chapter of I Kings, based on a deeper knowledge of conditions at the time.

The prince Adonijah, a contender to the throne as his father lay on his deathbed, proceeded in great pomp to the hallowed spring of 'Ēn-Rogel. There he "sacrificed sheep, oxen and fatlings by the Serpent's [Zohelet] Stone, which is beside 'Ēn-Rogel" (1:9). The anointment was not effected in an Israeli sanctuary "before Yahweh" in the accepted manner of coronations (Saul, David). On the other hand, the site and the Serpent's Stone seem to echo past traditions of a "holy place" hallowed by traditions held dear by the natives and their ancestors, and enhanced by the prestigious memory of Melchizedek. There is also reasonable ground to assume that this local tradition, rooted in pre-Israelite Jerusalem, endowed later recipients with the right to be recognized as the rulers of Jerusalem. Hebrew tradition required them, furthermore, to be anointed and crowned, subsequently, as kings over all Israel in a sanctified place "before Yahweh." The Serpent's Stone of 'Ēn-Rogel has left no trace.

To counteract the pretender, Solomon, accompanied by Zadok, the priest, who took with him the "horn of oil" from the tent of meeting on Mount Moriah, by Nathan the prophet, Bena'iah and the Cherethite and Pelethite bodyguard, went down to the Gihon spring while riding the royal mount. There he was anointed king over Jerusalem. This was the first step. We have another tradition in I Chronicles 29:22 saying: "And they made Solomon, the son of David, king the second time, and they anointed him as prince for the Lord, and Zadok as priest," thus making him monarch over all of Israel.

The King's Valley in the area near 'Ēn-Rogel is also the place where Absalom "built a monument to himself" (II Samuel 18:18). It has not survived but popular tradition has identified an impressive monument as the 'Tomb of Absalom.' The association is impossible historically, since the tomb dates to the Herodian era (1000 years later than Absalom) and is a considerable distance from the proper site. The king's wine presses were located in the vicinity as well (Zechariah 14:10).

Furthermore, the later sources gave their names to the gates of the eastern walls of biblical Jerusalem: the more ancient or 'East Water Gate' which faced the Gihon spring, mentioned by Nehemiah as being close to the Ophel (Nehemiah 3:26; see below), and the second or 'Fountain Gate' (see below, B, 7, a: The Water Gate, and B, 7, b: the Fountain Gate; Nehemiah 2:14; 3:15) at the southeastern end of the City of David. It is identified by many with the gate which led to 'Ēn-Rogel; it may refer, on the other hand, to the Siloam Pool when the term 'spring' was applied to the outlet of the tunnel after the Gihon was closed off (see Part V, A, 2: New Archeological Insights into the Book of Nehemiah).

Above: Reconstruction model of the southwestern and southern sections of the Temple Mount area, showing the vast stairway, the plaza, the wide staircase and the Ḥulda Gates. The basilical Royal Portico towered over the width of the southern area (see Part III, E and F), and included a section named the Ḥanuyot where Jesus is said to have clashed with money changers and dealers (see Part III, F, 1)
Below: The Temple Mount area seen from the west. The golden Dome of the Rock is seen, left. The Herodian retaining walls run south and southeast to the rear of the silver domed El-'Aqṣa mosque (see Part III, F, 1)

5. STRATEGIC POSITION OF THE CITY OF DAVID

The other reason for the selection of the southeastern ridge as the original site of Jerusalem was the strategic position of the hill and its magnificent natural defenses. The ridge descends at a steep angle from the Temple Mount, and is protected on three sides by the slopes of the corresponding valleys: the Kidron to the east which cuts between the Ophel and the Mount of Olives; the Hinnom to the south (these valleys meet near 'Ēn-Rogel); and the Tyropoeon in the center (mentioned frequently by Josephus), which cuts down through the present Old City from the Damascus Gate until it meets with the Hinnom valley, dividing the latter from the western ridge (see map 1).

a. The Exposed Northern Flank

Ancient Jerusalem could be guarded on three sides, east, south and west, by turning to account the steep declivity of the ridge and erecting the line of walls over the lower slopes. At the same time, the habitable surface over the declivity was secured and enlarged by the construction of terraces which were formed on the remains of earlier structures and reinforced with retaining walls (see below).

The northern side of the city was most exposed to enemy attack. Especially after the extensive building operations on the Temple Mount, including the Temple itself, the royal palace and associated structures, the Judean kings devoted major attention to strengthening the northern defenses. The threat of attack from the north was considered the most serious, and this concern is probably reflected in such biblical passages as "Out of the north evil shall break forth" (Jeremiah 1:14). Indeed, this is where two towers stood in the later days of the Monarchy, the Tower of Hananael and the Tower of the Hundred, which defended the northern gates: the Gate of Ephraim and the Gate of Benjamin. In the early days of the Second Temple, the citadel or *Birah* was erected northwest of the Temple in order to protect that part of the city, and the Temple in particular. The stronghold continued in use for many years; in Herod's days it was enlarged and reinforced and renamed the *Antonia* in honor of Herod's Roman patron, Mark Anthony (Part II, F: Herod's Period). On the other hand, no trace had apparently been left by then of the former citadel, the *Akra*, which stood on the other side of the Temple Mount in former days, south of it and overlooking the Lower City. It had been garrisoned with hellenist troops by Antiochus IV, and had been destroyed by the resurgent Maccabean princes (see Part V, C, 4: Where Did the Akra Stand?).

b. Earliest Defenses of Jerusalem on the East

It is evident that the earliest urban settlement in early Jerusalem was located on the southern side of the southeastern ridge; its northern border extended to the higher and narrower area between the slopes descending to the Kidron and Tyropoeon. At that site

160

The Temple Mount (above left) and the City of David (below) at an early stage of the excavations. The valleys bordering the southeastern hill are the Kidron (right) and the Tyropoeon (left, largely settled)

Above: Bird's eye view of the excavations southwest and south of Temple Mount. Left of the silver domed El-'Aqṣa mosque and beyond the transversal (Turkish) wall, are Moslem structures described in Part VI, C. Above them, to the left, is the site of the Upper City and reconstructed Jewish Quarter (Part I, G). The excavations in the foreground cover the *Ophel,* the monumental stairway to the southern gates and structures described in Part III, F, 4; below them are Byzantine structures (VI, B) and remnants of the Byzantine city wall abutting on the eastern wall of Temple Mount, right foreground, (see VI, B). A stairway that rose from an *eastern road* abutting this wall, once rose to the "Solomon Stables" (see pp. 123 and 151). The other two items of interest in this picture are: First, the ongoing excavations in the left hand corner where they hug the road approximate the course of the biblical First Wall (the eastern border of the Ophel as traced by the line marked 7 in Map 3, p. 207). In Herodian times this wall ran *parallel* to the eastern wall of the Temple area seen in the right hand corner. Secondly, two types of stones appear in this eastern wall. The rougher ones on the right are hellenistic, while those on the left are of Herodian style (see p. 121)

Below: Lower level of the Ophel excavations below the southern wall of Temple Mount. The walled *Hulda Double Gate* is situated beneath the El-'Aqṣa mosque. The walled *Triple Gate* is seen on the right. The structures in the foreground date from early Moslem times (see Part VI, C)

161

The lowest construction (bottom) is the salient of the Jebusite wall or tower (ca. 1800 B.C.) protecting the Gihon spring lying at the foot of the slope (below the stairs). The wall seen immediately above, an early Israelite construction, is also the easternmost defense of the City of David. It was built slightly in advance of a scarp hidden by the terraces. The latter, like the steps, are of recent origin and roughly suggest the more solid terraces or *Millo* of biblical times upon which the houses on the slopes were built

the remains of early walls are visible, among them parts of a thick wall discovered by R.A.S. Macalister (1923–25), which he attributed to Jerusalem's earliest phase. It may be remarked, however, that the precise nature of these structures and their date can only be determined by new excavations of a scientific and systematic nature, to be conducted at a future date. On the basis of present information, however, it can reasonably be affirmed that the pre-Israelite city was situated south of this line of defenses. Furthermore, Kathleen Kenyon's excavations have turned up evidence for the location of the most ancient eastern wall. She found part of a massive wall 8.2 feet (2.5 m.) thick, made up of rough boulders and built on the lowest part of the slope, at the edge of a rocky scarp. Kenyon assigns the wall to the early Middle Bronze period, that is, during the first quarter of the second millennium B.C. If this view is correct, then these walls were already in position in the days of the Egyptian Middle Kingdom (twelfth and thirteenth dynasties, in the twentieth-eighteenth centuries B.C.) This wall is positioned about two-thirds of the way down the slope to the Gihon Spring. It could not have been erected at the foot of the slope, although such a procedure would have brought the spring inside the city, because a wall constructed

a. The salient of the Jebusite wall (ca. 1800 B.C.), or possibly a tower to the Jebusite gate, made of rough unhewn boulders (center), leading to the Gihon spring which lies at the foot of the slope. The city wall protected the entrance to a shaft leading to the hidden spring. The wall was reused by David and his successors and was only replaced by another wall, seen on the right, in the eighth century B.C. *b.* Detail of the Jebusite wall salient seen in the center of picture *a*

at the level of the Kidron valley floor would have been in danger of erosion and collapse from the other side of the narrow valley. Safe access to the hidden spring was provided by a tunnel and shaft (see the description in Part II, A, 4, a: Ancient Fortifications and the Warren Shaft). These, in turn, were protected by the Bronze Age wall just described.

That Jerusalem was a city of some importance during this period is attested in Egyptian epigraphic sources, i.e. the Execration Texts, in which Jerusalem is mentioned (Part II, A, 4, b: Urban Development). Miss Kenyon rightly concludes, from the positioning of the ancient wall, that its builders meant to include within the city limits the entrance to the shaft giving access to the elaborate installations of the Gihon. Thus the people who had to descend a long and tortuous flight of steps to gain access to the spring could do so in safety. If this is true, the beginning of this water installation (or the *ṣinnōr* — pronounced *tzinnōr* — according to one of the current theories, see below) goes back to the early second millennium B.C.

This discovery provides evidence of the continuous exploitation of the natural rock terraces and particularly the eastern declivity of the eastern ridge since earliest times, in

Above: One of the most interesting discoveries of the Parker mission (1909–1918) at the lower end of the southeastern ridge was a find of painted pottery dating to the early Bronze Age or about 3000 B.C.

Below: Proto-Aeolic capital of an Israelite public building of the 9th–8th centuries B.C. discovered in the Ophel

addition to the occupation of the more level small area on the crest of the ridge. The erection of various retaining walls and other substructures was involved, in order to support the artificial platforms on which the residences stood. It was a constant struggle, however, against natural forces which threatened the permanence of the settlement. Earth tremors and erosion were the principal dangers. Foundations and supporting walls required frequent repair, and often houses and walls simply collapsed, their stones rolling down the hillside and creating an all but hopeless jumble of debris on the valley floors. Consequently, very little in the way of structures has survived from early times, though enough artifacts including pottery have turned up to confirm the existence of the community through the whole of the Bronze Age (third and second millennia B.C.) This evidence of early and continuous occupation was proven most dramatically by new discoveries made in 1974.

c. New Discoveries at the Upper Ophel

New and convincing evidence of early and continuous occupation was uncovered during excavations in 1974. They were made, to our surprise, at the upper part of the Ophel hill. They consisted of large quantities of ancient pottery starting with the Early Bronze Age, i.e. the beginning of the third millennium B.C., and going through to the last days of the Judean Monarchy, or the middle of the first millennium B.C. They were found among debris and refuse resting on bedrock which had accumulated below the floor of Byzantine buildings we were excavating. Curiously, this assemblage of artifacts was stratified in reverse order, with the oldest shards in the upper levels and the more recent pottery in the lower strata. In the normal process of stratification, the older material is at the bottom, and later items accumulate in successive layers toward the top. In this instance the debris had been dug up from a nearby spot and dumped in its present location as fill to level out a building site, thus reversing the layers of debris. The conclusion we have reached is that the northern edge of the Ophel was occupied since the Early Bronze Age (3000 B.C.). Further investigation is required before a final assessment of the significance of these finds can be made (see below, B, 3: The Millo).

d. Significance of the Historical Finds in the Excavations

In addition to these stratigraphic discoveries, there is a vast store of finds related to the long historical period from the Early Bronze Age (early third millennium B.C.) to the days of the Judean Monarchy, particularly the eighth and seventh centuries B.C., and of the destruction of the city by the Babylonians in 586 B.C. One of the interesting finds consisted of a proto-Aeolic capital (illustrated in our picture) which apparently had belonged to a public building of some kind in the ninth-eighth centuries B.C., but which had been totally destroyed. It has already been observed that these buildings on the slopes, together with all their contents, collapsed, eroded and were washed down into the Kidron valley by the seasonal rainfalls throughout all periods. A number of interesting discoveries were made by K. Kenyon at the foot of the ridge and in the tiers of terraces above them. Among these were the remains of a structure which

The shallow cave (above) enclosed by walls, discovered by K. Kenyon in 1962 and containing a fine deposit of pottery of ca. 800 B.C., was not a tomb. Nearby was a small compartment with two upstanding monoliths which must have supported the roof of an Israelite building (below)

A fertility statuette made of clay, dating to the days of the Judean kings

she interpreted as belonging to a shrine standing outside the city walls. Her inferences were based on the presence of two standing "monoliths" which she identified as ceremonial "maṣṣebot." A nearby cave contained a rich trove of pottery of the eighth century B.C. which, according to her, may have been a place into which remains of sacrifices were discarded. Another structure, square-shaped, was also discovered in the same complex, and Kenyon suggested that it had been an altar connected with the unofficial cults that certainly flourished during the period of the Monarchy, for which an extramural site would be appropriate. The building in question could also be a normal Israelite building, one of the rare remains that survived in the biblical city of David with its history of thorough destruction. It should be noted that these are speculative views and can only be tested by further excavations at the site to determine the true nature of these structures.

B. THE JEBUSITE STRONGHOLD AND KING DAVID

The archeological evidence shows that the ancient city was quite small but was not limited to the upper crest of the ridge. It extended over a series of terraces, built up on the slopes, which enlarged the space available for buildings and thus was able to accommodate an expanding population.

166

Above: Rooms of ruined Israelite houses, demolished during the destruction of the First Temple. They were excavated beneath the later Hasmonean tower and glacis

Below: A gate discovered by M. Crowfoot in 1927–28 on the western part of the City of David and above the Tyropoeon valley. It belongs apparently to the Persian (time of Nehemiah) and hellenistic periods (fifth-third centuries B.C.). This remnant has disappeared in recent years

1. THE ṢINNŌR AND THE CAPTURE OF THE JEBUSITE STRONGHOLD

The capture of Jerusalem by David was a vital turning point in its history; however, an interesting problem arises in relation to the biblical accounts of the capture. The story in II Samuel 5:6–10 is laconic in the extreme and full of obscurities, raising questions rather than providing answers. At that time, Jerusalem was in the hands of the Jebusites, described as inhabitants of the land, which probably included not only the city itself but the surrounding territory under its control. The citadel, which was captured by David, was called the 'stronghold of Zion' or 'the stronghold.' In the translations of the biblical narrative, David speaks of the impending attack on the city in these words: "Whoever would smite the Jebusites, let him get up the water shaft (II Samuel 5:8), whereas the equivalent Hebrew text for the last five words is "vayiga' baṣinnōr". The ṣinnōr (pronounced tsinnōr) has been connected by some scholars with the Warren shaft (see above, A, 5, b). It was believed that Joab crept through that passage to capture the Jebusite stronghold. This theory is discussed below.

a. The Debate over the Sinnōr

The translation and interpretation of the controversial verse "vayiga' baṣinnōr" or "let him get up the water shaft" as in a modern English translation, constituted a problem for ancient scholars who suggested various solutions. Several modern interpreters believe that the obscure 'ṣinnōr' referred to a water shaft, comparing the word with the term 'ṣinnōrim' which appears in Psalm 42:7 and is commonly translated as "cataracts" or "water-courses." It has become necessary to reassess the interpretation of the verse in question and the physical conditions at the site:

According to L. H. Vincent's interpretation, the Hebrew vayiga' baṣinnōr in this verse is presumed to mean that Joab, came through the ṣinnōr, i.e. that he climbed through the perpendicular shaft whose head led into the fortified city, a bold maneuver which would take the Jebusites by surprise and ensure the capture of the stronghold of Zion. Simple as it seems to be, this interpretation must be abandoned in view of the physical impossibility of such a feat, particularly when other means could achieve the same end.

We are inclined, to consider as more correct the late J. Braslavi's interpretation of the passage in II Samuel 5:8. He regards ṣinnōr as an actual water conduit similar in meaning to ṣinnorīm in the later literature, i.e. Psalm 42:7 in which the phrase means water conduits or water courses. He concludes that the gallery dug into the ridge of the stronghold does not conform with the concept of a dry water conduit; moreover, the bottom of the gallery did not gush water. The term ṣinnōr would correspond perfectly with the conduit which led the water of the Gihon spring to a natural pool below the shaft from which it could be drawn. It refers to anything but a perpendicular shaft!

The Hebrew rendering of vayiga' baṣinnōr is translated literally as "and he struck [and damaged]" the horizontal conduit which led the water of the spring below to the mouth of the spring shaft.

168

However, in order get to the conduit for this purpose, David had first to storm the well-protected city wall. According to the biblical story, Joab was the first to storm the wall, possibly at the lower end of the eastern defenses closer to the Kidron. The sequence of an attack on the wall defenses and the damage to the city's water supply offers a more obvious and more logical solution to the strategic problem of ensuring the city's capitulation.

The biblical account is further confused by folkloristic elements, including a curious reference to "the lame and the blind, who are hated by David's soul" (II Samuel 5:8). The parallel account in I Chronicles 11:4–6, on the other hand, is straightforward but diverges at certain points. The capture of the 'stronghold' is credited to Joab, David's commander. But no mention is made of the blind and lame, or of the phrase *"vayiga' baṣinnōr."* As a reward for the deed, Joab was named commander of David's army: "And David and all Israel went to Jerusalem, that is Jebus, where the Jebusites were, the inhabitants of the land. The inhabitants of Jebus said to David, 'You will not come in here.' Nevertheless, David took the stronghold of Zion, that is the City of David."

b. "The Stronghold of Zion"

It is clear, in any case, that the 'stronghold' (of Zion) is the walled city itself, the center of Jebusite power, which stood on the southeastern ridge. What is meant by this reference is the southern crest of the ridge with the Gihon on its eastern slope. The area of the city before David's time was larger than what former scholars had assumed, and covered over fifteen acres, a not inconsiderable area for the cities of Old Testament times. Megiddo, after its restoration by Solomon, covered a similar area. According to two biblical passages, David changed the name of the stronghold to the 'City of David' and established his official residence there (II Samuel 5:9; I Chronicles 11:7). In this way, the walled city of the Jebusites became the dynastic seat of the House of David, the capital of the United Kingdom.

c. The City of David

Both city and site were selected with deliberate care by the political genius, David. Jerusalem and its lands constituted an independent enclave outside of the territorial claims of any tribe, and exactly between the borders of the northern (Israel) and southern (Judah) nation-states, which were united under a single ruler in the person of the king, David and his lineal successors. The name 'City of David' was applied specifically to this part of the southeastern ridge, while the name 'Jerusalem' referred to the whole city including the surrounding areas (the Temple Mount and later, the quarter on the Western hill) as well as the suburbs situated outside the walls (see below: How Large Was Jerusalem in David's Time?).

2. DAVID AS BUILDER

The biblical sources credit David with the erection of certain structures in the city of David and in the area of the southeastern ridge. In particular, its northern extension as far up as the Temple Mount was annexed to the capital in order to accommodate there his large and growing household and his royal entourage, including civil servants, military officers and the like. In fact, a few remains were found belonging to a settlement in the area at the time of the United Kingdom, which was beyond the line of the northern wall of the pre-Davidic stronghold. There is not enough evidence to determine precisely when this settlement north of the Jebusite city was started, whether in the reign of David or Solomon, but we are informed that both kings encouraged the aristocrats of the land to build houses in Jerusalem and live there (cf. I Kings 2:36). This presaged the historic course of expansion which was to transform Jerusalem into the metropolitan center in biblical times.

3. THE MILLO

There is additional information concerning the extensive building operations of David and Solomon in Jerusalem, though we have as yet no direct chronological data to substantiate or supplement the biblical sources. We learn, for example, that "Solomon built the Millo, and closed the breach of the city of David his father" (I Kings 11:27). We do not know where this breach was, though some scholars think that the wall was breached during David's siege of the Jebusite city. But it is hardly conceivable that the king did not repair any damage to the walls after his capture of the city. It is more likely that David deliberately removed parts of the northern wall of his stronghold as part of a general plan to expand the building area in the direction of the Temple Mount. Solomon, however, reversed this plan, and rebuilt the wall in order to close off the City of David from his own royal acropolis on the Temple Mount (which included the Temple and royal palace). It may be supposed that this verse is to be connected with the remains of walls discovered by Macalister (cf. above: Earliest Defenses of Jerusalem on the East), and which he identified as belonging to the northern defense system of the early city. If our view is correct, however, David's building program was focused on the northern and northeastern sections of the ridge, including the slope which descended to the Kidron valley. That circumstance would also help to explain why David, and after him Solomon, devoted so much effort and expense to the construction of terraces and the expansion of available areas for building. A major undertaking in this respect was the Millo (see also below: The Kings Reinforced the Millo) upon which he erected magnificent structures, including his palace or 'House of Cedars' (II Samuel 5:11). Not only did building materials come from Lebanon, but King Hiram of Tyre (approximately 980–948 B.C.) also sent carpenters and masons to Jerusalem to build the palace for David. Here we have the earliest literary evidence of the strong impact of Phoenician art and craft on the United Kingdom. There probably was a close link between the royal palace and the

170

'Tower of David' (Song of Songs 4:4), a designation in all likelihood of his new strong-hold. The expression may be compared with the 'Tower of Shechem,' the stronghold of that city's rulers (Judges 9:46–49). It is possible that this stronghold, like the one in Shechem, was erected on a 'millo,' namely terraces supported by retaining walls and other substructures. The most probable location would have been on the eastern crest of the ridge situated southeast of the Temple Mount. This interpretation might help to explain the obscure verse: "And David built the city round about from the Millo inward" (II Samuel 5:9). It is agreed by some scholars that the 'Tower of David' was the great "projecting tower" mentioned in close proximity to the 'East Water Gate' (Nehemiah 3:26). The latter was the ancient gate which led to the Gihon spring and to the Ophel (see below) in Nehemiah's account (see also Part V, A, 2: New Archeological Insights into the Book of Nehemiah). The text does not make it clear whether they were still in use in his days or, what is more likely, that they lay in ruins but their names survived (cf. Nehemiah 3:26–27). It is also apparent that the same terraced area over the eastern slope was used as the platform for other structures which were related to the Tower and Palace of the king. One of these was the "House of David's Mighty Men" which was built south of the spring and served as quarters for David's officers. It was still well remembered in Nehemiah's time (3:16).

4. HOW LARGE WAS JERUSALEM IN DAVID'S TIME?

It may be deduced from the biblical sources that the population of Jerusalem, called the City of David, was made up in David's time of the royal household, including his family and attendants, the civil servants, the permanent Israelite garrison and Philistine mercenaries, the priests and levites — altogether perhaps fifteen hundred people. To these may be added the families of those with official responsibilities, the surviving Jebusites, and other members of the lower classes whose number cannot be determined. There is some reason to believe that many of the classes of people listed above lived in the neighborhood of Jerusalem, in towns and villages referred to as its 'daughters' rather than inside the walled city, and on farms. Others probably came from even further away, the different towns of Judah and Benjamin, to visit the capital and stay there for longer or shorter periods as circumstances required. It may be concluded that the City of David extended over the southeastern ridge, covering an area of over fifteen acres (see above: The Stronghold of Zion), with an initial population of about two thousand which increased considerably in Solomon's time as the city grew in size by annexing adjoining areas.

5. THE KINGS REINFORCED THE MILLO

The northern expansion of the City of David towards Mount Moriah continued throughout David's reign, along with buildings erected upon its substructures. The work

on the Millo was maintained by the early kings of Judah even after King Solomon had erected the royal acropolis and the Temple atop Mount Moriah. In other words, continuous attention was given to the reinforcement of the retaining walls which supported the terraces on the eastern slopes of the ridge upon which David had erected the 'Tower of David' (including the King's Palace = the 'House of Cedars'; II Samuel 5:11; cf. Nehemiah 12:37). That is why the court chronicler relates that "David built the city around about from the Millo inward" (II Samuel 5:9) and in I Chronicles 11:8: "and he built the city round about from the Millo in complete circuit," a somewhat obscure verse. Solomon followed the same plan of action (I Kings 9, 15 et al). It is also worth noting that Jeroboam rebelled for the first time against Solomon while the king "closed up the breach of the city of David his father." Jeroboam had been placed in charge "over all the forced labour of the house of Joseph" (i.e. of the tribesmen of Ephraim and Manasseh; I Kings 11:27–28). The work was evidently difficult and arduous, involving the maintenance and repair of the complex of retaining walls and the buildings erected on the terraces. In addition there was the closing of the breach of the northern wall of the City of David which had been pulled down when the city expanded northwards. The reconstruction was effected in order to keep the City of David separate from the new complex of buildings: the King's Palace and the Temple on Mount Moriah. Though the relevant biblical data lacks clarity, it remains true that the Millo and its imposing structures were maintained at least up to the days of King Joash (836–798 B.C.). It is said that he was killed at "the House of Millo, on the way that goes down to Silla" (II Kings 12:20) though we have no clear idea of what is meant by the expression "goes down to Silla."

172

The Ophel ostracon discovered in 1924 by J. J. Duncan in excavations dates from the end of the Monarchy. It lists a number of people bearing Israelite names and specifies the names of their fathers and grandfathers. Names such as Hezkiyahu and Ahiyahu appear, among others. The purpose for which the names were recorded remains uncertain

6. THE OPHEL REPLACED THE MILLO

The term Millo does not occur in the biblical record of later times. A different term is used instead, the *Ophel*, which designates the new fortress built by the Judean kings between the lower city of David and the royal acropolis of Solomon on Mount Moriah. The word apparently is a technical term for a specific type of fortress, namely the citadel of a royal city, as there are references to an 'Ophel' in Samaria, capital of the Northern Kingdom (Israel) and in Dibon, the capital of Mesha, king of Moab (east of the Jordan), as well as in Jerusalem. The meaning of the verbal root is 'to rise' referring to an elevated structure of considerable height. We do not know who erected this citadel, but it becomes clear that King Jotham (758–733 B.C.) "did much building on the wall of Ophel" (II Chronicles 27:3). It is related of Manasseh that he built an outer wall "and carried it round Ophel and raised it to a very great height" (II Chronicles 33:14). In contrast, the symbolic reference of Micah 4:8 baffles the reader: "And you, O tower of the flock, citadel [Ophel in Hebrew] of the daughter of Zion." It is not clear how a watchtower of the flock (Migdal 'Eder) is related to the Ophel of Jerusalem. One tradition, echoed in Genesis 35:21, locates Migdal 'Eder south of Jerusalem near the tomb of Rachel at Bethlehem, while another tradition places the burial place of Rachel at Ramah, north of Jerusalem, on the border of the tribal territories of Benjamin and Ephraim (see II Samuel 10:2 as well as Jeremiah 31:15).

In post-Exilic times the Ophel was settled by the 'nethinim' (servants of the Temple) due, no doubt, to its proximity to the Temple area. The name itself persisted through the period of the Second Temple. Josephus refers to the Ophel (in Greek Ophlas) as one of Jerusalem's quarters situated between the Temple Mount and the Lower City (see below).

7. THE CITY WALL AND STRUCTURES ON THE EASTERN RIDGE

Of all the archeological findings bearing on the City of David in the days of the Judean kingdom, the most important is the thick wall uncovered by K. Kenyon in 1962 on the eastern slope of the ridge (see above: Earliest Defenses of Jerusalem in the East) which probably remained in use up to the period of the monarchy. During the same period another wall had apparently been erected on the lower edge of the ridge, east of the wall Kenyon had discovered. The remains of the latter are buried in the accumulated debris of the floor of the Kidron valley. It would be reasonable to assume that the building and cave complex uncovered by K. Kenyon (see above A, 5, d: Significance of the Historial Finds) and only partially excavated, was situated within the eastern limits of the city. If so, then the remains of still another wall, standing above and to the west of Kenyon's thick wall, may be part of the wall of the Ophel, while the city wall was situated lower down, at the foot of the hill.

Cross-section of the early waterworks of Jerusalem. On the right: Section of the Warren shaft. On the left is Hezekiah's tunnel dug in 701 B.C. and ending at the Siloam Pool

King Hezekiah closed off the shaft entrance to the spring to prevent the overflow from running down the Kidron valley, and had a long and somewhat winding tunnel dug under the southeastern ridge (see picture of Hezekiah's tunnel). This brought the water directly to a pool in the lower Tyropoeon valley within the city walls, i.e. to the Pool of Siloam. It was then covered and made immune to Assyrian onslaught

Below: The construction of Hezekiah's tunnel was effected by two groups of workers, each boring from a different end and meeting in the middle. Near the far end of the tunnel, a Hebrew inscription was found carved in the wall. It recorded the joy of the two gangs of borers as they met underground (see No. 6 in above diagram). The printed line (bottom) is the fourth in the tunnel inscription and should be read, in English, from the left

a. The Water Gate

In any case, there are traces in the Gihon spring area of the line of wall belonging to various periods in the second millennium and the first half of the first millennium B.C. It is in this area, too, that we should locate the Water Gate, an important gate in the eastern wall since earliest times. The name shows that it must have led to the Gihon spring in the Kidron valley. It became less important in the days of the monarchy, especially after the construction of the Siloam tunnel, which brought the spring water inside the city walls during the reign of Hezekiah.

There are other important references to the Water Gate. It was probably through this gate that Zadok the priest and Nathan the prophet and their followers led Prince Solomon from the City of David down to the Gihon spring, there to anoint him king over all Israel (cf. I Kings 1:38–39) as they blew the trumpets. At the same time, the pretender, Prince Adonijah celebrated his own accession at 'Ēn-Rogel, reached by another route south of this site. The Water Gate was closely linked with building activities as early as David's time, for example David's Tower which is the Citadel of David. According to Nehemiah 3 such structures were situated south of the Citadel, or between it and the gate of the Gihon spring (see Part V, A, 2, a(2): The Water Gate).

b. The Fountain Gate

The section of the eastern wall which lies mainly southeast of the Gihon spring is the subject of considerable discussion and some controversy. One serious problem was occasioned by the discovery there of wall fragments by R. Weill and others, who attributed them to the period of the monarchy. The most interesting discussion centers around the attempt to locate at that site the *'Fountain Gate'* mentioned in connection with the Siloam Pool, which led to the King's Garden (Nehemiah 3:15; 12:37). R. Weill identified it with a gate he discovered in the eastern wall of the City of David, between the southern end of the city and the double wall of the Siloam Pool. Within this gate there was a square structure and steps carved in the rock. Despite this, it cannot be determined with any degree of certainty whether the Fountain Gate led to 'Ēn-Rogel (Bir Ayyūb) or whether it may more reasonably be assumed to be the point at which the Siloam tunnel emerged from underground. The King's Garden, on the other hand, is undoubtedly the area outside the city limits in which the valleys of Kidron and Hinnom converged.

c. "The Gate Between the Walls"

Another moot point is the possible connection between the Fountain Gate and the "Gate between the walls" through which King Zedekiah and his men fled by night from Nebuchadnezzar's forces, which had captured Jerusalem (II Kings 25:4). According to current theories, this gate was situated at the juncture of the ancient wall of the City of David with "another wall' (II Chronicles 32:5), that is, the one which King Hezekiah built to reinforce the Millo and to surround the area of the Siloam Pool (see below). If this assumption is correct, a link may be established between the Fountain Gate and the 'gate between the walls.' But this point can only be settled through an investigation of Hezekiah's plan of fortifications for the city.

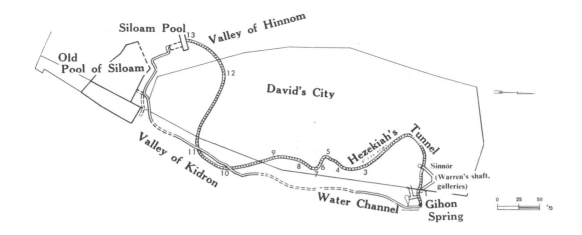

→ nqbh hkw hḥṣbm 'š lqrt r'w grzn 'l [g]rzn wjlkw

C. HEZEKIAH'S ACHIEVEMENTS

1. A REMARKABLE HYDRAULIC ENGINEERING FEAT

The Warren shaft referred to above (A, 5, b) was abandoned in time, and the Israelites dug an outside channel along the eastern slopes of the Kidron valley, which led the water of the spring to the old Siloam Pool. This installation, however, lay outside the city walls and was therefore accessible to the enemy in time of siege. This led King Hezekiah to carry out his ingenious hydraulic scheme.

Above: The upper platform of the Temple seen from the east. Its retaining wall (white, center) rests on the original blocks of the Ḥel rampart which are visible at the bottom (see Part III, D, 3, f.)

Below: The end of the Hezekiah tunnel as it emerges at the Pool of Siloam (see Part IV, C)

The decisive steps in the city's defensive arrangements, especially as these related to the City of David, were taken by Hezekiah (727–698 B.C.) on the eve of Senacherib's invasion of Palestine (701 B.C.), as shown by the most dramatic evidence. Several biblical accounts bear witness to Hezekiah's plan to ensure the capital's water supply by diverting the waters of the Gihon spring through an underground tunnel cut in the rock to the south of the City of David, to the Pool of Siloam (known as *el-Birkeh* in Arabic). The statement in II Kings 20:20 is explicit on this point: "how he [Hezekiah] made the pool and the conduit and brought water into the city," while II Chronicles 32:30 spells out the accomplishment in detail: "Hezekiah closed the upper outlet of the waters of Gihon and directed them down to the west side of the city of David." In fact, Hezekiah's tunnel is one of the most impressive engineering feats preserved in the land since biblical times, and a remarkable attestation of the technical skills of Jerusalem's early engineers. While the straight-line distance from one end of the tunnel to the other is 1,050 feet (320 meters), the conditions of the terrain required a variety of twists and turns making the actual length 1,750 feet (533 meters). A more complete account with colorful details is provided by a contemporary Hebrew inscription (ca. 700 B.C.) carved at the side of the tunnel near the southern issue at the Siloam Pool. The tunneling work was apparently performed with picks, with one team starting at the spring and another inside the city at what became the Siloam Pool. It was conducted with such great skill that it ended successfully with the meeting of the two teams of workers: "the quarrymen hewed the rock, each man toward his fellow, pick against pick, and the water started to flow from the spring toward the pool." The inscription was found in 1880 by children from the village of Siloam and transferred by the Turks to the Istanbul Museum.

2. HEZEKIAH'S GREAT WALL

Once the tunnel and water-supply system had been installed, Hezekiah built a new city wall in order to enclose the Siloam Pool within the city limits at its southern end. This view is in accordance with Professor N. Avigad's contention that Hezekiah's massive wall crossed the upper ridge of the Hinnom valley, following, approximately, later fragments of walls discovered by F. J. Bliss and A. C. Dickie in 1894–1895. This wall is to be identified with Josephus' First Wall; it encircled the present-day Mount Zion and was linked with the segment of the great wall discovered by Professor Avigad in the present Jewish Quarter of the Old City. The same wall also encompassed the new quarter called the *Mishneh* (Second) Quarter, on the Western hill in the latter days of the Judean Kingdom. Testimony to Hezekiah's achievement is recorded in the Bible: "[Hezekiah] built up all the wall that was broken down, and raised towers upon it, and outside it he built another wall" (II Chronicles 32:5). We cannot be sure that Hezekiah's "other wall" is the same as the wall uncovered by Avigad, but it is a plausible equation.

Isaiah's comments are of particular interest: "And you saw that the breaches of the city of David were many, and you collected the waters of the lower pool, and you

Above: View from 'Ēn-Rōgel spring to the south. The King's Gardens lie at the bottom of the Kidron valley and the village of Siloam is at the left

Below: Top arc of the Wilson Arch as it leans against the Western Wall (left). See details in Part V, D, 1

Eight centuries after Hezekiah's time, King Herod built a broad stairway leading directly to the Gihon spring. The broad stairs date from Herod's time

The Hezekiah tunnel near its outflow to the Pool of Siloam

counted the houses of Jerusalem, and you broke down the houses to fortify the wall. You made a reservoir between the two walls for the water of the old pool" (Isaiah 22:9–11). This statement indicates that Hezekiah executed a coordinated plan in organizing the city's defenses, and insured a water supply in times of siege: (1) by reinforcing the second wall and building a new wall to encircle the southern end of the southeastern ridge; and (2) by constructing the Siloam Pool and repairing the old pool (most probably the present *Birket el-Ḥamra* situated southeast of the Pool of Siloam at the confluence of the Kidron and Hinnom valleys). It is also evident that the overflow from this pool was used to irrigate the King's Gardens just outside the city limits.

The wall just described in the biblical account is none other than the massive city wall, 23 feet thick and built of large unhewn, unmortared stones, discovered, as stated above, at the upper level of the Jewish Quarter. It originally surrounded the Mishneh or Second Quarter. What remains today consists of two to seven courses of stone, reaching a maximum height of ten feet along a length of 128 feet; it should be noted that they represent only the foundations of the wall over bedrock. The city wall, according to Avigad's suggestion, continued southward, surrounded the Mishneh Quarter, and continued to the ancient walls of the City of David, joining them and encircling the Siloam Pool. Thus the pool was safely within the city walls, as the Bible, in recounting Hezekiah's careful planning, makes clear.

A thick wall 23 feet (7 m.) thick and about 132 feet (40 m.) long was uncovered in the Upper City (and preserved below the surface of the present Jewish Quarter of the Old City). It was constructed entirely of large unhewn and partly hewn stones stacked together without the use of mortar. Two or three layers have remained, reaching a height of 10.8 feet (3.3 m.) and these represent the foundation of the massive wall resting on bedrock. This wall terminates 917 feet (275 m.) west of the Temple Mount and it ran from northeast to southwest. It was built by King Hezekiah to protect the new quarters, the *Mishneh* and *Makhtesh*

3. OUTLET FROM THE SILOAM POOL

The present southern tip of the southeastern ridge of the City of David before the Pool of Siloam is cut by an artificial scarp. The outer side of an ancient rock-cut channel has been cut away and exposed by the scarp. At the base of the vertical cut is an overhanging rock (as shown in our picture), beneath which runs the overflow from the Pool of Siloam. The overflow then continues to the east and south in another enclosed channel along the flank of the southeastern ridge (which has also been cut). In the opinion of some scholars, the Siloam Pool itself was covered like a cistern in ancient times, rather than being open. Its overflow was concealed until it emerged again in the King's Gardens outside the city walls. Ultimately, the roof of the cistern must have collapsed and the pool assumed the open-air conformation which it has retained to the present day (see above B, 7, b: The Fountain Gate).

4. EXPANSION OF THE UPPER CITY WEST OF THE TEMPLE MOUNT

It is believed that the expansion over the Upper City on the Western hill during the days of the latter Judean kings coincided with the increase of the Judean population caused by an influx of Israelites fleeing Samaria after its subjugation by the Assyrians in the eighth century B.C. The excavations conducted by N. Avigad in the Upper City show that the population expanded there even before the erection of the massive wall surrounding the new quarter. Proof of this is found in remains of structures which were demolished when the wall was erected.

In the last century of the Judean kingdom, Jerusalem had increased threefold in size compared to its area in the tenth-eighth centuries B.C.

Contemporary biblical records, especially the book of Isaiah, lay stress on the continuous growth of the city and the consolidation of its defenses in Josiah's time, half a century after Hezekiah's days, including the construction of new gates and towers.

Above, right: An outlet from the Siloam Pool flows under the overhanging rock to the "King's Gardens". This is also the point where the Tyropoeon valley joins the Kidron valley, as indicated by the path (left). This seems to have been an important strategic position in biblical times

Below, right: Ancient stone outlet from the Siloam overflow into the "King's Gardens"

Left: A seal impression reading "Servant ('ebed = officer) of King Hezekiah"

ליהוזר
ח בנ·חלק
יהו עבד·ח
זק̇יהו
ליהוזרת בן חלקיהו עבד חזקיהו

Their identification raises many problems, though archeological research is helpful in some respects. Expansion continued in the days of Josiah's successors; it seems that the vast structure built by King Jehoiakim and described by Jeremiah was actually situated on the Western hill, protected by the thick city wall: "...a great house with spacious upper rooms and cuts out windows for it, panelling it with cedar, and painting it with vermillion" (Jeremiah 22:14). The prophet sees in his mind's eye the westward spread of the city right up to the hills of Gareb and Goah, but these cannot be identified with certainty. All the city's environs which will be joined up to that line "shall not be uprooted or overthrown any more for ever" (31:39–40).

In some such cases, biblical passages describing the city have been clarified in concrete detail by new discoveries. Thus, e.g., we can appreciate fully Jeremiah's realistic forecast of the expansion and growth of Jerusalem, since the prophet himself had witnessed a comparable expansion of the city which continued until the outbreak of the Babylonian wars around 600 B.C.: "Behold, I will gather them from all the countries to which I drove them in my anger... I will bring them back to the place, and I will make them dwell in safety... I will give them one heart and one way, that they may fear me for ever for their own good and the good of their children after them" (32:37–39).

D. REVELATIONS
OF ARCHEOLOGICAL DISCOVERY.
FROM PRE-ISRAELITE
REMNANTS TO THE SECOND CENTURY B.C.

1. THE MYTH OF THE JEBUSITE WALL

We have alluded in Part I, D, 1 (A Wave of Research after 1920) to R.A.S. Macalister's discovery of the remains of ancient walls on the Ophel overlooking the Kidron valley. His expedition brought to light a section of a wall rising over the northeastern brow of the hill, incorporating a glacis bulging outward like a vaulted slope, which resembled a steep flight of stairs. It was well-preserved and was flanked to the south by a large square tower which still stood to a considerable height. It was generally assumed at the time that the finds represented remains which belonged to the system of ancient fortifications of Jerusalem which, according to the excavators, was the Jebusite Wall, antedating King David's era. This theory was not accepted universally; some scholars attributed the wall, glacis and tower to the days of the Judean Monarchy, suggesting that they were built into the city wall of that period. Attempts were made by others to connect these remains to those uncovered in previous years by H. Guthe, R. Weill and others. Many years passed before it became evident, from K. Kenyon's excavations on the southeastern hill (Ophel) and her reassessment of previous discovery, that the fortifications discovered by Macalister

Handle of a vessel dating to the end of the Judean monarchy impressed with a seal of HWŠ'M HGY = Hoshe'am [the son of] Haggi

belong to the period after the destruction of the First Temple. A stratigraphic examination tion proved that the remains of the fortifications at the top of the Ophel ridge *could not* have been Jebusite fortifications, nor could they even be attributed to the days of the Judean Monarchy. It became obvious that at least the tower uncovered by Macalister in 1926–1927 was built over the debris of houses belonging to the end of the First Temple period, and that a determination of the proper chronological sequence of the relevant structures required far more careful investigation (see above A, 5, b: Earliest Defenses of Jerusalem on the East).

R.A.S. Macalister and J.G. Duncan were not able to determine the chronological sequence of the pottery which they had uncovered in their dig. Nevertheless. their important discoveries confirmed the fact that the Ophel had been in continuous habitation since the third millennium B.C. Some of their finds were of particular interest, among them a Hebrew ostracon (inscribed shard) listing a number of people bearing Israelite names and stating their place of origin. There were also a number of Hebrew seal impressions on jar handles; some bore the word 'Lamelekh' (of the king), supplemented by the name of a city (e.g. Hebron, Ziph, etc.) and the royal emblem. These date to the end of the First Temple period. Others bore the name YHWD (Judah) and date to the Persian period after the return from the Babylonian exile (fifth-fourth centuries B.C.), or YRŠLM (Jerusalem) and date to the early hellenistic period (third century B.C.). Excavations in the Ophel area explored by Macalister and Duncan were resumed by J. Crowfoot and C.M. Fitzgerald in 1927–1928, but this time on the *western* side of the Ophel overlooking the Tyropoeon Vale (see below Part V, B, 1, b).

2. THE CROWFOOT 'GATE'

They conducted a stratigraphic excavation to determine the successive layers and also carried out a systematic study of the structures and other remains found in them. The excavators found masonry blocks which stood on the cliffs overhanging the valley and, more important, a sizable structure in the western walls of the City of David which they took to be a gate. It had been reinforced by tremendous square towers; the remains of the southern one are still in place. Crowfoot assumed that this was the main gate giving access to the city from the Tyropoeon valley, going back to Jebusite times and continuing right up to the days of the Second Temple. Other scholars, especially A. Alt, tried to identify it with the 'Valley Gate' (Nehemiah 2:13). But as these theories were examined more closely, serious questions were raised, not only regarding the proper dating of this structure, but also the idea that it was the western gate of the City of David in pre-exilic times. K. Kenyon, who had inaugurated her excavation on the southeastern (Ophel) hill in 1961, paid particular attention to the eastern border of the City of David. She based her reassessment of the excavations in question on a logical assumption: If the fortifications discovered by Macalister at the upper level of the Ophel mark the city border facing the Kidron valley to the east, and if the presumed 'gate' uncovered by Crowfoot marks its western border over the Tyropoeon, the ancient biblical city would have been *too small*. In addition, the Gihon spring, the only spring providing water for the town, would be too far from the city wall. Kenyon made an important contribution to the investigation of the area by digging an excavation trench from the Warren shaft lying on the ridge, down to the lower end of the hill. There, over a rocky ledge, she discovered the remains of an ancient wall. The solution to the problem of the Crowfoot gate is outlined in Part V, A, 1, a: Identity of the Valley Gate.

3. THE RIDDLE OF THE MIDDLE BRONZE WALL

On the basis of pottery found in the trench, Kenyon dated this wall, which was about eight feet (2.5 meters) thick, to the Middle Bronze II age, and attributed its original erection to approximately 1800 B.C. Her dating would mean that this primitive wall served to protect the later City of David over a stretch of at least 1000 years, or until the eighth century B.C. when it might have become necessary to erect a new city wall west of the early wall. Such a conclusion is not warranted by the evidence; in particular it is difficult to deduce from the assorted shards uncovered in the trench that the Middle Bronze pottery there bears a chronological relation to this wall. Apart from this problematic phase of the work, however, it became evident that the buildings of this early town were erected over the slope of the Ophel and down to its bottom. The excavation cleared up another important question: Regardless of its origin and its age, why was the wall built along this line? The reason, evidently, is that the original builders of the wall had intended it to encompass the shaft which led to the Gihon spring, and thus to protect the primary source of water for the city.

182

E. ROYAL TOMBS IN THE CITY OF DAVID

Thus far, we have described the earliest remnants uncovered in Jerusalem and their relation to the countless generations who lived there. Another enthralling feature of the period just covered are the numerous remains of tombs dating to the period of the Kings of Judah.

David's enterprise in his new capital was not limited to its fortification, the building of David's Tower and the Royal Palace — the House of Cedars — and the tent-shrine to house the Holy Ark. One of his most important achievements was the establishment of a royal necropolis within the walls of the city which bore his name. We turn to a consideration of the relevant data.

The tombs of David (I Kings 2:10), Solomon (I Kings 11:43) and several of their descendants were cut into bedrock in the City of David. It is related of Hezekiah that he was buried "in the ascent of the tombs of the sons of David" (II Chronicles 32:33), that is, the crest of the ridge. On the other hand, some of the kings who preceded Hezekiah were buried in other places, among them Joram who was buried in the City of David "but not in the tombs of the kings" (II Chronicles 21:20), or Uzziah who was interred "in the burial field which belonged to the kings" (II Chronicles 26:23) which may be identified with the necropolis which we discovered recently opposite the Western Wall of the Herodian Temple, on the eastern slope of the Western hill (see below: The Burial Ground in the Tyropoeon). After the time of Manasseh, the kings of Judah were buried in the Garden of Uzza, close to Siloam village.

1. THE ANCIENT ROYAL BURIAL GROUND IN THE CITY OF DAVID

Very little information on the subject of the ancient royal burial ground has been preserved. Some clues may be found in the biblical notices concerning the death and burial of individual kings. We read the following about King Asa, for example: "They buried him in the tombs (the Greek translation, the Septuagint, has the singular form, 'tomb') which he had hewn out for himself in the city of David. They laid him on a bier which had been filled with various kinds of spices... and they made a very great fire in his honor." (II Chronicles 16:14). We may conclude that it was the custom of the kings to prepare their burial places during their lifetimes. It is also worth noting that the same necropolis was given different names: the Davidic Tombs (Nehemiah 3:16), the Tombs of the Sons of David (II Chronicles 32:33), the Tombs of the Kings (II Chronicles 21:20). We have Nehemiah's statement as to the location of these tombs (3:16), that they were in the southern part of the City of David, close to the eastern wall.

In view of this information, many scholars have accepted Raymond Weill's identification of a group of tombs which he discovered in the course of excavations in 1913–14, as the royal burial place. There are three principal tombs which, unfortunately, have

suffered considerable damage as a result of much later quarrying. It was possible, nevertheless, to determine the original layout on the basis of the remains found there. Among the tombs was a large one, cut into the rock to which access was provided by a shaft leading to a vaulted tunnel 54.4 feet (16.5 meters) long and 13.2 feet (4 meters) high. The latter ends at a stone bench in which a niche was carved, probably to hold a coffin. In R. Weill's opinion, these tombs and, more particularly, a fourth consisting of a vertical shaft and a burial loculus at the side, which he discovered in the course of additional excavations in 1923–24, support his theory that these reflect Phoenician influence which would be expected in the case of royal tombs, since the House of David was so much influenced by the art and architecture of its northern neighbor. The fourth tomb discovered by Weill shares certain features with some of the tombs we uncovered on the eastern ridge of the Western hill. It also bears resemblances to Phoenician tombs discovered in the ancient cemetery at Achziv, north of Acre (see below: The Burial Ground in the Tyropoeon). Apart from these limited observations, there is nothing conclusive that

Quarries seen below the tombs dating to the time of the First Temple.
The Israelite rock-cut tombs in the burial ground of the City of David were truncated
as a result of Roman quarrying. They were originally reached through a shaft
and tunnel

can be said one way or the other about the tombs, which Weill identified as belonging to the royal cemetery. The question, at least for the present, must remain open.

We find allusions to the royal tombs in later sources. The most interesting are Josephus' accounts of the treasures "discovered" by John Hyrcanus and after him, by Herod, in David's Tombs (*Antiquities* VII:392–394 et al); and the Talmudic traditions relating to the removal of the tombs from the city itself, with the exception of the tombs of the House of David which remained in place. How authentic the traditions are, and what their basis in historical fact may be, is uncertain.

2. LATER TRADITIONS OF THE TOMB OF DAVID

A significant shift in traditions concerning the site of the tomb of David and Solomon occurred several centuries after the destruction of Jerusalem by the Romans. In the tenth century A.D., current Jewish and Arab opinion located the so-called 'Tomb of David' at the present-day Mount Zion (in the Upper City). This tradition was also accepted by the Christians during the First Crusade (twelfth century A.D.), who fixed the exact site on the lower level of the Coenaculum, traditional scene of the Last Supper of Jesus and his disciples.

The meandering route through which the myth evolved may be traced to the Jewish traveler, Benjamin of Tudela (1167–1172). He reports that "the tomb of David and those of the kings who succeeded him, are to be found on Mount Zion." This statement is followed by a legend about a cave leading to a vast palace which rested on marble columns sheathed with silver and gold... This was the seat of David's tomb and left of it were the tombs of Solomon and his successors. The sepulchre, according to the legend, was closed or walled up by order of the (Christian) Patriarch and hidden from view to this day.

The Mount Zion tradition concerning the Tomb of David apparently was derived from an erroneous statement made by Josephus, that the City of David was situated on the Western hill. In other words, although this tradition is of ancient origin, it is without historical basis, and has no archeological support, even though it has been boosted on traditional or folkloristic grounds (like so many other sites in the Holy Land throughout the centuries) into a focus of pilgrimage. Vestiges of ancient structures are visible on this sensitive site on Mount Zion, though their age is uncertain. In 1949 the architect Jacob Pinkerfeld investigated the foundations of the 'Tomb of David' on Mount Zion, and concluded that the remains he discovered belonged to a church of the fourth century A.D., i.e. the Byzantine period (see Part VI, B: Byzantium and Jerusalem).

The later tradition which locates the Tomb of David at the place shown today is already mentioned in ninth century A.D. sources. Furthermore, several holy sites were pointed out on Mount Zion in Crusader times, for example the tombs referred to by Benjamin of Tudela, the tomb of St. Stephen the martyr and others. The actual building over the tomb was built in the fourteenth century A.D. as part of the Coenaculum con-

nected with the tradition of the Last Supper. In later centuries it was placed under the guardianship of the Moslem Dajani family. By the time the Turks rebuilt the city walls, the area of Mount Zion was left outside (cf. Part VI, F).

3. THE BURIAL GROUND IN THE TYROPOEON

On the terraces rising over the lower slopes of the Western hill, and on the western side of the Tyropoeon, facing the Temple Mount, we discovered an elaborate cemetery dating to the time of the Judean Monarchy, intended in all probability for the interment of the members of the royal court and the upper strata of society. Investigation showed that the rock-cut tombs there had been cleared out and used for other purposes in the days of the Second Temple. The type most commonly found consisted of a square shaft dug in bedrock and provided with an opening which gave access to the burial chamber. A rectangular chimney extends upwards from the roof of the burial chamber and the aperture is covered on top by stone slabs. The niche above the tomb is for the "nefesh," symbol of the spirit of the deceased. Like the tombs discovered in the City of David by

R. Weill, these tombs bear a close resemblance to those found in the Phoenician cemetery at Achziv. The Phoenician cemetery dates from the same period, the eighth century B.C., and the tombs are planned similarly. One of the tombs on the Western hill contained a rich collection of pottery, most of it dating from this period. Some of the vessels were inscribed with personal names in the Hebrew script of the time, one in particular bearing the name YŠ'YHW = Isaiah. Evidently, this cluster of tombs belonged to the latest phase of the Judean Kingdom, and is therefore to be distinguished from the cemetery of the House of David, referred to often in the Bible, or to the so-called 'Tombs of the Kings' situated over the ridge of the City of David (see above: The Ancient Royal Burial Ground in the City of David). Several biblical passages, however, mention burial places reserved for the capital's aristocracy, including even some of the Judean kings.

One of these passages (II Chronicles 26:23) mentions the "burial field of the kings" where Uzziah was interred, and this may be a reference to the cemetery we uncovered. Another burial field called the Garden of Uzza (II Kings 21:26) is described below.

It may be inferred that the tomb of King Uzziah was originally located there. In the Bible it is reported that the king was laid to rest "in the burial field which belonged to the kings" (II Chronicles 26:23). However, according to a much later Aramaic inscription found on a stone slab which had been in the collection of antiquities in the Russian church on the Mount of Olives and is now in the Israel Museum, his remains were transferred for reasons unknown during the days of the Second Temple. The Aramaic inscription reads: "Hither were brought the bones of Uzziah, king of Judah, do not open." Apparently it had been discovered and brought to the Russian church at the end of the nineteenth century A.D. Some scholars relate this find to the above-mentioned passage in Chronicles which relates that King Uzziah was a leper, and was therefore not buried in the tombs of the House of David, but somewhere else, presumably in the necropolis situated in the nearby Siloam village.

As it happened, the royal cemetery of the Western hill was moved in the days of Manasseh to a site known as the Garden of Uzza on the lower slope of the Mount of Olives, in the area of the village of Silwan (Siloam): And Manasseh ...was buried in the garden of his house, in the Garden of Uzza" (II Kings 21:18). The removal seems to have been the consequence of expanded building on the eastern slope of the Western hill, that is, the Tyropoeon Vale. The plan was carried out gradually and reached an advanced stage in the days of Josiah, grandson of Manasseh, not long before the end of the nation and the destruction of the Temple by the Babylonians.

Scholars have already noted that the meaning of 'Uzza is obscure. It is currently interpreted as an abbreviation of the name *Uzziah*. On the other hand, it may be related to the name *Peretz-'uzzah* (II Samuel 6:8) situated in the neighborhood of Jerusalem and named for the priest 'Uzzah, David's contemporary. In addition to Manasseh, King Amon was buried in the Garden of 'Uzza (II Kings 21:26), as was King Jehoiakim, according to the Greek (Septuagint) version of II Chronicles 36:8.

187

Tombstone of King Uzziah (769–733 B.C.) inscribed in Aramaic: "Hither were brought the bones of Uzziah King of Judah. Do not open".
The tombstone was not discovered in the royal necropolis where Uzziah was buried, according to II Chronicles 26:23, but in an ancient cemetery at the foot of the Mount of Olives situated in the grounds of the Russian Church. This anomaly is attributed to the fact that he was a leper

Nobleman's tomb of the First Temple period, popularly known as the Tomb of the Daughter of Pharaoh, hewn out of the rock in the village of Siloam, opposite the Kidron valley, with a Hebrew inscription above the entrance

4. THE TOMBS AT SILOAM VILLAGE

As early as 1872, C. Clermont-Ganneau surveyed ancient Jewish cemeteries which surrounded Jerusalem. He investigated a large group of tombs in and near the village of Siloam, situated on the upper slope of the Kidron valley and belonging to the later period of the Judean monarchy. Some tombs were carved in the rock and some were monolithic tombs. The most prominent of the latter type is a structure with a roof decorated by a pyramidal stone, known by a typically Arab-folkloristic name, "Tomb of the Daughter of Pharoah." The style of these tombs is influenced by Egyptian funerary architecture.

Nearby is an interesting cave-tomb; above the entrance is a hollow panel, inscribed with a few lines of archaic Hebrew characters, while another one-line inscription may be seen on a panel at the right side of the entrance. Clermont-Ganneau had already tried to interpret the larger inscription, which contained the expression: "who is over the house," as a reference to the highest civil official in the latter days of the Judean Kingdom. It was only in 1954, however, about eighty years later, that Professor N. Avigad was able to make a complete transcription: "This [is the burial...] of ...yahu who is over the house. There is no silver and no gold here but [his bones] and the bones of his handmaiden [slave-wife] with him. Cursed is the one who opens this [tomb]!" Both the title in the inscription and the date of the tomb might fit Shebna (the full form of his name would have been Shebnayahu) who was a contemporary of King Hezekiah and was "over the household" (cf. Isaiah 22:15 ff.), but the identification is not certain.

a. Burial Places of the Common People

The tombs of ordinary folk, on the other hand, lay in the Kidron valley; this is referred to in several passages. They are called "burial places of the common people" (Jeremiah 26:23), and they are certainly also the *shdemōt* (in the Hebrew text) in the passage "all the fields as far back as the brook Kidron" (Jeremiah 31:40), the fields meaning burial grounds, if the interpretation of *shdemōt* as cemeteries is correct (some interpret *shdemōt= śdē-māvet*, fields of the dead).

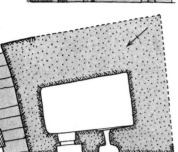

Above: Inscribed stone lintel (facade and structural plan of the tomb) of one of the First Temple period sepulchres hewn into the cliff of Siloam village. Below: The inscription is dedicated to the royal steward (in Hebrew: 'asher 'al ha-bayit') who was one of the highest officials in the Judean court

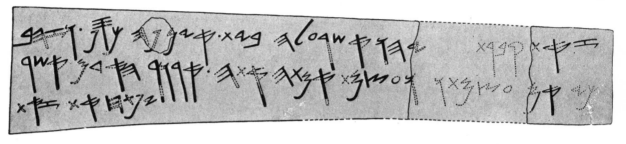

b. *An Eighth Century Cemetery on Mount Zion*

Early in 1975, two ancient cave tombs were discovered at the western foot of Mount Zion as bulldozers were widening the present Hebron Road, exposing the brow of the hill — a common enough occurrence in Jerusalem. One of them is a family tomb consisting of two rooms dating to First Temple days, namely the eighth century B.C. The buried remains and nearby objects found *in situ* were intact. They included various pottery items as well as a seal inscribed in archaic Hebrew characters indicating a woman's name. The second tomb had also been originally in use during First Temple days, but was used for secondary burial in Hasmonean times. A surface survey of the brow of the hill seems to suggest that it comprised a cemetery which had been in use in the latter part of First Temple days as well as between the Hasmonean period and the destruction of the Second Temple.

5. ROMAN QUARRYING OBLITERATED THE ORIGINAL ISRAELITE CITY

Quarrying in Roman and Byzantine times has been proposed by archeologists as one of the major reasons why remains of most of the buildings of the original Israelite city have not survived. The rock surface, when exposed, showed extensive damage to a large number of rock-cut structures, baths, cisterns and the royal tombs described earlier. Building remains above the surface were systematically removed over a large area to obtain stone for the construction of Aelia Capitolina. The Romans and their successors not only buried those parts of the earlier Israelite city which lay in this area, but cut away an important part of the rock foundation of the ancient City of David. Foundations of later buildings were laid on bedrock. Consequently, remains of ancient structures there were destroyed, often as low as their foundations.

189

PART V

JERUSALEM OF POST-EXILIC DAYS

While the Bible provides us with a good deal of information about the defenses of the City of David during the last days of the kingdom, including the various walls, gates, and towers, it is difficult to pin down specific names and places, partly because very few remains from pre-exilic times have survived, and partly because many changes occurred in the city between the end of the sixth century and the middle of the fifth century B.C., when we have Nehemiah's detailed and repeated description of the city and its walls. In some cases names were changed or shifted to other locations; in other cases new constructions replaced older ones, with changes in dimensions and in orientation. A fresh look at Nehemiah's data is therefore imperative, and a careful comparison of his topographical information with the descriptions and references in the earlier sources concerning the last phases of the Judean Kingdom, especially those mentioned in the book of Jeremiah (see map 1).

A. NEHEMIAH'S VITAL EVIDENCE ON THE CITY OF DAVID

Nehemiah's memoirs constitute the substantial account of a Jewish official in the court of Artaxerxes I, king of Persia (464–424 B.C.) and his mission to Jerusalem, together with his achievements there. According to Nehemiah's account, Artaxerxes I sent him to Jerusalem in the twentieth year of the king's reign (445 B.C.) as the *peḥa* or governor of Judah, armed with authority and with plans to repair the gates and walls of Jerusalem which had been broken down, and to repopulate and restore the city for "the survivors there in the province who escaped exile are in great trouble and shame" (1:3). The emphasis on the Judahites who had not been exiled, as compared with the Jews who had returned from exile more than two generations previously, is of special interest. Nehemiah took formal cognizance of the returnees and their leaders sometime after his arrival (cf. 7:5), probably when conditions became desperate. Another characteristic is worth noting in his memoirs. On the eve of his journey to Jerusalem, the king gave him a letter to Asaph, the keeper of the king's forest (apparently in Lebanon) to supply him with cedar timbers for the gates of the Birah, for the city walls, and for "the house which I shall occupy" (2:8). This structure, the governor's residence in Jerusalem, may be alluded to as well in a passage referring to the throne (translated "jurisdiction") of the "*peḥa* (governor) of the Province Beyond the River" (3:7), as the Persian satrapy west of the Euphrates was known. The Province of Judah formed part of this satrapy. The governor's residence is distinct from the Birah which stood northwest of the Temple Mount and housed a garrison. It was under the authority of Hananiah who was "governor of the Birah" and responsible for the administration of Jerusalem (7:2). This title survived until Herodian times.

1. HIS PLACE IN THE REVIVAL OF JERUSALEM

However, in spite of persistent difficulties in and around Jerusalem, as well as continued threats and charges by the governors of neighboring provinces, Nehemiah, with extraordinary singlemindedness and determination never slackened his efforts, and succeeded in carrying out his assignment of repairing the city walls and of accomplishing this in the short span of fifty-two days (6:15). This achievement was celebrated with great festivity (12:27 ff.).

A new look at the biblical text in the light of our knowledge of the terrain can help to explain the unusual course of events at this juncture. It is not only characterized by the short time required to feverishly accomplish the project, but also by its urgency and unusual circumstances. We have already referred above (Part II, C, 1: Restoration of Zion after the Exile) to the circumstances of Ezra's arrival from Babylon (458 B.C.), his insistence on reestablishing the exclusive character and inner unity of the Jewish community in Jerusalem and Judah, and the need to protect it against the inimical neighboring communities. As physical restoration progressed and as the observance of the Torah (Jewish Law) became more firmly entrenched — a process which involved the expulsion of foreign wives — the Samaritans rose to the attack. The message of the authority in Samaria to the Persian emperor Artaxerxes I accused the Jews of plotting a rebellion against Persia under the guise of restoration work; the Jews were accused, in fact, of an attempt to restore their own kingdom (Ezra 4:7 ff.). As a result of the campaign of slander, work was broken off in Jerusalem (446 B.C.) by order of the king, and the people of Samaria were sent there to ensure this "by force and power" (Ezra 4:23).

This episode provides the real background to the tense atmosphere portrayed in the opening verses of Nehemiah, an official of the imperial court of Artaxerxes I, as he hears of the problems of the survivors in Jerusalem for "the wall of Jerusalem is broken down, and its gates are destroyed by fire" (Nehemiah 1:3–4). This complements the story told in Ezra 4:24: "Then the work on the house of God which is in Jerusalem stopped" as a result of the humiliation of the Jews. In the second part of the same verse, the scribe then proceeds to relate this to an incident which occurred long before, during the reign of King Darius, ca. 521 B.C. "and it ceased until the second year of the reign of Darius king of Persia." The background to this last sentence is the story concerning the prophets Haggai and Zechariah who preceded Ezra and Nehemiah, but faced similar problems.

Nehemiah's concern, in summary, was to repair the damage recently done to the

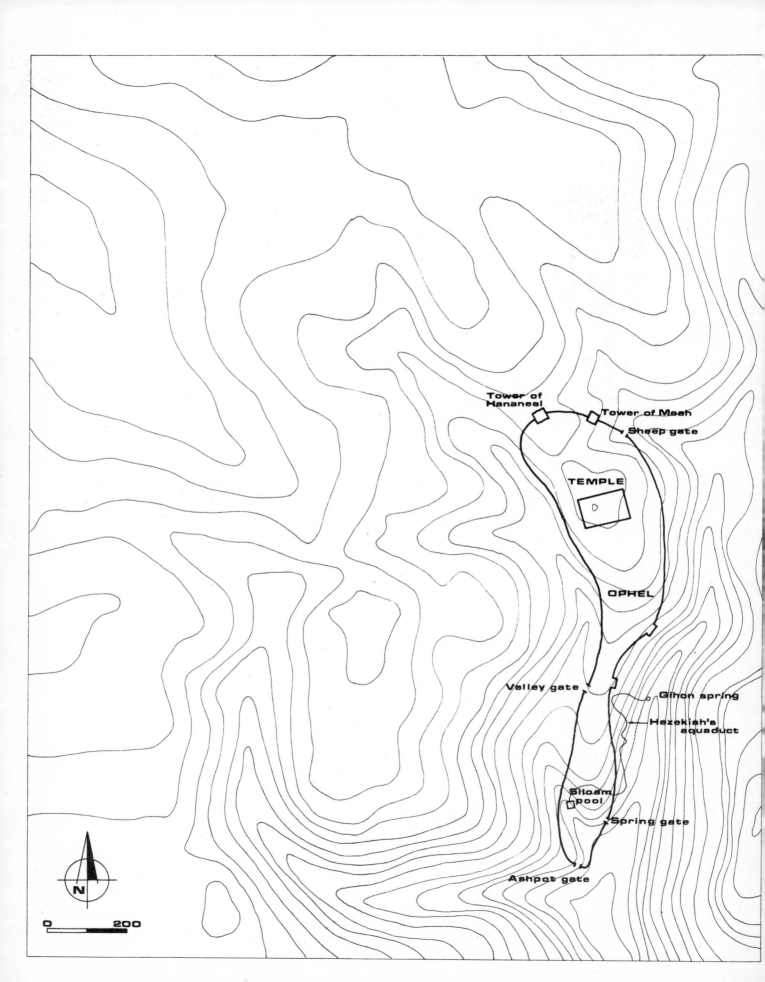

Tower of
Hananeel

Tower of Meah

Sheep gate

TEMPLE

OPHEL

Valley gate

Gihon spring

Hezekiah's
aquaduct

Siloam
pool

Spring gate

Ashpot gate

N

0   200

massive wooden gates of the city and sections of the city walls. This is why he was provided with timber and other building facilities referred to above (Nehemiah 2:8 ff). He thereupon proceeded to organize the work and completed it within fifty-two days.

A detailed examination of the record left by Nehemiah shows, however, that his work was restricted to the eastern hill alone, which included, beside the Temple area, the southeastern ridge. This evaluation of Nehemiah's work *fits well with the results of recent archeological excavations*. It is abundantly clear that barring a few isolated artifacts, nothing ascribable to the Persian period has been found in the Western hill (Upper City). Moreover, the City of David or rather its area of occupation was much reduced in size, in contrast to the extent of the city in the time of the Monarchy. Another curious feature of Nehemiah's memoir is his silence concerning repairs and renovations in the Temple proper or its immediate precincts. The omission can best be explained by the fact that Nehemiah, as the secular governor, was not empowered to interfere in affairs of the Temple, as this was the exclusive province of the High Priest.

Nehemiah, whose main interest was to restore a semblance of material security to the forlon people, took the lead in three building enterprises: 1) the *Birah* or citadel situated at the northwestern angle of the Temple Mount, which served as the seat of the local civil government; 2) the city walls; and 3) his own residence, the governor's palace.

A tragic picture of desolation emerges from his tour of the deserted city ruins by night: "I went out by night by the Valley Gate to the Jackal's Well and to the Dung (Ashpot) Gate" (see below). He found breached walls and burned gates everywhere (the walls were, apparently, not completely destroyed). He proceeds to the Fountain Gate and to the King's Pool "but there was no place for the beast that was under me to pass," and in the end he returns to the Valley Gate (2:3–15).

a. Identity of the Valley Gate

Any attempt to identify this structure is fraught with difficulty. One current theory identifies it with the gate of the Valley of Hinnom, which was in the wall of the southern city, on the slope of the present-day Mount Zion. Before we can accept this identification, two factors have to be considered: a) According to Nehemiah 3:13, the distance between it and the *Ashpot* Gate (see below) which lies at the southeastern end of the City of David, was a thousand cubits, or 1660 feet (half a kilometer). This gate is mentioned in the description of the fortifications erected by King Uzziah who is said to have "built towers in Jerusalem at the Corner Gate and the Valley Gate and at the Angle" (II Chronicles 26:9). If the Valley Gate is situated on the slope of the southwestern hill (now called Mount Zion) near and above the valley of Hinnom, the distance is too short; so it is necessary to assume that this southwestern hill was included in the city limits as early as the eighth century B.C. In view of these difficulties, Albrecht Alt proposed to identify the Valley Gate in question with a gate which had been uncovered by J.W. Crowfoot on the western side of the City of David, on the slope of the Tyropoeon (the valley which separates the City of David from the Upper City). This gate is about 12 feet (3.5 m.) wide and stands between two towers; its construction could only be attributed to a time when the City of David required protection on the western side. It must be noted, however, that Crowfoot's excavation (1926–27) failed to clarify the stratigraphic position of this gate (see Part IV, D, 2: The Crowfoot Gate); but the presence there of pottery from the period of the divided monarchy, as well as from Persian and hellenistic times, favors the theory that it was in existence in pre-exilic times, and was rebuilt in the days of Nehemiah, with continuing attention and maintenance in the hellenistic period.

Under the circumstances, we may conclude that the gate belonged to the old wall of the City of David, before the city expanded to the Western hill (the *Mishneh* quarter), and that it was put back in use by Nehemiah who "repaired a thousand cubits of the wall, as far as the Ashpot Gate" (3:13; translated "Dung Gate") thus limiting the urban settlement to the City of David. This interpretation would be appropriate in the light of the Hebrew text of Nehemiah 3:8 which says: "And they abandoned Jerusalem as far as the Wide Wall." The verb is often rendered 'restored,' but in Hebrew it clearly means 'abandoned.' The Wide Wall is understood as the one which N. Avigad discovered in 1973 in his excavations on the Western hill (present Jewish Quarter). While it circumscribed the wider expanse of the capital towards the end of the Monarchy, it was no longer in use after the destruction of 586 B.C. and the area remained unoccupied. Nehemiah did not attempt to effect any change there. Accordingly, judging by the biblical text, the extensive area of the Mishneh was not fortified by him, and that explains why he decided to repair the ancient western wall of the City of David and along with it the Valley Gate (see map 2).

b. Significance and Identity of the Ashpot Gate

Some interesting problems arise in connection with the identification of the Dung (Ashpot in Hebrew) Gate situated at the southernmost point of the defenses of the City of David. It must have had a strategic location, since Nehemiah mentions it repeatedly. It is reasonable to conclude that the gate site continued to be used in later times, and in fact such a gate was discovered by F. J. Bliss and A. C. Dickie in the First Wall described by Josephus. It guards the City of David at the southern end.

The Ashpot Gate is generally interpreted as the one through which the city's refuse was removed, but this is certainly wrong from any point of view. The attempt to justify the standard interpretation by identifiying it with the Potsherd Gate (Jeremiah 19:2) is at least doubtful. It is, in fact, one of Jerusalem's most important outlets to the valley of Hinnom and the 'Ēn-Rogel spring. Moreover, the Hebrew text of Nehemiah 3:13 reads "Gate of ShPt" (Shafot = שפות). It may therefore be worth determining etymologically whether the name does not derive from the root ShPT in the sense of 'hearth.' Compare it in this connection with the Hebrew MSʰPTAYM in Genesis 49:14 and Judges 5:16, in which the English translation is rendered, wrongly in our opinion, as 'sheepfolds.' This is one, but not the exclusive meaning of the term MSʰPATYM. The term SʰPT may be derived from the archaic ṬPT conceived as a by-form of 'Tophet' as suggested by some scholars. Indeed, many sources point to the Tophet or 'place of burning' in the valley of Hinnom, south of the City of David, where the popular rite of infant sacrifice to Molekh

194

Picture overleaf — above, left: Section of a wall and tower overlooking the Kidron valley, and incorporating a bulging glacis. It was considered ▶
a Jebusite tower or an Israelite fortress for a long time, but it later became evident that the tower had been built by one of the Hasmonean princes
in the second century B.C., on top of the ruins of a house destroyed by the Babylonians in 586 B.C. It was, in fact, one of the additions to
Nehemiah's wall or part of its restoration. On the right is a sloping ramp faced with stepped masonry and built later than the tower. It served for
the bolstering of a weak point in the city defenses and a rebuilding of the wall. Back of the structures is the wall of Nehemiah
Below: Detail of the Hasmonean fortification. The ramp or glacis described above, on the right; behind it is a wall bolstered by the glacis (center)
and at the left is a tower built in the form of a square.
Above, right: The meeting point of the wall and the tower

was observed in the days of King Manasseh (II Kings 23:10). The rite was abolished during the religious reform of King Josiah. Jeremiah voices his protest against this barbarous custom by saying: "And they have built the high place of Tophet, which is in the valley of the son of Hinnom, to burn their sons and their daughters in the fire; which I did not command, nor did it come into my mind" (7:31). He proclaims: "Therefore, behold, the days are coming, says the Lord, when it will no more be called Tophet, or the valley of the son of Hinnom, but the valley of Slaughter" (7:32). We may therefore conclude that the gate in question led from the City of David to the 'burning place' of Tophet in the valley of Hinnom (not to be confused with the present-day Dung Gate situated in the Turkish wall of the Old City, near the Temple area).

2. NEW ARCHEOLOGICAL INSIGHTS INTO THE BOOK OF NEHEMIAH

A fresh look at Nehemiah in the light of recent archeological discoveries (see above) has resulted in new proposals and in solutions to old questions, but has brought new questions as well. The latest archeological data concerning the eastern wall of the City of David and its gates is summed up below.

a. Structures in the City of David

(1) *The Fountain Gate:* In Nehemiah's memoirs, this gate is mentioned immediately after the Ashpot Gate, as stated. Opinions differ as to whether it is the gate which led to 'En-Rogel, or whether its name was derived from the outlet of the Siloam tunnel. It may have been called the Lower Gihon, in contrast to the Upper Gihon (II Chronicles 32:30), meaning the ancient Gihon spring. We have already seen that the gate was discovered by R. Weill in 1923–24 close to the steps cut in the rock. These may be "the stairs that go down from the City of David" (Nehemiah 3:15), that is, those leading to the Kidron valley.

(2) *The Water Gate:* This gate is mentioned by Nehemiah as the gate in the eastern wall which led to the Gihon spring (3:26; see map 2). Though the spring was no longer important as a source of water by that time, the site retained its hallowed associations with the past, for the area between the Fountain Gate and the Water Gate included all the structures which dated from the early period, chiefly the reign of David (see Part IV, B, 7, a: The Water Gate). It was also in this area that Ezra read the Law before the assembled people, i.e. in the square in front of the Water Gate, and this is where they erected their tabernacles (Nehemiah 8:1, 16).

(3) *Clues to the Palace of David and the Later Wall above It:* Nehemiah's description of the thanksgiving ceremony and dedication of the wall of Jerusalem (12:27–38) lays stress on certain revealing details: "At the Fountain Gate they went up straight before them by the stairs of the City of David, at the ascent of the wall [which is] above the house of David, to the Water Gate on the east" (12:37). This passage, in all likelihood, alludes to an ancient tradition which linked the area with David's palace. It also suggests

the possibility that the Water Gate had already been abandoned in Nehemiah's time, when the new city wall was built higher up, on the crest of the ridge. This view is indeed supported by archeological evidence uncovered by R.A.S. Macalister in 1923–25. His discoveries indicate that the wall, supported by a glacis on the crest of the ridge, as shown in our pictures, as well as the towers which are integrated into the wall, do not date back to pre-Davidic days or to the period of the Monarchy, but to a later period (as interpreted by archeologists who followed Macalister and reassessed his finds). Kathleen Kenyon later discovered, below these fortifications, some deposits which dated to the end of the Monarchy. They were remains of houses demolished during the destruction of the First Temple. On the other hand, it seems that the wall itself, on the basis of the dating of the pottery present there, was built in the Persian period. This is the period of Nehemiah.

(4) *The Towers:* The remains of towers uncovered in this complex, and chiefly the larger southern structure, pose another problem. It is not possible to determine whether it is hellenistic, or whether it had already been erected in Persian times. In the latter case, it may possibly be identified with the "great projecting tower" described by Nehemiah (3:26–27).

The description of this great projecting tower is confusing: "Palal the son of Uzai repaired opposite the Angle and the tower projecting from the upper house of the king at the court of the guard... the temple servants living on Ophel repaired to a point opposite the Water Gate on the east and the projecting tower... the Tekoites repaired another section opposite the great projecting tower..." (Nehemiah 3:25–27). It may be deduced that some extraneous material dealing with building activity on the Temple Mount has been introduced into the text. This was apparently due to confusion between the "great projecting tower" (3:27) and "the tower projecting from the upper house of the king" (3:25), i.e. the king's palace which had been destroyed during the Babylonian invasion.

(5) *The Ophel Wall:* It is now possible to explain the rest of Nehemiah's description which is characterized by the use of terms such as "angle" or "recess"= *miḳṣoʻa* (mistranslated as "sections"), and "the corner" (3:24) in reference to the walls as they turned northwest. These are actually the courses of walls whose remains were described as "the Ophel Wall" by Charles Warren in his early explorations of 1867–70. The same line of walls persisted in later centuries.

It is evident that Nehemiah reduced the city's area on the east side as well when he erected the eastern wall on the crest of the ridge, thus abandoning the ancient line of walls which lay further down the steep declivity. He had already determined for all time the course of the eastern wall of Jerusalem.

Nehemiah refers specifically to the "Ophel Wall," the citadel situated south of the Temple area as the continuation of the eastern wall of the citadel, and the eastern wall of the City of David. He points out, furthermore, that the Ophel was not completely ruined by the Babylonians as it could be used to house the *nethinim*, servants of the Temple, due to its proximity to the sanctuary.

It is believed by many that the segment of untrimmed stones uncovered by Warren southeast of the southeastern corner of the Herodian Temple area enclosure (or its retaining wall) is part of the Ophel wall (see map 1). This view, however, has not yet been verified by archeological evidence.

(6) *The Horse Gate:* Proceeding further north, Nehemiah mentions the Horse Gate (3:28) which was already known in Jeremiah's time: "all the fields as far as the brook of Kidron, to the corner of the Horse Gate toward the east shall be sacred to the Lord" (Jeremiah 31:40). In other words, this was the gate through which one went down from the Temple Mount to the Kidron valley.

b. Affluent Quarters

The gates mentioned so far by Nehemiah clearly belonged to the City of David, whereas the other gates referred to in the northern section of the Temple Mount such as the East Gate and the Muster Gate (3:29, 31) were the gates of the Temple area proper. It also has become evident that the homes of the more notable Jerusalem priests were located chiefly on the east side of the City of David and the Temple Mount, for example the vast and elaborate structures of Eliashib the high priest (3:20–21). A quarter of the city inhabited by the guilds of tradesmen and artisans, chiefly jewelers, was located to the east and southeast of the walls of the Temple Mount. In this connection, the existence is noted of a "house of Nethinim" i.e. servants of the Temple, in addition to those who had settled in the Ophel. From the account in Nehemiah 3:31–32, it may be assumed that this quarter ran westward as far as the Sheep Gate (see below), the northern gate of the city.

c. Rebuilding in the Temple Area

Archeological investigation in the Jewish Quarter of the Old City (facing the Western Wall to the west; see map 2) and on the present Mount Zion, demonstrates that this area was not reintegrated into the city in Persian times. But Nehemiah's descriptions indicate that he was instrumental in renovating or rebuilding not only in the Temple Mount area, but also in adjoining areas to the north and northeast. All of these were included within the city walls. Thus we hear about the Sheep Gate, the first to be listed in the account of the wall resorations (3:1). It was probably situated near the Birah citadel, at the northwestern corner of the Temple Mount (see above A, 1: His Place in the Revival of Jerusalem). This gate near the Bethesda Pool referred to in John 5:2 (the Piscina Probatica) was known in Jerusalem as late as the Second Temple period. It is reasonable to believe that it superceded the older Benjamin Gate which led to the land of Benjamin, and which dates to the time of the First Temple (Jeremiah 37:13).

d. The Fish Gate

This gate, mentioned after the Sheep Gate, raises a number of problems. It probably led out of Jerusalem to the main road descending to the coastal plain, the road to Beth-Horon and Ayalon. The gate was known in the days of the First Temple (Zephaniah 1:10) as one of Jerusalem's main entrances (II Chronicles 33:14). It may be the same as the Gate of Ephraim, so well known in classical times. In all likelihood, this gate was located at the northern part of Jerusalem, its most vulnerable point, and had to be reinforced constantly.

e. The Yeshana Gate

The name of the Yeshana Gate (so designated according to the Hebrew version of Nehemiah 3:6 and rendered 'Old Gate' in the translations) may be interpreted in two different ways: According to one idea, it received its name from the fact that the road from this gate led to the small city of Yeshana lying on the border between the provinces of Judea and Samaria in Persian times. According to the other view, it is a distortion of the name 'Mishneh' (the quarter) and designated the gate which led to that section of the city, having its origin in pre-exilic times (cf. Zephaniah 1:10).

3. JERUSALEM IN NEHEMIAH'S TIME

In all likelihood, Nehemiah did not fortify the whole populated area of Jerusalem, and the commercial and industrial precincts to the west may well have been located outside the city walls, including the bazaars of the goldsmiths and perfumers (Nehemiah 3:8), and the bakers along with the Tower of the Ovens (3:11). It is also interesting to note that by order of Nehemiah, the city gates were closed on Sabbath to the itinerant merchants among whom were the Tyrians who brought fish from the coast, forcing them to stay outside the walls and not to enter the city on the holy day.

The population of Jerusalem, following its settlement and the completion of the new wall, may be estimated at about 10,000. Some pertinent data on this matter may be gleaned from Nehemiah 11. The various enumerations add up to 3,044 men, among them 1,648 servants of the Temple (priests, levites and gatekeepers) and 1,396 other citizens of Judah and Benjamin. Moreover, a number of priests lived on their humble estates near Jerusalem. There would be about 12,000 other family members, adding up to a hypothetical figure of about 15,000. If an estimated 5,000 who live outside the walls are subtracted from the above, the total would come to 10,000. A comparison between these figures and the estimated population of Jerusalem in Herod's time (see below: Jerusalem's Population) is indicative of the city's expansion in the four intervening centuries.

4. NEHEMIAH'S FORESIGHT

It must be observed, in conclusion, that even the restricted area within the walls was sparsely populated and it devolved upon the handful of residents to organize teams of guards to man the gates and protect the houses in the city. The situation is described in this fashion by the chief witness: "The city was wide and large, but the people within it were few and no houses had been built" (7:4). Nehemiah therefore enjoined the notables of the province to "cast lots to bring one of ten to live in Jerusalem" (11:1) and thus swell

the population. This is how Jerusalem gradually became a fortified and populated city which could in time develop into the celebrated administrative and religious center of Judah, as described by the hellenistic authors. Nehemiah's foresight and determination were largely responsible for the material progress of the city and its environs which he had introduced in the middle of the fifth century B.C., enabling the people of Jerusalem to overcome the gloom and poverty which had prevailed since the Babylonian conquest and destruction of the city at the beginning of the sixth century B.C.

B. JERUSALEM OF HELLENISTIC AND HASMONEAN TIMES

1. SIMON'S WORKS IN JERUSALEM

Jerusalem appears to have reached a high peak of prosperity and urban expansion by 200 B.C. (see Part II, D: Jerusalem in the Early Hellenistic Period), as expressed in clear terms in the well-known treatise by Joshua Ben Sira (Sirach), author of the apocryphal work, Ecclesiasticus. He expounds (chapter 3) on the worthy deeds of the high priest Simon, the son of Yohanan, also known to posterity as Simon the Righteous, of Talmudic fame. Ben Sira lauds Simon highly for the services he rendered to his people, among them the strengthening of the city walls which had apparently been damaged in the war between Antiochus III and Ptolemy V. The city leaders helped Antiochus to capture Jerusalem and the fortress of the Temple, which had been occupied by a Ptolemaic garrison (*Antiquities* XII:138). Simon was equally diligent in strengthening the fortifications of the Temple and in building the great city pool to augment the water supply. It is likely that this is the reservoir mentioned by Ben Sira: "in his days the great water reservoir was dug, a deep pool as extensive as the sea" (Ecclesiasticus 50:1–3). The reservoir was named Beth-Hesda (in Aramaic, House of Mercy; later called the Pool of Bethesda) after the name of the new northern quarter of Jerusalem. In Roman days it was known as the Piscina Probatica or, to the Jews, the Sheep's Gate; its waters were reported to possess curative powers (as related in John 5:2–4). At a lower level more ancient remains, consisting of rectangular twin pools, were discovered at the back of the Monastery of St. Anne. The water may have been fed to the Temple area by means of canals (some connecting reservoirs are known to exist underground at the northern end of the Temple area). According to Father P. Benoit, the pools are identical with the Eshdatayim (twin pools) mentioned in the Dead Sea Scrolls. In the light of the 1956 excavations, they appear to have originated before the days of the Hasmonean (Maccabean) dynasty (162–35 B.C.).

a. *The Temple as Described by Aristeas*

The Letter of Aristeas pertaining to the period (see Part II, D, 1) imparts a description of the Temple, with its architecture, walls and gates, as well as the curtain at the entrance to the sanctuary. It tells of the thousands of animals sacrificed during the festivals, and lays particular stress on the seven hundred priests participating in the ritual with reverential mien and praiseworthy inner discipline. The high priest, impressively costumed, not only conveyed God's message and commands to the priesthood, but also headed the Jewish community which was represented by the *ecclesia*. This referred, probably, to the Great Assembly *(Haknesseth Hagedolah)*.

b. *Contemparary Coins*

It had hitherto been agreed by scholars that jar handles and coins of the preceding Persian period were the only ones to bear the imprint YHWD (Judah); those dating to the days of Ptolemaic (Egyptian) rule over Palestine (mid-third century B.C.) bear the imprint YRŠLM (Jerusalem). The few recently discovered silver coins bearing the legend YHDH (יהדה = pronounced Yehûda) and the portrait of Ptolemy I, date around 300 B.C. i.e. the beginning of the hellenistic period; they are of unknown provenance.

The plainer masonry of the stones along the so-called 'seam' at the southern end of the eastern supporting wall, underlines their Hasmonean origin (right) as compared with the Herodian stones (left) which are cut smoothly around the edges thus accentuating the bulges at the center (see also top color plate facing p. 161)

2. ARCHITECTURAL ACHIEVEMENTS OF THE HASMONEAN KINGS

The energetic Hasmonean dynasty, consisting of worldly rulers who had knowledge of western culture and technology, contributed vastly to the fortification and beautification of the capital, the repair of the Temple, and the expansion of commerce and trade. Jonathan began the work of erecting city walls and fortifying the Temple Mount, a task continued by Simon (I Maccabees 10:10–11). This is the period to which the remains of fortifications uncovered in the Citadel of today, near the Jaffa Gate, may be attributed. They belong to a section of the city walls which encircled both the Upper and Lower City. Hasmonean Jerusalem is indeed represented in the archeological picture as a period of expansion, a prelude to the glorious Herodian times.

Another interesting find dating to the same period is the remnant of a structure known today as Wilson's Arch. It is the eastern end of a causeway ending at the Western Wall of the Temple Mount, which spanned the Tyropoeon Vale and linked the Upper and Lower City with the Temple Mount. It was reconstructed in Herod's time (see D, 1 below: The Wilson Arch). Furthermore, it has been recognized that a section of the eastern supporting wall of the Temple Mount (facing the Mount of Olives), north of the seam referred to above and some 156 ft. (32 m.) north of the pinnacle of the Temple Mount — the Herodian southeastern corner of the Temple area — was erected at the time. The stone-cutting and masonry style resemble closely those peculiar to the Hasmonean stone rectangles found in the lower levels of the Citadel, as well as those of the Hasmonean fortress of Sartaba in the Jordan Valley. Whereas the huge stone rectangles of Herodian times were smooth around the edges with a wide boss in the middle, the Hasmonean stones were not cut as smoothly and had a rougher look, as will be evident from our illustrations.

It is interesting to note the expansion of the city northward and westward over the Western hill in this period of dynamic growth. The Hasmonean Palace was built at the eastern slope of the hill with a magnificent view over the Temple Mount and the entire neighborhood (*Antiquities* II:190). It was linked to the Temple Mount by means of a road and the causeway spanning the Tyropoeon Vale. Other important architectonic remains have been uncovered in the Jewish Quarter, among them the capital of a column carved in Ionic style (a Greek style distinguished by the spiral scroll-like ornaments on the capitals), as well as its Attic base (displaying simple elegance and delicacy), and several other sections which belonged, it is believed, to the Hasmonean Palace in the Upper City.

C. REDISCOVERING THE LOWER CITY OF THE HERODIAN PERIOD

Part IV and Section A of Part V sum up the investigation of the City of David in Old Testament times, and give a reassessment of the material uncovered to date. In the present section, we shall trace the developments in this and the adjoining areas in the later days of the Second Temple and the Herodian period, from the accession of Herod in 36 B.C. to the destruction of the Temple in A.D. 70.

1. THE LOWER CITY

We are indebted to Josephus for some of the most comprehensive descriptions of the city, its principal quarters and important buildings (*War* V:136–147 in particular). The observations of any contemporary, especially one trained as a historian, would be of the greatest importance, even though there are occasional distortions and contradictions in his accounts, partly due to accidents of transmission or the awkwardness of translation of his writing into the Greek. Only in recent years has it been possible to check by intensive archeological investigation the validity of his information and the precision of specific data (cf. Part I, A, 3: Josephus).

a. The Tyropoeon, or Street of the Vale

The central valley which he calls the Tyropoeon, separating the Eastern and Western hills, occupies a crucial place in his descriptions. The origin and significance of the name, meaning literally 'The Vale of the Cheesemakers,' have not been determined satisfactorily and remain obscure. We have been able, however, to identify it definitely in the light of Josephus' writings as the depression now called *El-Wād* (i.e. the Street of the Vale and the buildings abutting it on both sides) by the local population. This street crossed the present Old City from north to south, passing under the Wilson and Robinson Arches between two historic hills. In Josephus' time, it then proceeded south in the direction of the Siloam Pool and as far as the valley of Hinnom (see map 3). Josephus remarks that

These steps which lead from the Temple Mount area to the present El-Wad Street (the former Tyropoeon street) pass under an arched Arab construction which spans the ancient Tyropoeon street at this point. It is believed that this site lies along the probable line of the ancient causeway which ends at the Wilson Arch

the vale "extended down to Siloam" (*War* V:137–140). His description stresses the fact that Jerusalem, except for the Temple Mount area and the new quarters, was built upon two hills: the higher Western hill, i.e. the Upper City, and the eastern ridge, or former 'City of David,' lying south of the Temple Mount and called the Lower City, which he describes as having "the shape of a crescent." He speaks of it as the Akra (a reference to the hellenistic fortress in the southern part of this area). Both sections were surrounded by the "most ancient wall... well-nigh impregnable" (*War* V:142).

b. Continuation of the Tyropoeon Street in the City of David

In K. Kenyon's excavations of 1961–62 in the lower part of the City of David she cleared again the magnificent thick paving stones (6 × 4.5 feet) of the long Tyropoeon street which had been discovered in 1894–97 by the F.J. Bliss and A.C. Dickie expedition. Nearby was also a tumble of paving stones which came from an upper terrace.

c. The Three Walls of Jerusalem

We can accept at face value Josephus' statement that Jerusalem possessed only three walls prior to its capture: (1) The First Wall which surrounded both the Upper and Lower Cities; (2) The Second Wall which encircled the commercial quarter (the Upper Market) extending north of the First Wall; and (3) The Third Wall which protected the new quarters established north of the Second Wall (see map 3).

Josephus' estimate (*War* V:159) that the city's area on the eve of the siege (A.D. 66) was 33 *ris* (7,200 square yards) is supported by current analysis of topographical and archeological data which fixes the area at approximately 6,600 square yards. According to the same calculations, the First Wall enclosed an area of 4,800 square yards. Josephus' figures are remarkably good, especially in comparison with the wildly exaggerated numbers given in other ancient sources.

MAP 3

It will be noted that the First Wall (marked 7) which bordered the Ophel on the east, did not meet the southeastern corner of the walls of the Temple area (marked 1) but ran parallel to the walls on the east, above the Kidron valley (17) past a gate (p. 215) and up to an angle approximately facing the pool marked 20. At this point it merged with the Third Wall (marked 15). The northern and southern walls, of the Old City are indicated by thin lines

d. Archeological Links of the Central Thoroughfare

When he speaks of the Tyropoeon, Josephus refers only to the main street of the city which passed through the vale between the two hills, both sides of which were densely populated. Remains of this street, made of large and heavy paving stones, were discovered in the course of our excavations west of the Western Wall. This street apparently extended the entire length of the Tyropoeon and, south of the Robinson Arch, through the lower market in the Lower City. One branch of this paved street was discovered by F.J. Bliss and A.C. Dickie in the course of their excavations in 1894–97 (actually the Ashpot Gate, cf. above), while another branch turned off to the Siloam Pool. As stressed below however, no wall separated the Upper and Lower Cities along the line of the Tyropoeon. Presumably, therefore, Nehemiah's wall, which surrounded the City of David on the west side and included the Valley Gate (discovered by J.W. Crowfoot in 1927, see above, Part IV, D, 2: The Crowfoot Gate, and above, A, 1, a), was abandoned in Herodian times, as attested by the results of archeological excavations in the area. Furthermore, there is no evidence of any wall on the slope of the Upper City to protect it from attack from the direction of the Tyropoeon valley (which was far deeper in ancient times than it is today). This view is based on topographical data and in our judgment is not in conflict with historical data. The traditional argument is that there must have been a wall between the Lower and Upper Cities; otherwise, how could the Zealots have held out for a month against the Roman legionaries who had already occupied the Lower City? It is evident, in fact, that the fierce defensive action against the Romans took place on the steep rocky terrain of the Western hill (west of the Tyropoeon) and among the massive buildings erected on it. Hence, there is no need to look for some forgotten wall to account for the defense in this urban area during the period before the final Roman assault against the Upper City.

e. The City Was not Intersected

Contrary to the general opinion that the city was divided into two sections by a wall, Josephus presents a clear picture of a single integrated city, in which the two principal parts, the Upper and Lower Cities, were surrounded by a single wall. This so-called ancient 'Old Wall' was considered impregnable by the historian: "it was also strongly built... David and Solomon and their successors.. having taken pride in the work" (War V:142–147). The reference is evidently to the First Wall which enclosed an area of some 4,800 square yards (see map 3) as follows:

From the royal Herodian Palace and its three towers in the west, down to the wall on the upper slope of the Kidron valley in the east;

From the line of walls starting at the Hippicus Tower as far as the Xystos compound (see below) and the western porticos of the Temple to the north, and as far as the wall which extended over the slope of the valley of Hinnom to the south (as itemized above).

Outside the area of the First Wall were the Temple Mount, the commercial and craftsmen's quarter of the Upper Market (see above: The Three Walls of Jerusalem) situated north of the First Wall and enclosed by the Second Wall; and, finally, the New

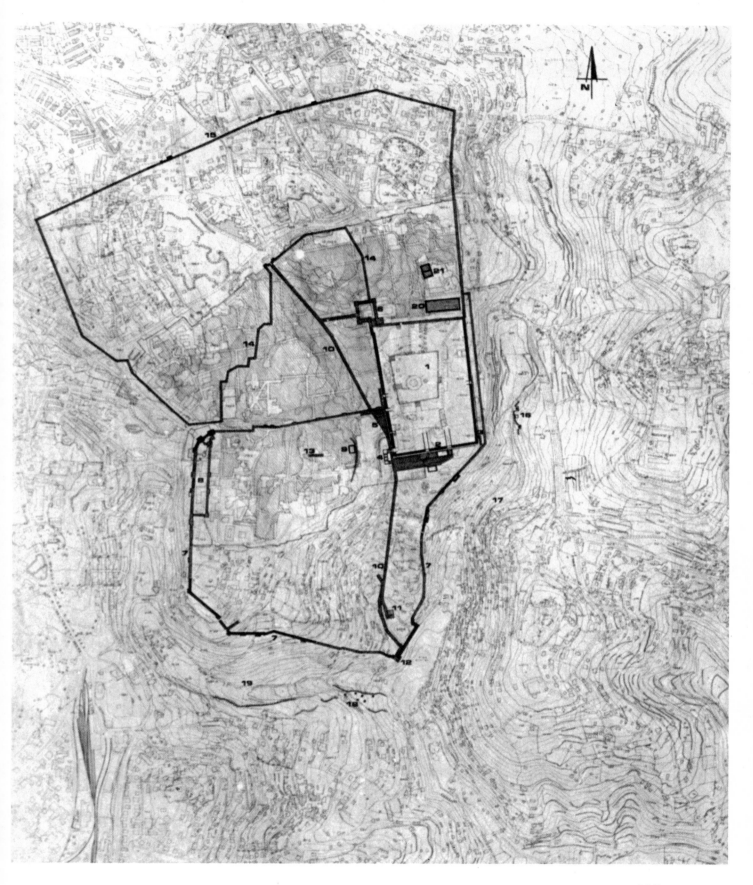

Town, still further north and protected by the Third Wall erected in the days of King Agrippa I (see Part II, F, 4, c: The Third Wall).

f. Expansion of the Walls

There is no doubt that Herod reinforced the Hasmonean wall which surrounded the Upper and Lower City (see above B, 2: Architectural Achievements of the Hasmonean kings), that is to say, the First Wall of Josephus, at the northwestern corner of which stood the palace and the three towers. Excavations in the present-day Citadel prove that the Phasael tower was built over the line of the original Hasmonean wall at the northwestern angle, which then turned east towards the Western Wall of the Temple Mount, north of the causeway which led from the Upper City to the Temple Mount (over the Wilson Arch).

The different quarters of Jerusalem had expanded greatly in Herod's time. Population was booming, there was rapid growth in the city's trade and crafts, and it was the acknowledged focus of pilgrimage from every corner of the country and the world. Interesting structures of the period were uncovered by Professor N. Avigad in the Upper City (today's Jewish Quarter), near the ruined Tifereth Israel Synagogue, among them the spacious home of a patrician family. It covered an area of 2400 square yards and was built in the early years of Herod's reign. It was larger than the average house; contemporary houses in urban centers, whether in Jerusalem or in hellenistic cities, averaged 250–350 square yards in area. It will soon be seen that urban development in the Upper City had increased in pace from Herod's time on, and lasted right up to the destruction of the Temple in A.D. 70. The structures bear witness to high architectural standards and to the manufacture of fine stoneware, pottery and glass. Pliny the Elder, a naturalist and contemporary of Josephus, described Jerusalem before its destruction as "longe clarissima urbinum orientis" — by far the most famous city of the East (*Naturalis Historia* V:15).

Herod also included the southern slopes of the Western hill within the city wall. This wall ran from the southwest corner of the present Old City walls and continued along the crest of the Hinnom valley. From there it proceeded across the lower Tyropoeon to complete its circuit of the city at the joint of the southeastern ridge (the Ophel). Segments of this wall were uncovered by F.J. Bliss and A.C. Dickie in 1894–1897. The western and southern walls of the city had been started in Hasmonean times, but Herod rebuilt them and in some cases extended them to include a larger area.

2. THE OVERALL PICTURE OF THE CITY

We are now in a position to reconstruct in large part the Holy City as it was in Herodian times, including a ground plan of its great walls and massive buildings, and other less durable but equally striking features. This picture is based on material found in literary sources, mainly Josephus, combined with the ever-growing mass of archeological evidence gathered from various parts of the city.

a. Dimensions of Jerusalem

The walled city was actually divided into three parts: the Temple Mount with the Antonia tower and fort standing near the northwest corner of its walls and serving, like its predecessor, the Birah, as the base for the military garrison; the Upper and Lower Cities, whose outer walls dated from Hasmonean days and were reinforced by Herod and his successors (the First Wall described by Josephus); and the commercial quarter to the north of the First Wall, which surrounded the markets at the upper end of the Tyropoeon and was enclosed by a new wall in Herod's time (the Second Wall). In addition, there were residential quarters beyond the western and northern sections of the Second Wall. These constituted the New City, including Beth-Zeta (Bezetha) which was unprotected until the time of Agrippa I when a wall was built around it (the Third Wall; see Part II, F, 4, c). By that time, the city extended over an area of some 450 acres.

The city owed its expansion and development to several factors. Its position as capital of an enlarged Judea under Roman tutelage led to increased population and prosperity, though an even more important influence was the ever-growing prestige of Jerusalem as a center of pilgrimage. The metropolis thus attracted merchants and craftsmen, chiefly stone cutters and masons, who were needed for the unparalleled building taking place.

b. Jerusalem's Population in Herodian Times

We have no reliable information about the population of Jerusalem in the time of the Herodian dynasty. Though its high density is beyond dispute, the figures cited by Josephus and other ancient writers are grossly exaggerated. For example, according to Josephus, 110,000 people died during the siege; 97,000 people were taken prisoner. He notes that most were Jews, though not all of them were Jerusalemites, as pilgrims flocked in masses to the capital for the Passover before the outbreak of the Roman attack (*War* VI:415–422). It may also be observed that Tacitus, in his *Historia* (V:13), states that as many as 600,000 people were beleaguered in Jerusalem. The Talmud mentions even higher figures. *Tosefta Pesachim*, Chapter IV, relates that when King Agrippa II wanted to determine how many people were in Jerusalem on the Passover, it was estimated that there were twice as many as the figure cited in the book of Exodus. This would mean a population of 1,200,000, besides those who had traveled to Jerusalem from distant lands or who were excluded for reasons of ritual impurity.

It is difficult to draw any conclusions on the basis of such data, except to wonder at the unusual density of population in a city covering only 450 acres at the height of its development, even taking into account a number of suburban areas outside the city walls.

These figures were not based, in any case, on a census or any objective evaluation. The difficulty applies equally to any estimate of the city's area, considering the facts that: (1) The city possessed many public edifices, extensive residences of the aristocracy and wealthier classes, a multitude of streets, markets, squares and other open public places; (2) There were many two and three-storied houses; (3) A considerable portion of the population lived in the suburbs and villages outside the city walls such as Bethpage and Bethany, known from the Gospels, e.g. Matthew 21:1, 17 etc.

Another factor in the total situation was the water supply (see below). The city's growth depended on the flow through the aqueduct, the proliferation of cisterns and rain catchments, storage pools, and so on. Water consumption reached a peak during the influx of pilgrims on the three holiday seasons of the year.

It is generally agreed that the population of Jerusalem, including the suburbs and outlying villages, came to 120,000 at most, though many consider that it was 100,000 or possibly less. With regard to the area of other cities in the country, it is commonly agreed that Caesarea and Ashkelon, each of them a maritime cosmopolitan center, covered an area of some 400 acres (half a kilometer square) and had a population of about 50,000 each.

c. The Economy of Jerusalem

The busiest trades and the ones for which Jewish craftsmen were famed were jewelry-making, iron-working, spinning, weaving, dyeing, tailoring, and shoemaking, as well and incense and perfume making. The busy and closely populated city required the services of numerous dealers in cattle, horses and donkeys, of bakers, manufacurers of oil, soap and perfumed ointments, food and sweetmeats, and other consumer articles. The pottery and tile making workshops were probably out of town, but their ware was sold in tremendous quantities in the city markets, as was stoneware, glassware and woodwork.

One of the most prosperous crafts in Jerusalem was stone working and stone carving, both for the booming building trade and for the making of ossuaries, decorated sarcophagi and household articles, equivalent to the multitude of objects now made of metal or its substitutes. An idea of the size of the building industry may be gathered from a factual situation mentioned by Josephus (*Antiquities* XX:54): When the building of the Temple was completed in the days of Agrippa II, some eighteen thousand building workmen became unemployed, whereupon the king kept them busy laying down the heavy pavements through the streets of Jerusalem.

Quarrying had attained a high peak of production in Jerusalem, both in the urban and suburban areas. The most famous was the underground quarry now known as the Cave of Zedekiah, close to today's Damascus Gate. This tunnel is some 660 feet (200 m.) in length, and 330 feet (100 m.) in width, and lies beneath the northern city markets. Josephus attributes the quarries to Solomon, calling them 'Solomon's Quarries.' Stone carving had long been a thriving trade, both in Hasmonean and in Herodian times. It was a necessary adjunct to the sophisticated architectural technique and advances in planning and decoration which reached the artistic heights we encounter in abundance in extant or excavated remains.

Another important trade was the accommodation and catering necessary for the multitude of pilgrims. The occupations including the maintenance of inns and hospices, and the sale of goods including ritual articles and art ware sought by the pilgrims.

d. The Water Supply

Supplying water for the expanding population of Jerusalem constituted one of the city's most complicated problems. The water of the Gihon spring which flowed to the

Siloam Pool was quite inadequate, and even with the cisterns and square storage pools carved in the rock on the Temple Mount and in various quarters of the city, there was not enough to meet the requirements of the people. Vast public cisterns were therefore constructed, among them the double Strouthion Cistern near the Antonia Fortress, the Pool of the Towers (now called the Pool of Hezekiah) north of the Citadel near the Jaffa Gate, and the Israel Pool at the northern edge of the Temple Mount. But the Temple Mount possessed other water resources. Large underground pools cut in the rock were recently discovered to the south of the Western Hulda Gates. Moreover, we discovered a very large reservoir on the lower slope of the Upper City, as shown in our photograph.

In spite of these efforts, it became clear that water would have to be brought from outside. The fundamental solution to the problem involved the construction of aqueducts which brought water by gravitation from higher localities in Judea, far south of Jerusalem. Three principal sources of water for this purpose are known: the Valley of 'Arub, Wadi Biyar, and the area known as Solomon's Pools. Although there is no record in available literary sources of any aqueduct specifically dated before the time of Pontius Pilate (A.D. 26–36; see below), there is a possibility that an aqueduct, mentioned in the Talmud, was built in an earlier period: "An aqueduct led to it [the Temple Mount] from Etam" (Jerusalem Talmud, *Yoma* 41:61). This would be the Lower Aqueduct which runs from 'En-'Etam near Solomon's Pools to the Temple Mount. The aqueduct, 13 miles (21 kms.) long, cut through two ridges by means of long tunnels, passed under the city of Bethlehem, and reached the slopes of Mount Zion (modern designation) and the Upper City; it then passed over the causeway which connected the Upper City to the Temple Mount

211

(the Wilson Arch) and ended in the underground cisterns beneath the esplanade of the Temple area, probably near the Water Gate in the Southern Wall of the inner enclosure of the Temple (see Part III, D, 3, b: The Balustrade; also subsequent sections). As only isolated remains of the original aqueduct were found, it is not quite certain that it was constructed in Herod's time. On the other hand, it is quite certain that the higher aqueduct built by Pontius Pilate with the funds of the Temple treasury is the one known as the 'Arub Aqueduct. It carried the water from the sources in the Valley of 'Arub to the vast Solomon's Pools for storage (about 700,000 cubic feet; 200,000 cubic meters); then a continuation of the aqueduct brought water to Jerusalem by a tortuous course some 42 (68 kms.) long.

3. THE HISTORIC STRUCTURES OF THE LOWER CITY

Within the area circumscribed in the Lower City were to be found the main public buildings of Herodian Jerusalem, including the theater, the stadium and the hippodrome. To these may be added the various structures, pavements, plazas and stairways leading to and from the Western and Southern Gates, as described in Part III, F: The Outer Walls and Gates of the Temple Mount. Nearby as well were the splendid private dwellings of the royal and patrician families. Among these were Herod's Palace, the palace of the Hasmoneans which was eventually occupied by King Agrippa II, the palaces of the royal house of Adiabene, and the sumptuous homes of the high priests (see below).

a. The Lower City during the Siege

Josephus provides decisive evidence regarding the most ancient quarter of the capital. For example, he describes those sections of the city which were held and defended during the siege by Simon bar-Giora and John of Gischala: "Simon occupied the upper town, the great wall as far as the Kidron, and a portion of the old wall from the point where it bent eastward at Siloam to its descent to the courthouse of Monobazus, king of Adiabene beyond the Euphrates... he held also the fountain and part of the Akra, that is to say the lower town as far as the palace of Helen, the mother of Monobazus." The rival leader, John, "held the Temple with much of the environs, Ophla [Ophel] and the valley called Kidron. The region between them they reduced to ashes and left as the arena of their mutual conflicts" (cf. *War* V:250).

212

Though this description lacks clarity, it provides certain specific data concerning the Lower City. It mentions the Old Wall situated to the east, or more specifically, the wall Nehemiah had built and which had been reinforced during subsequent times and was still in use in Herodian times. Mention is also made of the Fountain, i.e. the outlet of the Siloam tunnel, the capital importance of which as the city's main municipal water supply has been stressed in these pages. Also of major interest among the items mentioned by Josephus are the palaces of King Monobazus and Queen Helen of Adiabene, near the Siloam Pool. This section of the city had attracted high-placed Jews and Judaizers from abroad, who presumably formed the membership of the well-known synagogue of Theodotus whose dedication plaque was discovered by R. Weill (see Part II, F, 5, d: Synagogues). In this, as in other writings, Josephus identifies the Lower City with the (former) Akra. He seems to regard the Ophel, on the other hand, as a special quarter abutting on the public square close to the Temple Mount (see map 3).

The description is supplemented by an account of the inception of the revolt against Rome in the summer of A.D. 66. After setting fire to the house of the high priest Hananiah (Annas) and the Palace of Agrippa II in the Upper City, the Zealots went on to burn the House of the Archives (which was in the Lower City) and thus destroy the outstanding promissory notes filed there for safekeeping (*War* II:427). In this account of the final destruction of the Lower City in the summer of A.D. 70, Josephus declares: "On the second day, they set fire to the Archives, the Akra and the Council Chamber [Buleterion], and the region called Ophlas [Ophel], the flames spreading as far as the palace of Queen Helen which was in the center of the Akra" (*War* VI:351–353). We are not yet able at this juncture to pinpoint the site of these structures, though we can place them generally on the south of the western ridge.

b. The Council House

The Council House (*bule* or *buletērion*) and the Records Office (Archaia) is identified by some with the *Lishkat Ha-gazit* (Hall of Hewn Stone) where the Sanhedrin met before it was transferred to the *Hanuyot* (see Part III, D: Herod's Temple), presumably in the basilica-like Southern Portico.

c. The Ophel

It should be noted that the ancient name 'Ophel' (in Aramaic, *Ophla*, in Greek *Ophlas* in Josephus) was preserved through the centuries right up to the end of the Second Temple. Whereas it had been originally the Citadel (of the City of David) which protected the king's palace and the Temple, it became the quarters of the *nethinim*, servants of the Temple from the time of the return from exile. In Josephus' day it served as a residential quarter lying close to the Temple. His description of the First Wall (see above 1, e) is most helpful in locating the Ophel: "...after passing a spot which they call Ophlas finally joined the.... eastern portico of the Temple" (*War* V:145). From this statement, it is clear that *the Ophel extended as far as the southeastern corner of the Temple Mount walls*. The particular place called the Angle of the Ophel was situated

213

right below the pinnacle of the Temple mentioned in Matthew 4:5 (see map 3). The southeastern angle is presently about 92 feet (28 m.) high. It is made up of 35 Herodian courses of stones reaching to 158 feet (48 m.) in height.

We also suggest on the basis of recent observations, that a gate was situated in the eastern wall, close to this Angle giving access to the Temple Mount courts from the Kidron valley. This is described above in Part III, F, 5.

Maps of both the City of David and the Ophel, as well as of greater Jerusalem on the eve of its destruction in A.D. 70 must be redrawn on the basis of newly acquired evidence. The changes are due in part to a reassessment of previous excavations, including those conducted by K. Kenyon and, more particularly, as a result of our own excavations. The revised maps are published in this book (see pp. 56, 192, 207).

d. The Xystos

The Xystos compound seems to have been an open-air porticoed plaza paved with polished flagstones, and used for public assemblies. It faced the wide expanse of the Western Wall, between the present Barclay Gate and the point where the plaza meets the First Wall south of the causeway which passed over the Tyropoeon (the Wilson Arch). In describing the northern line of the First Wall which ran perpendicular to the walls of the Temple Mount, Josephus specifies that it started at the Hippicus Tower of the Citadel, reached the Xystos, then linked up with the *bule* and ended at the western portico on the Temple Mount (*War* V:144). The Xystos was probably the site of the earlier hellenistic *Gymnasium* (II Maccabees 4:9; cf. Part II, E, 1: Impact of Hellenization on Urban Jerusalem), which was no longer in use during the Herodian period. To the west and above it, on the slope of the Western hill, stood the Hasmonean palace, rebuilt later and used by King Agrippa II and his sister Berenice.

Josephus relates the following incident which took place when King Agrippa II tried to pacify the Jerusalem crowds during the Florus riots: "He summoned the crowd into the Xystos and placed his sister Berenice conspicuously on the roof of the Hasmonean palace." The Xystos was linked to the Temple by the causeway over the Wilson Arch (*War* II:344).

e. The Theater and Hippodrome

Josephus mentions several other monumental structures which he attributed to Herod. Herod was not content to limit his building programs to the magnificent buildings, the Temple and the Palace, or to the reinforcement of the fortifications and economic development of the city. True to the hellenistic standards of the day, he built a theater southeast of the Upper City, as well as an amphitheater, apparently at the lower end of the Tyropoeon Vale (*War* XV:268–9), and a stadium or Hippodrome south of the Temple Mount (*War* XVIII:255). We are not yet able to pinpoint the location of the theater, although progress of excavation and the common view is that it was on the eastern slope of the Upper City. We have better clues to the site of the Hippodrome which probably resembled the one erected by Herod at Samaria. Josephus refers (*War* II:44) to the three

Roman army camps put up by Titus when he besieged Jerusalem: One lay north of the Temple area (that is to say on Mount Scopus); the second lay to the south, close to the Hippodrome, and the third was west of the Palace and Citadel. The Hippodrome was probably outside the First (southern) Wall, in the valley of Hinnom. Another reference (*Antiquities* XVII:255) locates the Hippodrome south of the Temple Mount perimeter.

2. WHERE DID THE AKRA STAND?

The Akra, erected by Antiochus IV Epiphanes (see Part II, E, 2) in 168 B.C. as a stronghold of Seleucid power and as the nucleus of the hellenistic *polis* of Jerusalem, was remarkable for its powerful fortifications, its walls and towers. Because it rose above the Temple Mount (*Antiquities* XII:258), it was instrumental in the Maccabean (Hasmonean) wars against the Syrian Seleucids and the hellenizers until it was razed in 141 B.C. by Simon, the Hasmonean high priest, one of the brothers of Judah the Maccabee. It stood at a distance of a few hundred yards from the Birah, the older fortress situated northwest of the Temple which had served as a garrison since Persian and Ptolemaic times. According to Josephus, the Akra stood in the lower city, that is to say the Ophel, the top of the Southeastern hill. In the time of Herod and his successors, the entire hill (ancient City of David) was called the Akra.

A theory advanced by some scholars situating the Akra on the Western hill, today's Jewish Quarter, must therefore be rejected, particularly in view of the utter lack of any remains whatsoever of the Seleucid period in that area. Another recent theory is that the Akra stood southeast of the Temple, in the area later incorporated by Herod within the Temple Mount compound, and was connected to a section of the Eastern Wall, north of the "seam," the spot where this ancient wall section was joined to the Herodian extension of the wall in a southerly direction. But this idea is equally unacceptable in the light of recent observations (cf. above: B, 2: Architectural Achievements of the Hasmonean Kings).

It is more likely that the powerful, towering Akra stood on the spur at the top of the Ophel ridge, on both sides of the Herodian Southern Wall, in the area of the Hulda Gates, where it could easily command both the Temple Mount and the Lower City, i.e. in the area generally indicated by Josephus. Simon the Hasmonean, the confirmed commander of the people had razed it. In the ensuing century the whole area was filled in and leveled by the builders of Herodian times who erected there the huge southern supporting wall of the Temple Mount, with its gates and underground chambers cut in the rock, and with a paved road which ran along the Southern Wall. (See Part III, F, 4, f: The Road along the Southern Wall.) In support of this view, it may be noted that a considerable number of remains of the hellenistic period were uncovered by J.W. Crowfoot in 1927 on the western slope of the Ophel, including coins and pottery especially Rhodian jars of the third-second centuries B.C. The pottery included jars from the Island of Rhodes, the handles of which had stamps bearing the names of local high priests, thus indicating the date of manufacture in the third and second centuries B.C.

Top arc of the Wilson Arch, where it joins the retaining Western Wall (left). It represented the ultimate end of the causeway which spanned the Tyropoeon valley and Herodian pavement which skirted the Western Wall. The top arches were rebuilt by the Ommayad caliphs some seven centuries after the destruction in A.D. 70

D. EXPLORATION OF THE WILSON ARCH AND THE NORTHERN EXTENSION OF THE WESTERN WALL

1. THE WILSON ARCH

The visible top of the Wilson Arch leaning on the Western Wall near the Xystos (which includes the present site of Jewish prayers and assemblies facing the Wall and is part of it) is the last and upper end of a series of arches supporting the causeway which spanned the Tyropoeon valley and brought water to the Temple Mount through the Lower Aqueduct (see above, C, 2, d: Water Supply). The water flowed by gravitation from 'En-'Etam "higher than the floor of the inner courts [*Azarah* of the Temple] by twenty-three cubits" (39 feet or 12 m.; Babylonian Talmud, *Yoma* 31:71).

The vaulted subterranean arch stands 594 feet (180 m.) north of the southwestern angle of the walls. The visible top arch which is apparently a later restoration of the original (see below) consists of smooth stones whose edges fit together and lean against one another without any cementing. It stands some 25 feet (7.6 m.) above the present pavement, and is 45 feet (13.4 m.) wide. The original archway, however, which had rested over the bedrock of the Tyropoeon valley stood some 74 feet (22.25 m.) high. It consisted of two superimposed arches resembling Roman bridges or causeways of the times. This implies that at least 48 feet (14.6 m.) of the lowest tiers lie underneath, partly filled by its remains and other debris. It is doubtful, whether this can be excavated and exposed without damaging the structures standing over it. Nevertheless, the exposed and unexposed sections can be gauged from our diagrams.

Picture taken in 1870 of the clearing of Wilson's Arch by Charles Warren

2. THE BATTLE OVER THE BRIDGE

The causeway is the setting for the dramatic scene during Pompey's siege of Jerusalem in 63 B.C., as described by Josephus (*War* I:143). Aristobulos, one of the last Hasmonean princes, was fighting his last battle. As his men retreated into the Temple area, "they cut the bridge," i.e. the causeway which spanned the Tyropoeon valley and led to the principal gate of the Temple, the one standing over Wilson's Arch (see Part III, F, 1, b: What Were the Gates of the Western Wall?). The Temple was captured on a Sabbath, and the priests were killed while conducting their ritual (*Antiquities* XIV:67). Pompey respected the Temple, however, and did not plunder its treasures. He appointed Aristobulos' brother, Hyrcanus, high priest under Rome's tutelage.

3. EXCAVATIONS NORTH AND WEST OF THE WILSON ARCH

Exploratory digs initiated by the government Ministry of Religions have been carried out since 1968 in two directions from this point:

a. The first dig, in a northern direction, was performed in order to clear the Western Wall through a horizontal corridor about 530 feet (160 m.) long, skirting the Wall. The height and depth of the sections cleared in the corridor range from 10 to 26 feet (3 to 8 m.).

218

This operation exposed continuous layers of stone rectangles of enormous length, chiselled to a smooth edge at their sides and with protruding bosses in the middle, in the familiar style of Herodian ashlars in other parts of the vast retaining walls of the Temple Mount. The picture here is similar to that of the imposing layers under the Robinson Arch, as they are a continuation of the same stretch of wall, as shown in our pictures.

b. The second direction of the clearing operation (which is not a regular stratigraphic excavation due to the precarious condition of the area underground and the structures standing over it) is to the west and northwest of the visible Wilson Arch. The excavation has cleared the lower part of a pier which stood opposite the present visible pier of the arch. It is similar in structure and origin to the vast pier which faces the Robinson Arch in the Tyropoeon valley (cf. Part III, F, 1, a: The New Significance of the Robinson Arch).

c. The work of excavation has also uncovered several wide halls covered with vaulting and formerly filled with rubble and fetid rubbish, which stand west and north of the upper pavement under the Wilson Arch. This area lies under the Arab houses and narrow alleyways of that section of the Old City.

d. Still further on and at a lower level are remains of vaulted halls and rooms built of large, smooth stones. They are filled with debris and earth which abut the deeper and more ancient tiers of the Wilson Arch. The debris originates from different periods, beginning with the Herodian and ending with the Arab period (see Part VI, C: The Moslem Period).

4. THE 'MASONIC HALL'

One of the paved halls lying at a lower level could be more adequately cleared despite the precarious conditions of the underground. It lies lower than the present pavement of the Wilson Arch and is 86 feet (26 m.) to the west of it. Discovered before Charles Warren's time in the nineteenth century, this relic has been imbued ever since with esoteric mystery. On the basis of primitive folklore which connected it with the arcane rites of Solomon's Temple, it was patronized for some decades by the Masons and dubbed the 'Masonic Hall.' It has been abandoned for the last forty years, however.

This hall is part of a complicated system of underground vaults running under the present Street of the Chain (see diagram). Warren had also discovered there another room which had existed before the vaults were constructed. The interior measurements of the so-called Masonic hall are 46 × 84 feet (14 × 25.50 m.). The original walls of the structure are three feet (1 m.) thick. The stones of the exterior walls are of typical Herodian style (with margins and bosses) while the interior walls are built of plain dressed stones, without mortar. A double doorway flanked by two ornate pilasters stands in the eastern wall of the beautifully decorated room, and another column stands in the center. The double doorway 7.4 feet (2.25 m.) high leads to an additional room which has not yet been excavated.

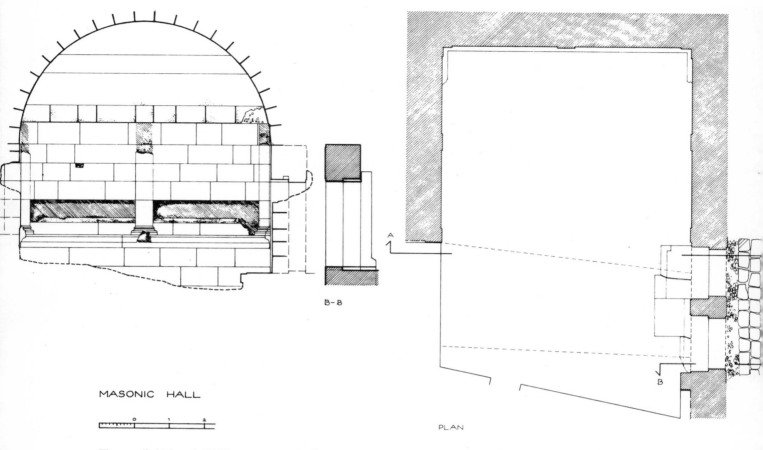

B-B

MASONIC HALL

0   1   2

PLAN

The so-called Masonic Hall is a most remarkable underground structure. It is located west of the Wilson Arch and must have antedated it, as it possibly formed part of the hellenistic *gymnasium* for athletic games, at the *Xystos* compound. The hall (left) was beautifully decorated by pilasters flanking the eastern doorway. The column standing over a pedestal in the center was intended to support the vaults joining the ceiling.

The Xystos was first cleared as a platform for assemblies and games. Stone benches, arcades and portals were added later to accommodate the public

a. Link with the Gymnasium

This important structure was certainly used in Herodian times, but it is not improbable that its antecedents lie in the previous period and might originally have been part of the *Gymnasium* of the hellenistic period (preceding Hasmonean times) and adjoined the *Xystos* and other public edifices at this level of the Tyropoeon valley (see above: C, 3: The Historic Structures of the Lower City).

A puzzling feature of the hall is its northwest orientation. Other half-hidden chambers located nearer to the Western wall or abutting it, lie perpendicular to the Wall, in contrast to the so-called Masonic Hall's orientation. The reason may possibly be sought in the general direction followed by the high causeway above, which may have been later than the Gymnasium, and which spanned the Tyropoeon valley and did not run at right angles to the Western wall, but met it obliquely, perhaps because of the bedrock profile of the valley.

220

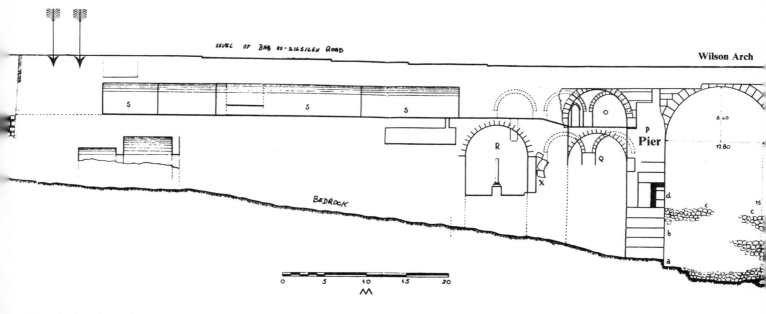

Warren's plan of the subterranean structures situated below the level of the Street of the Chain (Bab el-Silsileh, top) and ending at the Wilson Arch (right).
c, b, a: Buried sections of the arch down to bedrock.
P, d, b: The huge pier which supported the eastern end of the Wilson Arch.
O, Q: Upper and lower arches, presumably joined to the eastern pier (P) of the Wilson Arch.
R: The so-called Masonic Hall which had apparently stood there when the arches were erected.
X: The eastern doorway and pilasters of the Masonic Hall.
S, S, S: Secret passage below the present Street of the Chain.
A. Remnants of the presumed casemated First Wall.

5. WHAT IS THE AGE OF THE UPPER WILSON ARCH?

It has been noted that the upper and visible arch is made up of much smaller stones than the huge rectangles and square stones found in the debris which we uncovered below the Robinson Arch (dug down to bedrock). The stones situated deep below the Wilson Arch were also standard Herodian ashlars which had tumbled from the crumbling top of the huge retaining wall (the Western Wall) in A.D. 70. The chiselling of the smaller stones was different from the familiar Herodian style. The destruction of the arches of the causeway is attested by the early homiletic Midrash *Ekha Rabbati* 4:7: "Said Rabbi Abba bar-Cahana: The aqueduct which came from 'Etam was destroyed one day by the Sicarii" (rebels of the A.D. 66–70 war against Rome).

Evidently, the upper part of the Wilson Arch was rebuilt some time after A.D. 70. The existence of tumbled ashlars scattered over the pre- A.D. 70 Herodian pavement, discovered *at a lower level*, lends proof to this idea. It would be absurd to think that the original top of the arch had collapsed and been repaired in Second Temple times (before A.D. 70) as no one would have left the debris of fallen arches and piers lying over the Herodian pavement and yet rebuilt the top arch to span the ruined pavement. The top of the arch as we see it actually spanned a pavement whose level was thirteen feet (4 m.) *higher* than the Herodian pavement; in other words, the restorers of the upper arch built it over the debris which had fallen from the more ancient arch. This higher level of

221

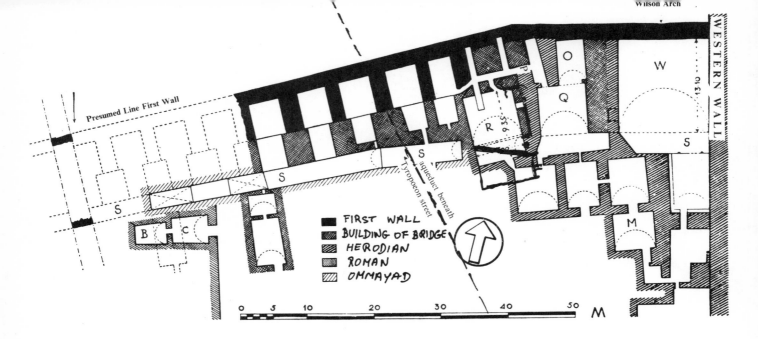

construction corresponds, in fact, to the Moslem Ommayad levels which we uncovered at the southern end of the Western Wall, along with other Ommayad pavements and buildings also lying thirteen feet higher than the debris which had fallen from the Herodian Robinson Arch and lying over the pavement which had passed under it (see Part III, F, 1, c: The Paved Road along the Western Wall).

We have gathered sufficient data about the building plans of the Ommayad period (see Part VI, C: The Early Moslem Period) over and near the Temple Mount to suggest that they too undertook the restoration of the archway which supported the aqueduct that brought water to the area. The restoration of the upper arch, particularly at the point where it joins the retaining Western Wall, was so precise that it requires a trained eye to recognize its close imitation of Herodian masonry.

6. UNDERGROUND REMNANTS OF BYZANTINE AELIA AND CHRISTIAN JERUSALEM

Another long and interesting — though not as ancient — underground area faces the Wilson Arch due west. It lies approximately at the level of the present pavement of the arch (apparently of later Arab origin) and consists of a complex of vaulted chambers of all shapes and dimensions. There are storehouses, recesses, cisterns, and even stairways, all of them flanking both sides of a narrow subterranean alley which runs for a distance of some 330 feet (100 m.). This alley, which may be found to extend further west should it be excavated, actually runs several feet under the present Street of the Chain which leads to the Haram es-Sherif (Temple Mount). More than fifteen hundred years ago, it ran over the ancient west-to-east Via Praetoria of Christian Aelia. It may even have been in use as late as Crusader times (twelfth-thirteenth centuries A.D.). The alley and the structures which line it on both sides are, in a way, a living witness of this part of the city as it may have looked in ancient days. Although this discovery helps to illustrate the successive levels of habitation in the western precincts close to the Temple Mount, no stratigraphic or other precise data have been gathered thus far in the area (see passage marked SSS in diagrams of Warren's survey).

222

Warren's survey (1867–70) of the causeway spanning the Tyropoeon valley between the Upper City and the Western Wall (right). It indicates the successive building periods in the area. In black above: The presumed line of the First Wall of First Temple days; the shadings under the black suggest the successive periods from the building stage of the causeway, through the Herodian and Roman periods, and down to Ommayad times, when the upper part of the Wilson Arch was rebuilt (W).

Legend: O, Q: Superimposed vaults.
        R: The Masonic Hall, originally hellenistic and enlarged in Herodian days.
        S, S, S: The secret passage leading west under the present Street of the Chain.
        M: Basement of the Mameluke madrasa (the later Mahkameh) built at the site of the Wilson Arch.
        B, C: Halls oriented eastwards.
        P: Water passage.

The diagonal across is the probable line of the underground drainage channel, recently uncovered, which ran under the Tyropoeon street and crossed diagonally under the causeway which ended at Wilson's Arch. A segment of a water passage P was uncovered over the causeway

E. THE NECROPOLIS OF JERUSALEM

We have mentioned above (Part IV, E: Royal Tombs in the City of David) the tombs in the Tyropoeon valley and in Siloam. One of the characteristic features of ancient Jerusalem was its vast necropolis, the City of the Dead — a ring of cemeteries which completely surrounded the city. This phenomenon was already known to a certain degree in the days of the monarchy, and became even more prominent in the period of the restoration after the Babylonian exile.

This necropolis of Jerusalem assumed even greater proportions in Hasmonean times, and the process reached a climax in the Herodian era. The cemeteries were expanded to their greatest extent during the first century A.D., until the destruction of the Temple in A.D. 70.

1. THE CHARACTER OF THE NECROPOLIS

Archeological excavations have uncovered thousands of tombs, and found that some of the burials date to the time of the Hasmoneans and Herod, while the rest are of a later date. The typical family tombs were cut in the rock, forming underground loculi (burial places) consisting ordinarily of one sepulchral chamber or more in which were carved niches for ossuaries *(kokhim)* or benches carved under vaulted recesses *(arcosolia)*. After the flesh of the deceased had disintegrated completely, the bones were gathered into an ossuary which was placed on a shelf in the recess. Occasionally it might be stored in a special cubicle of the underground tomb. The preservation of bones in ossuaries was the prevailing Jewish custom at the time. The ossuaries were made of stone and shaped as rectangular containers. Conventional decorations were usually carved on them, and frequently they would be inscribed with the names of the deceased — sometimes with additional information — in Hebrew, Aramaic or Greek. The tombs of notables contained large sumptuous sarcophagi, decorated with elaborate carvings. Some of the facades and entrances were elaborately decorated, while a few were surmounted by a monument

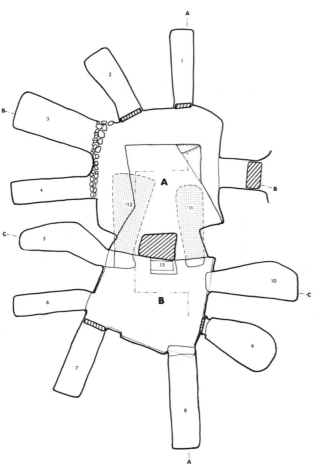

Above, left: A familiar scene in the great necropolis of Jerusalem: cave tombs uncovered underground, with ossuaries and sarcophagi taken out of their niches

Below, left: Cross section of one of the tombs at Giv'at Hamivtar necropolis. It comprises an upper burial chamber (A) with four loculi (1–4) and a lower chamber (B) with eight loculi (5–12). Number 13 is a child's tomb

Above, right: "Absalom's Tomb" (ca. A.D. 50), as it is called, is part of a monumental funerary complex of a high priestly family of Herodian times. It is a cubical monolith carved out of the surrounding rock and topped by a pointed cone made of smooth stone blocks. A group of cave-tombs behind it has been called the "Tomb of Jehosaphat." The monolith in the front is, in fact, the funereal monument or *nefesh* of the funerary complex of Jehosaphat

Below, right: Cross-section of the interior of Absalom's Tomb

(nefesh) commemorating the deceased. Some of the decorated monuments constitute an invaluable repertoire of local motifs with strong hellenistic and Roman influences. Others, more characteristically, bore the geometric designs and floral themes combined with an absence of human figures which marked the Herodian era. Moreover, the numerous inscriptions on the tombs provide a vast library of information concerning Jerusalem's varied population, its spiritual values, its social and economic achievements, and not infrequently the place or origin of the deceased outside the city's precincts.

224

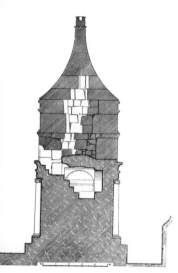

2. TOMBS IN THE KIDRON VALLEY

A number of tombs of special importance are attributed to the Hasmonean and Herodian periods under consideration. One set consists of burial chambers called the Tomb of Jehosaphat, and is joined to its specific commemorative monument known as Absalom's Tomb. They belonged to one of the leading families, probably that of high priests. The tombs are cut into the rocky ridge on the lower slope of the Mount of Olives, facing the Temple Mount, where the tombs of the family of Bnei Hezir and the one known as the Tomb of Zechariah had been carved in an earlier period (see Part II, E, 4: The Mausoleums in the Kidron Valley.) The large rock-cut alcove, measuring 8 × 10 feet (2.5 × 3 meters) of the Tomb of Jehosaphat is a typical example of Herodian construction. It is covered by a richly carved triangular pediment in the east hellenistic style of the day, as shown in our illustration. Absalom's Tomb, on the other hand, possesses a peculiar architectonic character all its own. Its lower section forms a cubical monolith carved out of the surrounding rock. It is ornamented on all sides with columns cut lengthwise in half, and pillars topped by a frieze of Greek Doric type. Its rounded upper part is constructed of ashlars composing a pediment and a carved conical roof. Below there is only one burial place whose inside plan is simple.

225

3. OTHER TOMBS

Jason's Tomb, discovered on Alfasi Street in Jerusalem's Rehavia quarter, west of the Old City, was designed in the form of two courts, a porch, and two burial chambers. The porch was topped by a pyramid; the walls of the porch are decorated with drawings of ships, Greek graffiti, and a lament in Aramaic over the deceased, Jason. The tomb, situated some miles west of the city walls, apparently served as the burial ground of a seafaring family in the first century B.C.

Many of the decorated fronts of these tombs are influenced by the architectural style of the Greco-Roman west and the hellenistic east; the combination created a hybrid style which may be defined as Jewish art of the Second Temple period (cf. below: The Family Tombs on Mount Scopus).

4. THE FAMILY TOMBS ON MOUNT SCOPUS

Innumerable places of burial of various types have come to light on Mount Scopus (Giv'at Hamivtar), among them a number of primary importance in illuminating the Herodian period.

a. Nikanor the Alexandrian

A Greek inscription on one of the ossuaries found there testifies that it contains the bones of the family of Nikanor the Alexandrian, who had donated the magnificent decorated copper gates to the inner court of the Temple. In Hebrew are inscribed the words *"NKNR 'LKS'"* (Nikanor Aleksa), clearly referring to Nikanor of Alexandria (*Middot* 1:4 etc.).

b. Mattathi, Son of Judah

Not far off, a monumental inscription written in archaic Hebrew letters (quite similar to the Samaritan script) came to light. It proclaims: "I Abba, son of the priest Eleazar, son of Aaron the high (priest); I Abba, an oppressed and persecuted man, native of Jerusalem, went to Babylonia and brought (the bones of) Mattathi, son of Judah, and I buried him in the cave which I acquired by writ." The ossuary discovered in the cave proved to be one of the finest found in the necropolis. A mystery lurks behind the return of the remains of Mattathi, an important and revered person, from exile and their inhumation in native soil. The matter has aroused considerable speculation, but no conclusion has been reached at the time of writing. In spite of its obscurities, the inscription of Abba emphasizes, like so many others, the importance of Jerusalem for Jews everywhere as the goal of migration (or return), and the ultimate desire to be buried in the area of the holy city. The burial in a new tomb of a person who is not a relative of the owner is permitted in ancient rabbinic law. This is illustrated in the case of Jesus who was buried in the unused tomb of Joseph of Arimathea (cf. Luke 23:53 and parallel passages

1 ‫אנה אבה בר כהנה א-‬

2 ‫לעז בר אהרן רבה אנ-‬

3 ‫ה אבה מעניה מרד-‬

4 ‫פה די יליד בירושלם‬

5 ‫וגלא לבבל ואסק למתת-‬

6 ‫י בר יהוד וקברתה במ-‬

7 ‫ערתה דזבנת בגטה‬

The inscription mentioned in Part V, E, 4, b proves a heated source of discussion. Abba, son of the high priest, had brought back the bones of Mattathi, son of Judah. Mattathi is presumed by many to be Mattathias Antigonus, the last Hasmonean prince, who was usurped by Herod (see Part II, F). The decorated ossuary, one of the finest in the necropolis, was well-hidden under the inscription, and suggests the burial of a person of note, under extraordinary circumstances. However, the evidence is inconclusive at the time of writing

in the other Gospels). A catalogue of such burials is a veritable atlas of the Diaspora, in which figure Jews of Palmyra, Delos ("Maria the convert from Delos"), Anatolia, North Africa, and other distant regions of the ancient world.

c. Simon, Builder of the Temple

Another burial tomb of particular importance bears an Aramaic inscription: *"Smwn bn' hklh"* (Simon, builder of the Temple). This statement evidently describes the crowning achievement in the life of an architect or master-builder who, along with others, worked on Herod's masterpiece. Still another tomb which attracted considerable interest was that of a Nazirite (ascetic) family, as attested by the inscriptions carved on the ossuaries and one sarcophagus. These may be assigned to the period before the destruction of the Second Temple.

d. The Crucified Jew

A dramatic find in the burial caves of the Giv'at Hamivtar necropolis was the skeleton of a Jew of unknown origin among thirty-five other skeletal remains preserved in fifteen ossuaries. He was a male in his twenties who had been crucified in the first half of the first century A.D. Both heel bones had been transfixed by a large nail to which a plaque of wood was still attached, and his shins had been deliberately broken. The man's knees had been doubled up and laid sideways, one on top of the other, and the two feet thus transfixed by the same nail at the heels, with the legs adjacent. Impalement or crucifixion was a common form of punishment in the ancient near east, widely practiced by the Romans, especially among subject peoples. In Roman law it was applicable to crimes against the State or Emperor (lèse majesté); Roman citizens were exempt from this form of execution.

228

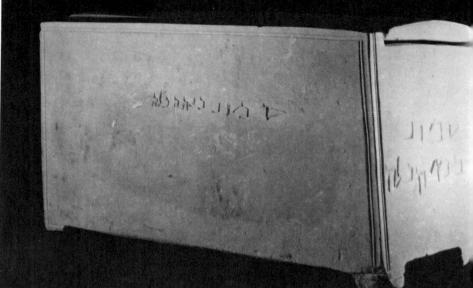

Above, right: Inscription in Aramaic characters on an ossuary found at Giv'at Hamivtar reading: "Šimon, bn[é] hykl [a]" = Simon, builder of the Sanctuary (namely a master builder or architect)

Above, left: Restoration of the position in which an unknown first century B.C. Jew – with the legs adjacent – was crucified. This was determined from the skeletal remains found in his tomb in the Giv'at Hamivtar necropolis

Below, right: Entrance to the cave-tomb of Herod's family near the modern King David Hotel, with the rolling stone which sealed its entrance

Above, left: Ancient stairway, still extant, leading to the great court of the Tomb of the Kings of Adiabene, Jewish converts of the first century A.D. ▶

Below, left: Sarcophagus of Queen Zaddan of Adiabene found in the cave-tomb. Below, right: Ossuary found in the cave-tomb

Above, right: Restoration design of the imposing funerary monument standing near the entrance of the burial chambers of the royal house of Adiabene. Three pyramids topped the funeral monument or *nefesh*. The wide stairway is shown at the left

5. THE MAUSOLEUM OF QUEEN HELEN OF ADIABENE

The lure of Jerusalem, the realization of a lifelong dream to live and die and then be buried in Jerusalem, recognized no social distinctions. A remarkable example of this attraction is to be seen in the story of Queen Helen of Adiabene and her family, who hailed from a kingdom in northeastern Syria and east of the Tigris. Josephus relates that the royal family converted to Judaism at about this time and built themselves a palace in the Lower City, in the heart of the Ophel (*War* VI:395 etc.). North of the Third Wall, they hewed out a structure of great magnificence to serve as the burial place for the family. The site is known today as the Tombs of the Kings. According to Josephus, the area was marked by three pyramids (*Antiquities* XX:95) and was famous throughout the ancient world for the wealth of its architectural and artistic embellishments. A wide, descending stairway, with water courses along the side, leads to a cistern used for ritual purposes. The broad rock-cut forecourt and the once columned vestibule of the tomb itself are of monumental proportions, and are decorated with relief carvings of wreaths and grape clusters peculiar to Jerusalem art in Herodian days. At the southwestern corner of the vestibule is the entrance to thirty rock-hewn chambers and niches. The entrance was sealed by the rolling stone still to be seen there. Important personages were buried singly, in most ornate and sealed limestone coffins known as sarcophagi. Among the decorated sarcophagi found in a sepulchral chamber was an elegant stone coffin with a bilingual inscription: *ZDN MLKT'* (Zadan Malkata') in Aramaic and *ZDH MLKTH* (Zada Malkatah) in a Syrian dialect, meaning "Queen Zadda(n)" and referring most likely to Helen of Adiabene herself (dialectic reasons account for the discrepancy in spelling).

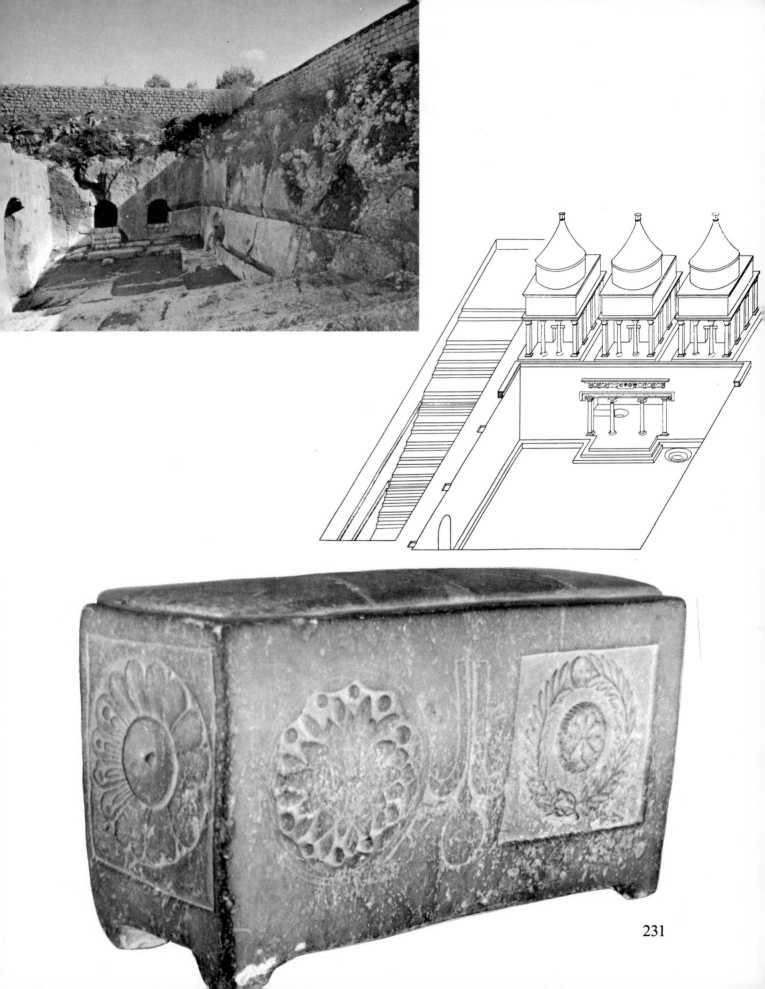

231

PART VI

ARCHEOLOGICAL DISCOVERY IN JERUSALEM AFTER A.D. 70

A. THE ROMAN PERIOD

The ruthless destruction of the Temple by the Roman legions is recounted in revealing detail by Josephus; confirmatory and supplemental data have been supplied by numerous writers, Jewish and non-Jewish, along with reactions, interpretations and assessments, ever since the disaster. The overall record, moreover, has clearly been substantiated by the archeological excavations in Jerusalem.

Destruction of the Upper City was complete. The houses which had been burned in the conflagration collapsed and remained buried under the debris, which was never cleared. This is also true of the accumulation of rubble near the Western and Southern Walls. Fallen masonry blocked the Tyropoeon valley; torrents of water from winter rains swept down the slopes, and the waters churned up the debris of earlier occupations, silting up the valley. The latest Jewish coins found among the ruins date from the "Year Four" of the "Redemption of Zion," that is, A.D. 69 (see Part II, G, 2: Testimony of the Coins). Furthermore, the vast cemeteries, including the magnificent mausoleums, were abandoned during the days after the destruction.

Titus quartered the Tenth Legion Fretensis in the ruins of the city under the command of a Roman legate, whose headquarters were in Caesarea. This person, who bore the title of *legatus Augusti*, was in charge of the administration of the entire province of Judea.

1. THE ROMAN COLUMN OF THE TENTH LEGION

Few remains of the period between A.D. 70 and the founding of the imperial Roman city of Aelia Capitolina have been discovered. These few include the fragments of a column bearing a Latin inscription memorializing Vespasian, Titus and the commander of the Tenth Legion, as well as numerous tiles and bricks stamped LXF *(Legio Decima Fretensis)*, some of them bearing the figure of a wild boar, the Legion's emblem. The inscription is fairly well preserved except for its right side and fifth line, which was scratched out, leaving only the first letter 'L'. The transcription of the text (reproduced in the picture), spelling out the abbreviations, reads as follows:

IMPCAESAR
VESPASIAN VS
AVG IMPTCAE
SARVESPAVG
L FLAVIVS SILVA
AVG PR PR
LEG X FR

IMPERATOR CAESAR
VESPASIAN[US]
AUGUSTUS IMPERATOR T[ITUS CAE]
SAR VESP(ASIANUS) AUG(USTUS) [f(ilius)
L[UCIUS FLAVIUS SILVA]
AUG(USTI) PR PR (PRO-PRAETOR)
LEG[IO] X FR[ATENSIS]

The first four lines commemorate the Emperor Caesar Vespasian Augustus (A.D. 69–79) and his son Titus Caesar Vespasian Augustus (A.D. 79–81). The last three lines mention the commander of the Tenth Legion Fretensis, apparently Lucius Flavius Silva, whose name has been scratched out for unknown reasons. He is Silva, the commanding officer who captured Masada after a bitter siege in A.D. 73, and served as governor of the new Roman province of Judea from A.D. 73–80. What has survived may be only part of a larger commemorative inscription erected during the reign of Titus. The true significance of this inscription lies in its allusion to the new status of Jerusalem which was transformed from a flourishing metropolis and revered holy place into a devastated ruin, hardly more than a military base for the Roman garrison.

2. THE COINS OF ROMAN VICTORY

There is an abundance of Roman coins from this period to commemorate the downfall of Judea, in particular those struck by the Flavian emperors; e.g. the bronze pieces with the emperor's portrait on the obverse and, on the reverse, a Greek legend *IUDAIAS EALOKIAS* (Captive Judea); and a series of gold, silver and bronze coins, also with the emperor on the obverse and on the reverse the figure of a Jewish woman, her hands tied, seated under a palm tree, with the legend *JUDAEA DEVICTA* (Defeated Judea) or *JUDAEA CAPTA* (Captive Judea). The latter were struck not only by Vespasian and

a   b   c

Roman coins commemorating their victory. From left to right: a. a mourning captive Jewess sitting under a palm tree and the legend JUDAEA CAPTA (Defeated Judea); b. JUDAEA and the Roman Eagle; c. DE JUDAEIS [Victory] over the Jews

Titus but also by Domitian (A.D. 81–96), showing how much importance the Flavian emperors attached to that historic event. Dating from the reigns of Vespasian and Titus, these coins were, in fact, the regular means of exchange for the Roman Tenth Legion which was garrisoned in the ruins of the city. The recovery of these coins has proved that during this period, the camp of the Legion was located on the Western hill, with the Praetorium at its center. In previous years this had been the site of the Palace and Citadel (see Part I, G, 5: The True Site of Pilate's Praetorium); and it is clear from the evidence that Titus preserved from destruction the three towers which stood north of the palace. Although the architectural remains are problematic, the coins, tiles and pottery which we recovered in the excavations south and southwest of the Temple Mount walls, may show that some of the Legion's units were stationed there. Moreover, the column with its imperial Latin inscription was found there.

3. HADRIAN'S AELIA CAPITOLINA

A review of the traditions concerning the foundation of *Aelia Capitolina* as a Roman colony (following the pattern of other provincial cities in the east, it was named after the emperor: Publius Aelius Hadrianus) may help to clarify certain historical ambiguities involving Roman-Jewish relations and the activities of the Jewish revolutionary movement.

Talmudic sources of the years which followed the destruction of the Temple attest that Jews continued to visit the Temple Mount and cherished ever-growing hopes of rebuilding the ruined Temple. The volatile combination of persistent Jewish disaffection and resentment of Roman rule, and urgent messianic expectations of Jews in Palestine and the Diaspora which led to the great uprisings of Jews in the east around A.D. 115, must have weighed on Hadrian's mind when he visited Jerusalem, Judea, and the Asian provinces in A.D. 130–132. Since Jerusalem seemed to be a source of the troubles and the key to the situation, a drastic solution was proposed. In an effort to settle the problem once and for all, the decision was made to obliterate Jewish Jerusalem and establish in its place a Roman colony, Aelia Capitolina. Hadrian planned to erect a temple to Jupiter Capitolinus in the Temple area in order to put an end to Jewish aspirations. It has become evident that the final decision was reached after his last visit there in 130. It was carried out in brutal fashion when the legate Tinus Rufus ploughed the city's confines (*pomoerium* in Latin) as shown on Roman coins. This, to the Jews, was an ominous sign forecasting the doom of the city prophesied by Micah: "Zion shall be ploughed as a field" (3:12). The Roman action precipitated the uprising in A.D. 132.

The reversed inscribed base of a Roman statue, apparently Hadrian's, was found embedded in later repairs effected in the wall above the right side of a lintel over the walled-up Double Hulda Gate. It reads:

TITO AEL HADRIANO	(To Titus Aelius Hadrianus
ANTONINO AUG PIO	Augustus Pius, the Father
PP PONTIF AUGUR	of the Fatherland, Pontifex Augur
DD	By decree of the Decurions)

4. BAR KOCHBA'S RULE OF JERUSALEM

A number of sources refer to the dramatic events which took place in Jerusalem and Judea during the time of Simon Bar Kochba's violent uprising. The Roman historian Dio Cassius (A.D. 155–235) asserts that Hadrian erected his temple to replace the sanctuary of the god of Israel. But his information does not establish clearly whether Tinus Rufus, as directed by Hadrian, had carried out the plowing of Jerusalem before the outbreak of the rebellion. It is also difficult to determine accurately the length of time that Jerusalem remained under Jewish control, or to decide whether Bar Kochba was able to initiate a reconstruction of the Temple or a restoration of the city walls. We know that he was able to capture the city in A.D. 132 and that he took prompt measures to reinstate the sacred rituals, including preeminently the resumption of sacrifices at the High Altar. This explains why Eleazar was appointed high priest in association with the *Naśi'* (prince, leader in both a military and civil capacity) Simon Bar Kochba (his actual name was Simon Bar Kosiba). The dual leadership — civil and ecclesiastical — is rooted in ancient biblical tradition, and is confirmed in this instance by coins struck in 132/33, i.e. the first year of Bar Kochba's rule, which have the legend *Simon Naśi' of Israel*, and *Eleazar the Priest*. A principal role of the latter would have been to preside at the official worship services at the Temple Mount. Furthermore, the appearance of the word Jerusalem, and more particularly the phrase "To the Liberation of Jerusalem," on the coins of the first and second

Coin of Bar Kochba marked by a palm tree with the legend: Shimon (i.e. Simon bar-Kosiba)

years of Bar Kochba's rule, emphasize the importance of Jerusalem as a Jewish city, civic and religious capital of the commonwealth.

It should be noted at the same time, that only two such coins were found in the excavations south of the Southern Wall of the Temple Mount, and nothing else that could be attributed with certainty to this period. It may be inferred, therefore, that Bar Kochba's lieutenants ruled the city for a short time only, just the years 132–133 and that owing to the exigencies of the war, they were barely able to begin work on the reconstruction of the Temple, if indeed they did even that much. When Roman rule was restored after quelling the uprising (A.D. 135) the authorities proceeded with the establishment of *Colonia Aelia Capitolina*. Several sources have provided details of Hadrian's plan. Moreover, archeological evidence helps us to understand more clearly the topography and ground-plan of the new city, and to follow its development during the second and third centuries A.D.

5. THE CHRONICON PASCHALE ON AELIA

One of the most interesting of the ancient sources is the anonymous Christian work known as the *Chronicon Paschale*. Though it was written late in the Byzantine era, it was based on earlier records and preserves important information about Roman Aelia. It relates, among other things, that Hadrian "pulled down the temple *(naos)* of the Jews at Jerusalem and built the two *demosia* (public baths), the theatre, the *Trikameron* (the Temple of Jupiter, divided into three parts with statues of Jupiter, Juno and Minerva), the *Tetranymphon* (one of the public baths), the *Dodekapylon* (the colonnade)... formerly known as the *Anabathmoi* (the 'Steps') and the *Kodra* (the square podium of the Temple Mount); and he divided the city into seven quarters (unidentified to date)..."

The opening statement raises a problem in that it speaks of the destruction of the temple of the Jews by Hadrian. Dio Cassius asserted also, as we saw, that Hadrian built his temple to replace the sanctuary of the god of Israel. We may infer, consequently, that the author of the *Chronicon* has in mind the destruction of a partly restored sanctuary of the time of Bar Kochba by Hadrian, rather than suppose that he has erroneously attributed the destruction of the Temple in A.D. 70 by Titus to the later monarch. On the other hand, we have found very few material remains of the Bar Kochba regime in the course of excavation, leaving a problem which only the discovery of new data could resolve.

6. ROMAN REMAINS

There is evidence to show that the city was not fortified in any way at first, its defense being entrusted to the Tenth Legion. Its walls were not erected until the end of the second or beginning of the third century A.D. Throughout the period from Hadrian's reign until the end of the third century, there was steady growth, and the populated area was extended to the foot of the southern wall of the Temple Mount. The material remains include numerous Roman bricks and tiles stamped with the seal of the Tenth Legion *LXF, LEG X FRE, LEG X FR,* etc., dating to the second and third centuries A.D., while some bore the legend *Ael*(ia) *C*(olonia) *C*(apitolina). In addition there were large quantities of Roman pottery, glass and coins. Most of the latter were local Roman city coins, including those struck in Aelia Capitolina. South and west of the Temple Mount walls we found fragments of marble statues, decorative objects such as *gemmas* (gems), seals and bronze figurines, including an artistic representation of a barbarian horseman. A fragment of a monumental Latin inscription includes the names and titles of the emperor Septimus Severus and his son Caracalla, who commemorated the completion of an important building project in *Colonia Aelia Capitolina Commodiana.*

Fragments of statues found south of the Southern Wall of the Temple Mount belong to this period of Aelia, and are related to the temple of Jupiter erected on the Mount (see above, section 3). One large fragment of the statue of a youth preserves the body and part of the hands and feet, though the head is missing. Another fragment is that of a woman dressed in typical second–third century costume, standing on a pedestal engraved with the Latin dedication: "Valeria Emiliana dedicated [it] by her vow."

The evidence of the coins which were struck in Aelia, as well as bricks, tiles, etc. shows that the city was administered by the Tenth Legion from Hadrian's time until the reign of the emperor Diocletian (A.D. 284–305). The Legion left the city probably in A.D. 285 and was stationed at Eilat ('Aqaba). In addition to the central city or planned city center of Aelia (see below), there were several other quarters inhabited by artisans, tradesmen and workmen who supplied the needs of the Legion.

7. THE JEWS AND AELIA

According to a current opinion, Hadrian forbade the Jews from living in the city and his decree remained unbroken for many decades. Nevertheless, the restrictions were relaxed by the local authorities and as early as the middle of the second century A.D., i.e. one or two decades after Bar Kochba's uprising, a small Jewish community had established itself there and was known as "the holy community of Jerusalem," numbering several famed scholars, a fact supported by Talmudic references dating back to the end of the second and the third centuries A.D. The Jews prostrated themselves over the Temple Mount ruins on the ninth of 'Ab (date of the destruction of the Temple) and occasionally during the three pilgrimage festivals. It appears also that the Jewish farmers from Judea

237

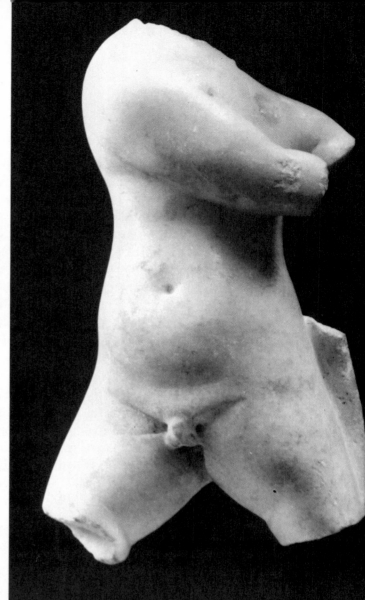

and even Galilee brought to the site the traditional offering of the first fruits to the Temple (Deuteronomy 26:1–11). Some stayed on, to follow trade or business there and apparently to settle down to normal life in the city. This partial relaxation of the ban occurred following Hadrian's death in A.D. 138, in the reign of Antoninus Pius (A.D. 138–161). Further liberalization took place under the rule of the Severi, when the Jews were permitted to resume autonomous community life throughout Palestine.

This period is apparently referred to by Epiphanius, one of the church fathers of the fourth century A.D. He states that seven synagogues existed on Mount Zion and that one of them survived to the days of Emperor Constantine.

8. AELIA'S PLAN

Aelia had turned into a garrison town housing its legionaries in brick houses. It was planned as one of the provincial military camps of the empire, and was located in the western part of Jerusalem. Its center, the Praetorium (see above) was the seat of the *legatus* who commanded the Tenth Legion as well. It was located in Herod's former palace; in this locality at least (as indicated in Part I, G, 5: True Site of Pilate's Praetorium) Aelia's topography did not seem to have changed significantly since the time of Pontius Pilate a century before. There were extensive changes, however, in the inner perimeter of the new city. Two main streets intersected it. One, the *Via Principalis* (main street) ran north to south, i.e. from today's Damascus Gate to the neighborhood of the modern Zion Gate. (In its place today, but several feet higher, is the Khan el-Zeit bazaar and the route of the Street of the Jews in the Jewish Quarter.) The second street was the *Via Praetoria*, running west and east, from the Praetorium to the Temple Mount (along the line followed by today's David Street and its continuation, the Street of the Chain).

a. Main Structures

The city was not fortified at first, but a new wall was erected during a later period of Aelia. Some remains were discovered by R.W. Hamilton in 1931–37 and J.B. Hennessy in 1964–66 in the present northern wall of the Old City, near the Damascus Gate. They uncovered a gate from this late Roman period under the Damascus Gate, as well as sections of walls on both sides, probably dating to the fourth century A.D. Under the Roman foundations were found the remains of the Herodian gate of the Second Wall. A decorated area was found over the facade of the foundations of the eastern tower of the Roman gate. It bore a Latin inscription on a reused block, reading: "By order of the Decurions of Aelia Capitolina."

239

The royal tombs south of the City of David were hacked away when the area was quarried by the Romans. Nearby is a maze of cisterns, baths, and other rock-cut structures truncated by quarrying

A Roman building of Aelia Capitolina outside the southwestern angle of the Temple Mount (cf. p. 243)

As this stone was in secondary use, the excavators were led to the conclusion that the wall was erected a long time after Hadrian. Other interesting remains were uncovered in different parts of the city. We have already described (see above, Roman Remains) some of the sites we excavated south and southwest of the Temple Mount. The outstanding monument north of the ruined sanctuary was the tripartite triumphal arch known as the *Ecce Homo*, which had been investigated by C. Clermont-Ganneau in 1873–74. The central archway, 17 feet (5.2 m.) wide and 20.5 feet (6.25 m.) high had survived, spanning today's Via Dolorosa. The northern arch also survives, over the altar of the church in the Convent of the Sisters of Zion which was built around it, as well as a pavement under the building which covers an underground cistern. Another tripartite arch was discovered in 1964 located some 1155 feet (350 m.) north of the Damascus Gate, bearing a Latin inscription commemorating Hadrian.

Scholars have also devoted much attention since the middle of the last century to the Roman Forum of Aelia. Its Hadrianic foundation walls are situated in the basement of

Hadrianic foundations of the Roman Forum of Aelia in the basement of the Russian Hospice near the Church of the Holy Sepulchre

Above: Coin dating to the last years preceding the destruction of the Temple, and bearing the image of Emperor Nero, a contemporary of Paul of Tarsus. Below, sides of a half-shekel of Tyre, a common coin in Jerusalem

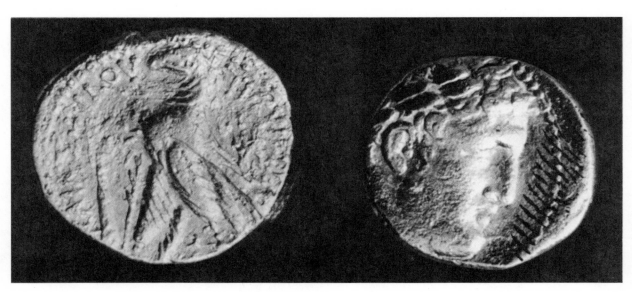

the Russian Hospice bordering on the Church of the Holy Sepulchre. On the grounds of St. Anne's Church, two plastered pools were found, joined by an underground passage decorated with frescoes. They are called the Pools of Bethesda on the basis of the tradition of John 5:1–18. Some scholars assume, however, that this was an underground sanctuary dedicated to the worship of a pagan god or goddess.

Over the ruined Temple Mount, as noted, Hadrian had put up a temple to Jupiter Capitolinus. South and west of the Temple Mount walls we unearthed considerable evidence of extensive building activity, including many bricks and tiles stamped with the Tenth Legion's insignia, as well as coins of the period and large amounts of pottery.

A most important discovery was a structure situated to the south of the southwestern corner of the Temple Mount. In addition to various coins struck in different cities of the empire and Roman pottery dating from the second and third centuries A.D., we found, over the plastered floor belonging to the earlier stage of building, other significant artifacts related to the everyday life of the legionaries, e.g., dice and bronze figurines. A structure of still greater interest was found south of the great pier at the foot of the Robinson Arch (see Part III, F, 1, a: New Significance of the Robinson Arch) and in it we uncovered a baking oven lined with bricks stamped with the Tenth Legion's insignia. The coins found in the earlier building stage of this structure date to the period from Hadrian to the beginning of the reign of Diocletian (284–305), at which time the Legion left Aelia and moved south to Eilat.

The structures in question belonged, in fact, to a whole complex built by the legionary establishment. This period is probably contemporaneous with the earlier stage of the Roman baths we found northwest of the Robinson Arch and which were still in use in Byzantine times. A considerable number of Roman bricks were found in the area, stamped with the seal of the Tenth Legion.

Ultimate lines of a monumental memorial stela dedicated to Septimus Severus and his family (early third century A.D.)

The ancient depiction of the domed *Anastasia* (Church of the Resurrection) mounted on a gold ring was unearthed in 1974 on the second story of a sixth century A.D. Byzantine building south of the Temple Mount. The ring is contemporaneous with the church erected by Emperor Constantine in the fourth century, a circular and domed small building that stood over the traditional tomb of Jesus before its renovation and inclusion under the Crusader-built Church of the Holy Sepulchre. Gold pendants, bronze vessels, and a bead were found nearby. Other similar depictions are found in the Louvre and in the Benati Museum, Athens

b. Christian Aelia

The Roman town was still very much alive after the Legion's departure, and soon experienced a major transformation. The great change in its character and topography occurred after A.D. 325, the date of the Council of Nicea. Makarios, Bishop of Jerusalem, had convinced Emperor Constantine and his mother Helena that they should erect a magnificent basilica on the traditional site of the Tomb and Resurrection of Jesus. The building of the Church of the Holy Sepulchre, then called the Anastasis, close to the Roman Forum situated in this northwestern section, coupled with the sanctification of the nearby Rock of Golgotha — the place of Crucifixion — turned the site into the holiest shrine of Christendom, attracting pilgrims from all over the Christian world.

The Church of the Holy Sepulchre underwent many structural changes through the centuries, chiefly during Crusader times. Since religious considerations have always prevented excavations at the site, there is no way to reach definitive conclusions about the nature and extent of the various building phases, or to reconstruct the different churches which stood on the site, including the original Constantinian basilica. Detailed surveys could only be made on those occasions when the church required extensive structural alterations or repairs. However, additional information concerning the early phase can be gleaned from a close study of the Madeba mosaic map (see Part I, B, 3: The Madeba Mosaic Map) and from writings of Byzantine times. An imaginative reconstruction of the grandiose basilica of Constantine was published by Father Vincent in his *Jerusalem Nouvelle* but it suffers from the lack of hard data, and in the nature of the case is rather speculative. Further exploration is necessary in the light of many new items of information which are now available.

Thanks to the extension of archeological research in Jerusalem, we have gathered important data on the city's development during the Byzantine period, beginning with the reign of Emperor Constantine and closing with the Moslem conquest (fourth-seventh centuries A.D.).

B. BYZANTIUM AND JERUSALEM

The fourth century A.D. inaugurated the great period of church building in Palestine. Emulating the example of Constantine and his successors who dipped into the imperial coffers to build monumental structures as testimony to their faith, private donors also poured out their wealth in an orgy of building unmatched in the history of the country. As a result, there was general and remarkable prosperity, along with a marked increase in population, both Christian and Jewish (excepting only in the Jewish ghetto in Jerusalem).

244

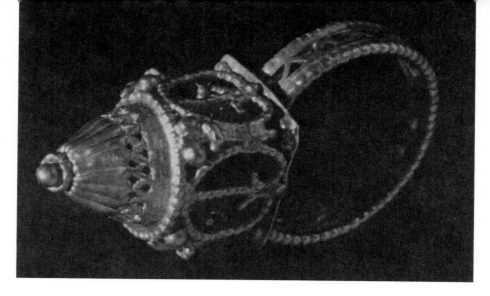

1. EARLY BYZANTINE CHURCHES IN JERUSALEM

The churches, in many cases, were not simple affairs, but richly adorned edifices. Many of them were decorated with intricate mosaic pavements, an art in which the Byzantines excelled. The most notable examples in the Byzantine world are found in Palestine, and many of them still survive in whole or in part. The most important churches were erected on sites identified with central events in the life of Christ.

a. The Anastasis in the Church of the Holy Sepulchre

As the basilica erected by Emperor Constantine in A.D. 335 was incorporated in later centureis into the vast Church of the Holy Sepulchre, the question of the location and dimensions of the original structure is of continuing importance. West of the rock of Calvary and its cloister, Constantine had built a circular church with the tomb of Jesus in the center. Egeria, who visited the basilica about a century after its completion, saw the tomb chamber cut out of solid rock inside a large building. Several groups of scholars sponsored by various Christian bodies in recent years (see below: D, 2), have worked on a number of problems connected with the structure of the early shrine. The investigation has been aided significantly by the discovery, south of the Temple Mount, of a golden ring with what appears to be a representation of the dome of the original shrine, the Anastasis (Resurrection). It was generally supposed that a row of columns and piers supported the dome around the traditional tomb in Constantine's basilica, with open spaces between the piers. This picture has now in fact been supplemented by the golden ring we found which probably depicts the domed structure and its columns and piers in that arrangement.

It is rewarding to report that the Greek architect, Oekonomopolis, engaged in current restoration work in the adjoining area of the church, has successfully exposed the edge of the apse of the Constantinian basilica which stood east of the tomb, as well as part of the eastern stylobate which supported a row of pillars in the court surrounding the rock of Golgotha.

To recapitulate the successive building stages in the Holy Sepulchre in Byzantine times: Charles Couasnon in his "Church of the Holy Sepulchre in Jerusalem" (London, 1974) believes that a basilica for the Christian community was built first and that the Rotunda (Anastasis) over the tomb of Christ was completed later, in the fourth century A.D. The chapels of the Cross and of Calvary were built as autonomous units east of the

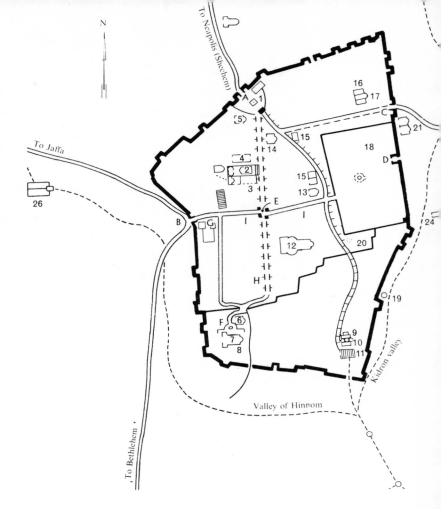

The holy city in Byzantine times according to J. T. Milik. Its walls followed the contours of the present Turkish walls on three sides, but whereas the latter runs now north of the line between F and 20, the Byzantine city wall surrounded also the southern part of the Western hill and contoured the ancient Lower City (from 11 to the Temple area).
A: Stephanus Gate (present Damascus gate). B: David Gate (present Jaffa Gate). C: Probatica Gate. 16: Beth Hesda Pool (Pool Probatica). E-H: the old Roman Cardo street. 15–15: structures along the ancient Tyropoeon street. D: Golden Gate. G: The Citadel. 18: Temple Area. 12: Nea Basilica (present Jewish Quarter on the Western hill). 2: Church of the Holy Sepulchre. 7: Hagia Zion church. 9: Basilica of Siloam. 24: Church of the Agony at the foot of the Mount of Olives

Anastasis. Constantine's splendid edifice was destroyed by the Persians in A.D. 614. When the Rotunda was restored soon after, it conformed to the original measurements and architectural standards of the day.

A collection of metal ampoules (flasks) from Jerusalem, dating to the beginning of the seventh century A.D., features the Church of the Holy Sepulchre in twelve different representations. They are on exhibit in the cathedrals of Monza and Pobio in northern Italy and were in great demand by Christian pilgrims.

b. The Hagia Zion

The Hagia Zion, mother of all churches, was built by Maximus, Bishop of Jerusalem in A.D. 340 on the traditional site of the Last Supper, the Coenaculum, on Mount Zion. Part of its original wall was uncovered when the foundations of the Basilica of the Dormition were laid in 1898–99.

c. The Church of the Ascension

The Church of the Ascension (Ascensio), built by a pious Roman lady named Pomenia on the Mount of Olives, marks the traditionally accepted site of Jesus' ascension into heaven. It was excavated by Father V. Corbo in 1960. An inscription by Patriarch Modestos was found there, commemorating the restoration of the church after its destruction by the Persians in A.D. 614. The octagonal church was destroyed in 1009 by the Caliph Abdel Hakim, rebuilt by the Crusaders, then destroyed again by Saladin in 1187 and rebuilt as a mosque.

246

d. The Basilica Eleona

The Church of the Mount of Olives, the Basilica Eleona, was established in A.D. 326 by Queen Helena, mother of Constantine, at the same time as the Church of the Holy Sepulchre and was built above the cave (known as the Crypt of the Credo) to commemorate the site where Jesus taught the Lord's Prayer to his disciples. The original church, uncovered by excavation, was partly restored by the White Fathers in 1910 as the shrine and Basilica of the Sacred Heart.

e. Church of the Agony

Another brilliant example of the basilical style (an oblong hall with a double colonnade and apse) is the church erected by Emperor Theodosius I (A.D. 385) on the site traditionally identified as the Rock of the Agony of Jesus. Here he prayed alone on the night of his arrest at Gethsemane at the base of the Mount of Olives. The church was uncovered by Father P.G. Orfali during the years 1909–1920. Parts of its Byzantine mosaic pavement protected by padded mats, may be viewed in the imposing Basilica of the Agony which was rebuilt on the same site in recent years.

2. MONUMENTAL ROMAN AND BYZANTINE STRUCTURES NEAR THE TEMPLE MOUNT

Interesting structures of the period were uncovered in the course of our excavations near the southwestern corner of the Temple Mount. They include two buildings originally erected in Roman times, which had been restored and renovated according to new plans during the Constantinian period (fourth century). One of them is particularly well preserved with its arches, carefully constructed doorways and windows. It not only reflects the fine quality of craftsmanship in those days, but also supplies important information about an obscure episode in Jerusalem's history. We have discovered that the latest phase of occupation in this building dates from the time of Constantine and his successors, as shown by their coins. The latest coins found there belong to the very end of the reign of Julian the Apostate (362–363 A.D.). A thick layer of ashes which was uncovered in certain rooms indicates that the building was burned at that time; the date of destruction is supported by additional evidence. A plausible inference is that the buildings, located near the Western Wall, and going back to the time of Constantine and his heirs, were destroyed by Jews who had settled in Jerusalem in response to Julian's invitation to return and rebuild the Temple. Interesting evidence of Jewish enthusiasm at this time is provided by the Hebrew inscription discovered on one of the huge ashlars of the Western Wall below the Robinson Arch (described in Part II, H, 1: The Isaiah Inscription). The interlude was brief, however, and Jewish hopes ended with the death of the emperor. The subsequent period in Jerusalem's history was even more prosperous than the previous one, and there was a new spurt in building activity.

A dyeing plant of the Byzantine period with vats, left, was uncovered in the upper part of the Ophel facing the Southern Triple Gate

3. THE PERIOD OF CHRISTIAN BYZANTINE JERUSALEM

Jerusalem rapidly became the focus of the empire's religious interest, attracting hordes of pilgrims and inducing patrician families to make their homes in Jerusalem. The greatest impetus was provided by Emperor Theodosius II and his wife Eudokia, whose concern with Jerusalem became even more pronounced after her estrangement from her husband. Jerusalem had become a Holy City of beauty and splendor with a plethora of churches, monasteries and guest houses for pilgrims, a picture brilliantly illustrated by the sixth century Madeba mosaic map (see Part I, B, 3: The Madeba Mosaic Map). As a result of Eudokia's munificence, several churches were built or restored and the city walls were expanded. Remains of this wall were discovered south of the southeastern corner of the Temple Mount by F.J. Bliss and A.C. Dickie in 1896;

View of the structures excavated below the walled-up Triple Hulda Gate and the Byzantine building in the foreground. The area covers the upper level of the Ophel

lower down, at the southern end of the southeastern ridge (the Ophel), they found a gate which led to the Hinnom Valley. Near the Siloam Pool they also discovered a basilica which had been built during Eudokia's first visit to Jerusalem in 438–439. The dimensions of this impressive church were 116 × 53 feet (35 × 16 meters). The atrium (covered portico) faced north and the central hall ended at the apse. The center of the church was covered by a vast vault resting on four piers. The discoveries show that as a result of Eudokia's activity in Jerusalem, the city's borders were extended once again in a southerly direction.

249

Above, left: Top floor of the Byzantine monastery lying close to the Triple Gate and Southern wall of the Temple Mount

Below, left: The stairway leading from the first to the second floor
Right: The stairs leading down three flights to the bottom floor of the monastery

Left: The Byzantine complex viewed from the top of Temple Mount showing the Ophel ridge (the site of the City of David, right), the Kidron valley (lower background) and Siloam village (upper left)

Above, right: The Byzantine complex southeast of the Triple Gate, viewed from the north

Below, right: Same complex with the monastery in the foreground

a. The Convent below the Pinnacle of the Temple

The impressive building we discovered in the area south of the Triple Eastern Hulda Gate and the Single Gate turned out to be the cloister described by the historian Theodosius in A.D. 530. He located it below the corner of the Temple Mount (whose top is known as the Pinnacle of the Temple; Matthew 4:5). It was built to accommodate six hundred nuns as permanent residents. Once admitted to the premises they never left, and when they died they were buried there. The gate was opened only on rare occasions; goods were delivered over the walls and water was drawn from their own cisterns. During the second phase of its existence in the sixth century A.D., the building was a three-storied structure surrounded by walls, with only one gate on the west side. We found two cisterns and a number of tombs in the basement from which bones had been removed long since. We deduce, therefore, that the building served a different purpose in the initial phase of its existence, i.e. the fifth century, and that it may originally have been Eudokia's palace which was turned into a convent in the days of the emperor Justinian.

b. Other Remains of Eudokia's Building Activities

Another structure ascribed to the queen was a church dedicated in A.D. 460 to the protomartyr Stephen outside the northern gate (the present Damascus Gate). Its remains were discovered in the years 1885–93 by the Dominicans who erected their monastery of St. Stephen there along with the Ecole Biblique, an illustrious academic institution devoted to the study of the Bible and the exploration and excavation of the Holy Land.

Another well-built structure, excavated by M. Avi-Yonah at Giv'at-Ram near the present Hebrew University campus, proved to be a hospice for the aged *(Gerokomion)* with a chapel dedicated to Saint George. Its church was built in basilical style and is distinguished by prayer cubicles in the aisles and a mosaic pavement with an inscription reading: "Lord, god of Saint Georgios, remember the donor."

4. WHAT WAS JEWISH LIFE LIKE OUTSIDE JERUSALEM?

Though they were treated as second-class citizens in Byzantine Jerusalem, the Jews were fruitful and multiplied and prospered in their communities throughout the north of Palestine, the upper Jordan valley, the Golan Heights and various parts of Judea. They enjoyed a significant measure of autonomy under the institution of the 'Patriarchate' which controlled internal Jewish affairs. Their academies and synagogues flourished as we know from excavations of their remains. Many magnificent buildings have been uncovered, identified, and investigated for evidence of Jewish religious life and culture. The rich art of the synagogues attests to the vigorous condition of the Jewish community and its faith. The Jews, like the Christians, decorated their religious edifices with rich mosaic pavements. They left behind monumental structural remains, as well as numerous cisterns, olive and wine presses, and other remnants. They took a significant part in commerce and industry with due concern for the country's rural economy. Patrician

e heart of the Byzantine *Anastasis* (Holy
pulchre) is occupied by the tiny traditional
rtuary chamber of Jesus (6.8 × 6.4 ft. –
7 × 1.93 m). A marble slab, right, is presumed
hide the funereal couch upon which Joseph of
imathea is said, according to the gospel tradtion,
have laid the body

Jewish sepulchre is seen north of the Anastasis
thin the basilica) with a range of rock-cut niches
okhim) and pits for ossuaries. It is popularly
own as the sepulchre of Joseph of Arimathea.
d records relate that architects in Byzantine
es, or later, cut away the rock to make room for
basilica around the *Anastasis,* thus isolating it
m the rest of the original hill

families from Palestine and the Diaspora settled everywhere. They buried their dead in vast catacombs like those discovered at Bet She'arim in southern Galilee, and in a cemetery in Jaffa in the coastal area. Nevertheless, by the time the era of general prosperity reached its peak in the fifth-sixth centuries A.D., the Christians had become a majority in Palestine.

5. THE JUSTINIAN PERIOD

There was a new phase of expansion in Jerusalem during Emperor Justinian's reign (mid-sixth century A.D.). The Holy City's prestige had been affected adversely in preceding years by a split between the two principal theological camps of Christendom, the eastern or oriental Christians who held to the Monophysite position (the belief that Christ had only one single nature), and the western Christians who adopted the opposing view (that Christ had two natures, divine and human), the tenet which ultimately prevailed and became normative. The situation was also aggravated by an uprising of the Samaritans of central Palestine against Byzantine rule. Justinian was able to weather the crises. He afterwards embarked on a vast building program ranging as far south as the Sinai desert (the Monastery of St. Catherine) and eastward to the wilderness of Judea where hosts of hermits had settled (e.g. in the canyon Monastery of Mar Saba and other retreats of the 'Grand Laura'). His most elaborate project in Jerusalem was the church called Nea (New Church of St. Mary) dedicated in November 543 and described in detail by the church historian Procopius. It was destroyed by an earthquake in mid-eighth century. Its extensive remains were partly discovered by N. Avigad in the course of his excavations in the Jewish Quarter on the Western hill. The foundations consisting of huge stone ashlars rested on bedrock. An apse facing east measured 16 feet (5 m.) in diameter and proved to be the smallest of three apses of the basilica. These remains are now carefully preserved under the basement underpinnings of one of the high-rise apartment buildings which dot the restored Jewish Quarter of the Old City.

6. THE LATE BYZANTINE PERIOD

Additional building remains discovered in the Jerusalem area can be ascribed to the late Byzantine period, especially those discovered on the Mount of Olives and its slopes outside the city walls. Of particular interest are the Byzantine structures, mostly dwellings, excavated in the southeastern ridge by R.A.S. Macalister and S.W. Crowfoot and, quite recently, remains of buildings discovered in our excavations south and southeast of the Temple Mount. They prove that the area was thickly populated from the late Byzantine period to the Moslem era. Some of their plastered walls, well-built doorways and

windows, their arches and pillars supporting the roofs, the stone paving blocks of the courts and mosaic pavements of the rooms, were well preserved. It is interesting to observe the Greek markings and insignia on several kinds of bricks and tiles left by the craftsmen, as well as the Greek inscriptions, most of them blessings or commemorations. The buildings were mostly destroyed during the sudden Persian attack in A.D. 614 at which time a section of the southern wall of the Temple Mount enclosure was breached west of the Double Hulda Gate. A major portion of Byzantine Jerusalem fell in ruins as a result of the invasion.

There is an interesting question about a wall standing back of the traditional Tomb of David on Mount Zion, as mentioned in Part IV, E, 2: Later Traditions of the Tomb of David. Two or possibly three niches were found there, facing north. J.P. Pinkerfeld who examined the area closely suggests that, judging by the orientation of the structure, the wall represents a previous level, and is all that remains of a fourth century A.D. church mentioned by Byzantine sources in connection with the Coenaculum, traditional scene of the Last Supper.

a. Jews During the Persian Domination

A two-storied house of this period, situated south of the southwestern corner of the Temple Mount deserves special attention. Depiction of two menorahs (seven-branched candelabra), painted in red, were found on the door lintel of the northern wall, on both sides of a cross which protruded at the center of the lintel. The people who drew the menorahs may have disregarded the cross, or perhaps they had covered it with plaster. Two other menorahs, flanked by a shofar (ritual ram's horn) and an ethrog (citron), were also painted in red in the entrance hall, on the upper part of the outer wall facing the entrance. It is very surprising to find Jewish symbols in the entrance of a building which had been a Christian dwelling. It may be inferred that the building was occupied by Jews following the Persian invasion in A.D. 614. The Jews would have been delighted with the opportunity to live near the Western Wall. They used the building for public purposes during the short-lived era of Persian dominance (see Part II, H, 2: A Third Rebuilding Attempt). Christian sources bear witness to feverish partisan activity in Jerusalem during this period. They aver that the Jews helped the Persians occupy the Christian city of Jerusalem. It is true that the Jews were in control of the city for a limited period. In this connection, we found in 1974, graffiti of two menorahs on the wall of a Byzantine building located south of the building referred to above. These can also be attributed to the period of Persian conquest.

b. Signposts on the Madeba Map

A careful check of the details provided by the Madeba mosaic map (see Part I, B, 3: The Madeba Mosaic Map) and contemporary Byzantine literature on the one hand,

Clockwise: Reconstruction of a Byzantine wooden coffer based on bronze pieces found near the Triple Gate; a bronze artifact found there; an oil lamp and base of an oil lamp (?)

The Byzantine city wall (left) meets the southeastern angle of the Temple Mount. The courses of stone at the (right) are Herodian. View from the east

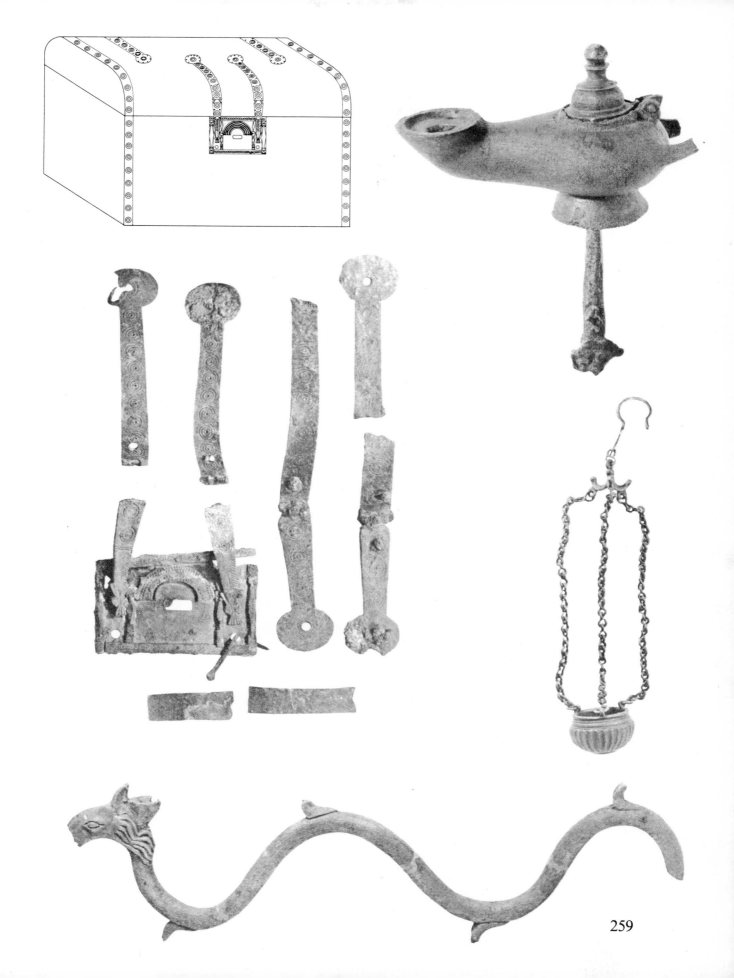

and recent archeological discoveries on the other, enables us to draw a basically accurate picture of Jerusalem's topography and character. The presence of the Nea (New Church of St. Mary), built in A.D. 542, on the map shows that the latter could not be dated earlier than the middle of the sixth century; the map cannot be dated later than the death of Emperor Justinian (565 A.D.) for other reasons. Among the outstanding features of the map are its two main streets — the Cardo Maximus, running north to south (from the present Damascus Gate to the Zion Gate of the Old City), and the Decamenos (west to east, or from the Jaffa Gate to the Gate of the Chain). They cross at the Tetrapylon whose traces are still visible at the crossing of David Street and the cluster of bazaars. The third, eastern street, more germane to our study, is the old Tyropoeon which started at the Damascus Gate and ended at the Siloam pool, at the gate which once gave access to the Hinnom valley, and which was standing in the Herodian period. The Tyropoeon continued to be an important thoroughfare in the Byzantine period, though its course had been altered somewhat during the passage of time.

Several churches were located along this street, notably St. Sophia north of the Wilson Arch and the Basilica lying adjacent to the Siloam Pool which was discovered by F.J. Bliss and A.C. Dickie. It should be observed that the Madeba mosaic gives special prominence to the Church of the Holy Sepulchre, though it does not detract from the importance of the other churches throughout the city (see diagram on p. 246).

c. End of the Byzantine Period

Disaster befell Byzantine Jerusalem as a result of the Persian invasion (A.D. 614). The excavations south and southwest of the Temple Mount have shown that several large buildings had been razed and burned, and the Temple walls breached nearby. When Byzantine rule was restored by Emperor Heraclius in A.D. 628, only sporadic efforts were made to rebuild the areas which had been levelled. Shortly thereafter the Moslem Arabs captured the Holy City and inaugurated an entirely new era in the city's history.

C. THE EARLY MOSLEM PERIOD

1. THE ARAB IMPRINT ON THE TEMPLE MOUNT

The capture of Jerusalem by the Arabs in A.D. 638 brought only gradual changes in the character of a city which remained basically Byzantine-Christian in design. On the basis of later traditions and legends about the conqueror of Jerusalem, Omar ibn el-Khattab, it appears that the city passed into Arab hands without much disturbance, and that the new settlement of Moslems in the Holy City, and the accompanying increase in the number of Jews there, did not bring about at first any serious change in its appearance. But the Temple Mount was regarded as sacred by the Moslems (see background in Part I, B, 7: Arab Restoration of the Temple Mount), and the caliph Omar erected a mosque on the deserted site. It stood on the south side of the enclosure which is now occupied by the El-'Aqṣa mosque (see below). According to the evidence of the Christian traveler Arculf who visited Jerusalem in A.D. 670: "...in that renowned place... placed in the neighborhood of the wall from the East, the Saracens now prepared a quadrangular place of prayer which they have built rudely constructed by setting beams on some remains of ruins..." and capable of holding 3000 worshipers. This was known as Omar's mosque.

The application of the concept *Beit el-Makdes* (the Holy Sanctuary) to Jerusalem as a whole echoes a distant memory dating back to Second Temple days, i.e. the apocryphal book of Enoch in which the concept of holiness does not apply only to the Temple but to Jerusalem as well. The city's symbol is a *House* with the Temple as its tower. Abu-Hureira quoted the prophet Mohammed as saying pithily: "Among all cities, Allah had singled out four for special esteem, and they are: Mecca — the city of all cities; Medina which is like a palm tree, Jerusalem which compares to an olive tree, and Damascus which is like the fig tree."

The Caliphate was founded in Mecca in A.D. 633, and immediately became the occasion of strife among the followers of Mohammed in the first decades after his death, during the great expansion of Islam. The caliph Moawiya, founder of the Ommayad dynasty (which lasted until A.D. 750), had made Damascus the capital of the empire in 661. Nevertheless, he went to Jerusalem and in solemn ceremony there, had himself officially crowned Caliph of the vast Arab empire. The reason he chose Jerusalem for this purpose rather than Damascus was that Jerusalem was the holy city of biblical tradition, and retained this status in Islam. This fact accounts for the origin of the name *Beit el-Makdes*, the Arab translation for the Hebrew *Bet-Hamiqdash* (the Temple). The name applies not only to the Temple Mount but to the city proper, which the Arabs call *el-Quds* (the Holy) to this day.

a. Why Were the Dome of the Rock and the El'Aqṣa Mosque Erected?

It was in this spirit that the later Caliph Abdel Malek (A.D. 685–705) and his son El-Walid (705–715) erected two monumental edifices on the Temple Mount, the Dome of the Rock (completed in 691) and the El-'Aqṣa mosque, thus further enhancing Jerusalem's prestige in the eyes of the Moslems. This policy served three purposes: (1) It memorialized the scene of one of the most controversial visions of the Prophet Mohammed as recorded in verse 1 of Sura 17 of the Koran, whereby the messenger of Allah was transported from Mecca to the "distant shrine" (the most remote) mounted on a magic animal called el-Buraq, accompanied by the Angel Gabriel. He then ascended to the Seven Heavens by a magic ladder. This verse was originally interpreted by Moslem scholars as designating the holy place in Jerusalem, and more specifically the Foundation Rock, in Arabic *es-Sakhra*. According to a recent interpretation, el-Buraq meanwhile had been tethered to the Western Wall (the exposed section known to Jews formerly as the Wailing Wall). This is why the Western Wall was called el-Buraq by the Moslems and the closed Barclay Gate designated *Bab en-Nabi* (Gate of the Prophet). The designation was a deliberate political step to counteract its obvious focal character to the Jews.

This situation may be further supplemented by other considerations: Mohammed did not specify in the above Sura the location of El-'Aqṣa, the distant shrine. This has consequently left room for doubt.

The Moslem commentators could not determine whether the nocturnal journey referred to Jerusalem or whether the prophet rose straight to heaven. It is obvious that the first interpretation gained precedence, the more so when the Ommayads promoted Jerusalem to a religious center.

The holy place was apparently located at the south of the Temple, namely the site over which Abdel Malek erected the El-'Aqṣa mosque — and not over the hallowed rock *El-Sakhra* (see below, b.). The extrapolation of el-Buraq to the Barclay Gate, as stated, was a later accretion.

It may be finally observed that Mohammed may have been influenced in his 'prophesying' about the journey to the site by his Jewish companions and their feelings for the Temple Mount, before the days of Jewish conversions to Islam.

(2) The Dome of the Rock competed in beauty and attraction with the magnificent Christian basilicas which filled the city, inspiring the awe and admiration not only of Christians, but of Moslems as well. In particular, it served as a balance or counterweight to the holiest sanctuary of Christendom, the Anastasis or Holy Sepulchre. The Dome of the Rock was built with eight sides to match the octagonal structure of the Church of the Holy Sepulchre. In the face of this competition for grandeur between Christian and Moslem, the Jews were left without any monumental building of their own. All they had left was access to the remains of the tremendous retaining walls of the Temple Mount, and more particularly the Western Wall.

(3) As a result of Arab building activities, Jerusalem became more than ever a magnet for pilgrims. Moslem historians relate that Caliph Abdel Malek was very apprehensive about the annual Moslem pilgrimage to Mecca which brought thousands of pilgrims to an area that was under the influence of his rival, Abdallah ibn Zubayr, the Meccan caliph. Jerusalem provided an alternate attraction which would divert the stream of pilgrims and weaken the position of the rival caliphate. Strenuous efforts were made to induce the travelers to come to Jerusalem which was strategically located in the heart of the Ommayad empire. In fact, since Abdel Malek's time and that of his son, El-Walid, the great builder, an ambitions plan was put into effect to expand, improve and beautify several sections of the city and in particular the Temple Mount area. Our archeological expedition had the good fortune to uncover the impressive remains of a vast building complex erected south and southwest of the Temple Mount walls. Most of these structures were intended to house upper-class pilgrims, as will be described below.

b. What Did the Dome of the Rock Represent?

The elegant building erected by Abdel Malek, one of the most beautiful in the whole of the Middle East, was intended primarily to shield the holy rock *Es-Sakhra* which is identified with the Foundation Rock of Jewish tradition; for this reason the edifice is called *Qubbet el-Sakhra* (Dome of the Rock). The name Mosque of Omar which is

The Dome of the Rock in the late afternoon of a spring day, when the olive trees are in bloom. View from the east. In ancient times, the Temple which stood there faced east

mistakenly applied to this building gained currency all over the world but has no historical basis, as it refers to the older mosque described by Arculf (see above).

The outstanding feature of the Dome of the Rock is its outer wall in the shape of a regular octagon, completely encased in marble and covered with myriads of rare blue tiles. This wall encircles two inner concentric ambulatories which are separated by an intermediate arcade supporting the inclined inner ceilings. A drum, pierced by a row of coloured windows, rises over the base of the central arcade encircling the Rock. It is covered with enchanting Byzantine mosaics on a field of gold.

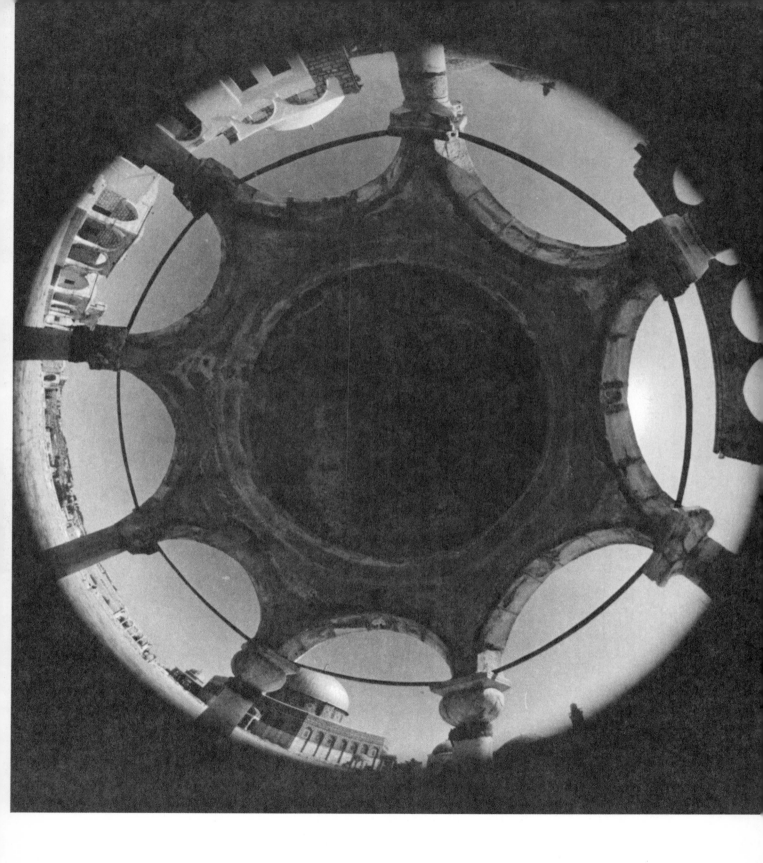

A small Islamic eighth century A.D. hexagonal open edifice — the *Qubbet el-Silsileh* or Dome of the Chain — adjoins its lordly companion on the east (right) and is a miniature prototype of it. This sweeping view taken from under the open hexagon offers a striking picture of the northern end of the esplanade and of several edicules erected by pious grandees in Mameluke days

264

Arabesques inside the top of the Dome

Four portals flank the outer octagonal walls at the four points of the compass. Despite many restorations since Ommayad times, the building has preserved its original magnificent decorative motifs, including elegant arabesques which are endlessly repeated, architectural decorations, wonderful antique mosaics, mother-of-pearl encrustations and other gems of Islamic art. All of these elements blend into a riot of color, yet still maintain the harmony and balance of the initial construction.

c. The El-'Aqṣa Mosque

The erection of this monumental building may have been initiated in the days of Abdel Malek, but it was carried through to splendid completion by his son El-Walid. Unlike the Dome which had withstood the ravages of time, the 'Aqṣa had undergone a

variety of basic alterations and reconstructions. R.W. Hamilton, who has made a thorough survey of the edifice, has drawn attention to six building stages beginning with the oldest Ommayad period. The second stage relates to the aftermath of the 747/8 earthquake which destroyed the mosque along with a number of other buildings in the area (see below). It had originally been built in basilical shape, consisting of a central nave with seven parallel aisles flanking it on each side. At the head of the central nave and against the south wall is a *mihrab* (prayer niche) oriented to Mecca. In front of the latter and above rose the dome of the mosque. Underneath the whole length of the central nave runs a wide underground passage called the *'Aqṣa el-Qadima* (the Ancient). In Herodian times and later, in Ommayad days, this passage began at the entrance to the Double Hulda Gate (which has been walled up since Crusader times; see Part III, F, 4: The Monumental Southern Gates); it proceeds as far as the front entrance to the mosque. One can still see the inner vestibule of the ancient Double Gate with its two immense standing Herodian columns. The dimensions correspond to those given by Josephus (*Antiquities* XV, 430) i.e. 4 feet (1.25 m.) in diameter, for the columns of the Southern Royal Portico, which collapsed nearby and were reused by the builders of the 'Aqṣa.

Among other decorations of the mosque, carved wooden plaques can be seen above, encased in the architraves (beams) which connected the top of the marble colonnade of the aisles, the whole blending in harmonious motifs. Some of the plaques are on exhibit at the Rockefeller Museum in Jerusalem.

266

Left: The Ommayad Palace. Compare with diagrams on pp. 268–270. The heavy wall (left) was built of reused blocks of the Western Wall and the foundations (center) of the cut-up columns which tumbled from above.

Right: Remnants of the buildings and pavements of the Ommayad period adjacent to the Southern Wall of the Temple Mount.

2. THE OMMAYAD STRUCTURES NEAR THE TEMPLE MOUNT

In addition to these two magnificent structures and vast complex of buildings erected south and west of the Temple Mount walls, there was intensive building activity on the part of the Ommayad Caliphs throughout the city. Written reports of the period confirm the finds and supplement them with accounts of the restoration of the city walls, the erection of the governor's palace *(Dar Imara)*, and the establishment of Moslem and Jewish settlers in Jerusalem. It is known that Christians as well as Jews played an active part in the realization of the Moslem building plans, as well as in the execution of the exquisite decorations and embellishments which characterize the architectural monuments. The decorative motifs derive principally from the Byzantine tradition, but were also influenced by the Sassanid artistic practice (see below).

a. The Ommayad Palace

The vast building complex of the Ommayad period which we have gradually uncovered south and southwest of the walls of the Temple Mount conform with the plans laid down by Caliph Abdel Malek and his son El-Walid — the builders of the great mosques on the Haram es-Sherif — to transform the area around the shrines into a Moslem religious center. The most remarkable of the six buildings we have so far uncovered is also the largest and most elaborate (identified as Building II in our diagram), measuring 280.5 × 313.5 feet (85 × 95 m.) and with thick walls. It is situated south of the Southern Wall of the Temple Mount, lying between it and the Turkish city wall. The side facing the Herodian wall starts close to the southwestern corner of the Temple Mount and ends near the Double Gate. A narrow paved street leading to the gate separates it from the Herodian Southern Wall which it skirts. Another western street ran north to south along the Western Wall, proceeding further south, apparently in the direction of the Pool of Siloam. This road ran at a higher level than the pavement of Herodian times. In fact, the Ommayad caliphs rebuilt this part of Jerusalem without being aware of its history (see Part V, C: Rediscovering the Lower City of the Herodian Period).

The palace, a large square structure with a vaulted court in its midst, bears a close resemblance to other Ommayad palaces in Syria and Palestine, e.g. the winter palace in Jericho, built by Hišam ibn Abdel Malek (A.D. 724–753), now called Khirbet el-Mefjer. Unlike its Jericho counterpart, the Jerusalem palace is not flanked by towers at its four corners. It consisted of two stories and — as indicated by M. Ben-Dov who studied the Ommayad structures in this area — the upper story still shows traces of a bridge which linked its roof with the El-'Aqṣa mosque, thus assuring direct access to it through its southern wall, the one facing Mecca (termed *kibleh* in Islamic parlance). This fact leads our investigator to believe that the palace was built by Caliph El-Walid I to allow him direct access to the mosque. Further evidence may be found in a Greek papyrus found at Aphrodito in Egypt which mentions artisans employed by this same caliph when he built a palace in Jerusalem.

The building, like other large and sumptuous structures in the area, made consider-

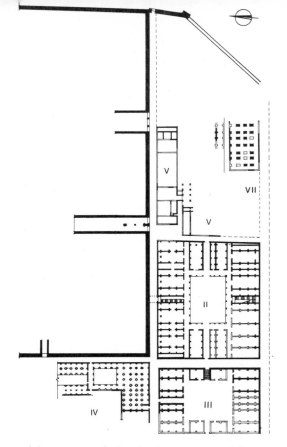

Diagram of the Ommayad Islamic quarter southwest and south of the Temple Mount (details in the following diagram). The recess left of V was the reopened Double Gate

able reuse of the large stone ashlars and columns of previous periods, chiefly of Herodian times. Striking evidence of this is seen in its western outer wall which looks almost like the Herodian wall of which it is an imitation. The Moslem structures were built over the former Byzantine buildings which were leveled (see above B, 3: The Period of Christian-Byzantine Jerusalem). The Islamic structures were well-equipped with all amenities to accommodate them for a large number of residents, more specifically, for the numerous pilgrims and high-placed guests from all parts of the Ommayad empire. Another local feature distinguishing them from the more elaborate architectural decorations of other Ommayad palaces is their characteristic pattern of geometric and floral forms.

The court of the palace was surrounded on its four sides by covered galleries whose ceilings rested on the walls of the adjoining long halls of the palace as well as over a row of evenly-spaced columns which surrounded the court, as shown in our diagram. There are three principal gates to the building: the main gate on the east, the second on the west and the third, on a higher level, to the north. All the gates are located in the middle of the outer walls thus establishing perfect symmetry.

b. Significance of the Islamic Quarter

There is no doubt that this vast building complex, so closely associated with the erection of the Dome of the Rock and El-'Aqṣa mosque, represented an ambitious socio-political and religious plan intended to heighten the prestige of the House of Ommaya in the Moslem world. This refutes a view of the Arab historian el-Muqqadasi who regarded the building of the sanctuaries of the Haram es-Sherif (Temple Mount) as nothing more than a work of art intended only to overshadow the Holy Sepulchre built by the Byzantines. And indeed this sumptuous quarter stood in glory in the period of the Ommayad caliphate whose center was Damascus. When the Moslem capital was moved from Damascus to Bagdad under the Abbassid caliphate, the quarter finally crumbled.

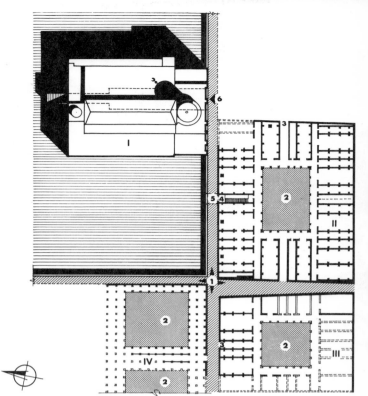

Layout of the Islamic structures near the southwest corner of the Temple Mount:
  I. El-'Aqṣa mosque.
 II. Large building south of Ḥaram.
III. Large building on southwest.
 IV. Building with large court.
  1. Paved streets between buildings and Temple Mount.
  2. Paved courts in the three buildings.
  3. Eastern gate of building II.
  4. Exit gate from building II, to street.
  5. Traces of bridge joining building II and Ḥaram.
  6. Double Gate, entrance to Ḥaram beneath El-'Aqṣa mosque.

The time of this final deterioration can be dated on the basis of archeological evidence to about the middle of the eighth century A.D. The city was hit by a severe earthquake in 747/8 which also severely damaged the El-'Aqṣa mosque.

The catastrophe is amply recorded in old literary sources and is known in Hebrew annals as "the year of the seventh" or the seventh Jubiliee (the fiftieth year which follows seven Sabbatical years, as ordained in Leviticus 25:3–8 and the Talmudic tractates *Sheviith*, when cultivation is prohibited, slaves are freed and land purchased, since the previous Jubilee year reverts to its original owner). The commandments of the Jubilee year were valid when Jews were resident in their land and were observed throughout Palestine and Syria. It is not possible at this stage to trace the precise chronological "seventh" Jubilee sequence in relation to the earthquake year, but a correlation did exist.

The Abbassid caliphs who succeeded the Ommayads did not lavish the same love and care over Jerusalem and were content to limit themselves to repairing El-'Aqṣa and other buildings of the Ḥaram es-Sherif which they maintained thereafter.

c. Reconstruction of the Double Gate

The plans of the Ommayad palace, as revealed by our excavation, bear a direct relevance to the ultimate fate of the Double (Hulda) Gate. A bridge now led from the palace to the Herodian gate which had not been in use for centuries. The ancient gate and its ancient inner vestibule (see above C, c: The El-'Aqṣa Mosque) had not been completely destroyed. The Moslems repaired it, mainly at the upper sides of its flanking walls, replacing the ruined huge ashlars with smaller ones, and adding typical decorative geometrical features of the ceiling which they repaired as well. They restored the underground passage which had led from the Herodian gate to beneath the Southern Royal Portico (see Part III, F, 4: The Monumental Southern Gates). The gate became once more the hub through which traffic flowed from the lower city to the Temple Mount.

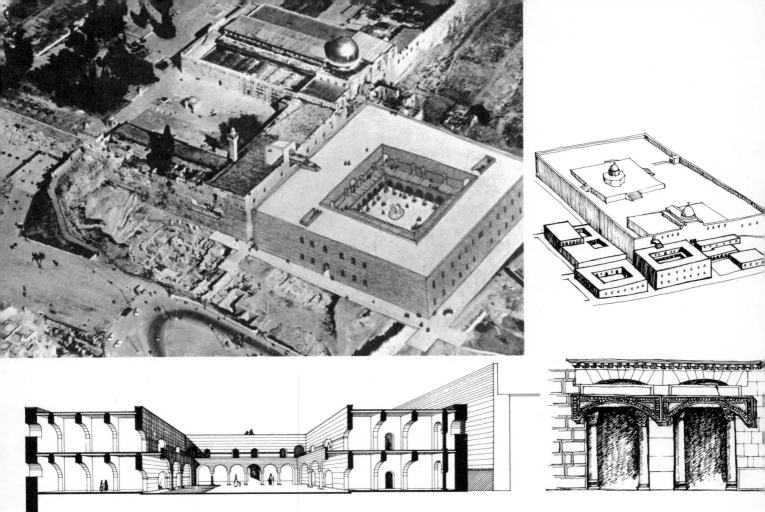

Above, left: A reconstruction (on the right) of the cube-shaped Ommayad Palace (described as building II) as it once stood south of the Temple Mount esplanade. Its roof communicated with a wing of El-'Aqṣa mosque (center)

Above, right: Reconstruction of the Ommayad structures around the Temple Mount

Below, left: Cross section (north-south) through the center of building II. View facing west

Below, right: Reconstruction of the Double Gate

d. The Ultimate Period

Our excavations in the Ommayad Islamic building levels indicate that the quarter was not restored after the middle of the eighth century. There was, however, some haphazard construction of houses, hovels, or even parts of buildings which reutilized Ommayad architectural members such as columns, capitals and lintels. The finds from the humbler living quarters are mostly from the ninth century, living evidence of the waning importance of Jerusalem as a great Moslem center after the end of the Ommayad caliphate (A.D. 750) and the rise of the Abbassid caliphate which centered on Bagdad, a great distance away from Jerusalem. It corresponds also with the decline of the imperial regime which had characterized the Ommayad realm; by then Jerusalem no longer enjoyed universal prestige as the ancient holy city.

In the course of time this section of Jerusalem supported a poor and sparse population and became a forgotten, crumbling slum. By the eleventh century the whole area had turned into a source of valuable building materials for restorations and repairs of the El-'Aqṣa mosque and other buildings of Jerusalem. The few who remained there made no attempt to erect real dwellings. This is what we found in 1967 south and west of the vast retaining walls of the Temple Mount.

270

Pictures Overleaf, right: Wood panel discarded during repairs of the Ommayad El-'Aqṣa mosque ▶

Left: A *sebil* or edicule at the southern end of the esplanade of the Haram es-Sherif and, in front of it, a row of reversed capitals which supported roofs of Islamic shrines prior to renovations and repairs in later centuries. They are stacked outside the Islamic Museum

The use to which the other buildings were put has not yet been determined fully. It appears that one structure (III in our diagram) found south of the palace was a hospice for wealthy pilgrims. Other colonnaded buildings were situated west of the Western Wall, stretching from the outer southwestern angle of the Temple Mount to the Barclay Gate and separated from the ancient wall by a narrow lane (IV in the diagram). Their function is still not clear.

e. The Ommayad Pillared Structure

The vast structure marked VII in our diagram constitutes an interesting problem. Found opposite the Triple Gate and at a lower level, it is surrounded by thick walls and is characterized by a row of mighty pillars. It may have survived, after undergoing restorations, up to the Fatimite Islamic period in the tenth and eleventh centuries A.D. The building is of interest because it may be identified with a structure called *Dar el-Akhmas*, mentioned in a guide to Jerusalem, a document discovered in the *geniza* (reliquary) of the ancient synagogue (built in A.D. 882) in old Cairo, Egypt. This document, now in the Cambridge University library and published by the late Yoseph Braslawi, is couched in Arabic, but written in Hebrew characters, a custom followed by oriental Jews at the time. It mentions the southern gates of the Temple Mount by both their Hebrew name, the Hulda Gates, and by their Arabic name, *Abwab el-Akhmas*. Before them stood a structure called *Dar el-Akhmas*, known to medieval Jews as the *Ḥaṣar bat* which must probably be complemented as Bat[sheva] court.

From Arabic sources, chiefly the Arab historian el-Muqqadasi, it is learned that the caretakers of the Temple Mount were referred to as *el-Akhmas*, meaning "the fifty." This name clings to the designation of the Moslem caretakers of the Haram es-Sherif sanctuaries since the days of their founder, Abdel Malek.

3. JERUSALEM ON THE EVE OF THE CRUSADES

In his *Diary of a Journey through Syria and Palestine* (1047) Nasir I-Khusrau, a contemporary of the Fatimite caliphate preceding Crusader rule, related that many Moslem pilgrims visited Jerusalem, chiefly those who could not get to Mecca. He reports, "Christians and Jews came from all lands, the first to visit the Holy Sepulchre and the others the synagogues found there." He estimated the city's population at about 20,000.

The *Gaon* or president of the Jerusalem *Yeshiva* (council of divines) was until the end of the eleventh century the recognized highest religious authority of the Jews in the Fatimid empire (successor to the Ommayads) during the first century of its existence. The office lapsed after the Turkoman invasion of Palestine, when it was moved to Cairo (A.D. 1071). Jerusalem's elegant quarters were abandoned and remained bare for several centuries.

D. JERUSALEM OF CRUSADER TIMES

1. CHARACTER OF THE CRUSADER RULE

The capture of Jerusalem by the Crusaders in July 1099 A.D. effected a drastic change in the life of the city. The Christian armies broke through the defense lines at Herod's Gate in the northwest quarter, and then systematically massacred all the Moslems and Jews in the city. This action was followed by an edict forbidding Moslems and Jews to settle there. The new population of the city was varied, with a majority of Europeans, mainly French (Franks), and a minority of eastern Christians split up among a number of communities. Each of these groups clustered around its churches, each spoke its own language and followed its traditional way of life. This parochial religious pattern has survived to the present time in the Old City: The most striking example is the Armenian community which continues to live within its walled compound established in Crusader times, and to worship at the Cathedral of St. James near the Zion Gate and the Jewish Quarter (the former Upper City).

The Crusaders ruled over the walled city of Jerusalem for nearly a century (A.D. 1099–1187). During that time there was considerable building activity for both military and communal purposes, including fortifications and religious institutions such as churches and monasteries.

Although the contours of the Old City remained unchanged and the Temple Mount compound retained its traditional and unique features for the most part, the city as a whole underwent a revolutionary change during this period. Once again Jerusalem was transformed into a Christian city of special sanctity, with the Church of the Holy Sepulchre at its heart. Other churches were erected or rebuilt, showing distinctive European influences. It may be noted, however, that comparatively few remains of the Jerusalem of Crusader times have survived and only a small number of contemporary structures have been uncovered by excavations in the city and its vicinity (see below: The Seat of Power).

2. THE CHRISTIANS CHANGED THE CHARACTER OF THE TEMPLE MOUNT

The most significant changes occurred on the Temple Mount. The vast Herodian retaining walls and main structures were left unimpaired physically for the most part, but the religious institutions were altered to express the faith and worship of the new Christian masters. We discovered in the course of our excavations south of the Temple Mount that the Crusaders had blocked the entrance of the Double Hulda Gate (see Part III, F, 4, a and Part VI, C, 2, c). This was due chiefly to the abandonment of the Ophel ridge and its total depopulation. In its place they opened a small gate near the far south-

274

eastern angle of the retaining walls — the Single Gate — to gain access to the subterranean vaulted halls and galleries of the so-called *Solomon Stables* (see Part III, E, 3, a: Archeological Links with Structures under the Haram). The walled arch can still be seen near the wall angle; it lies at the southern end of the sixth gallery of the inner halls. The Crusaders used the halls as stables for many years, as is evident from the rings fixed in the stone pillars to which horses and camels were tethered, and the numerous feeding troughs.

a. The Shrines Change Hands

The Islamic Dome of the Rock shrine built by the Caliph Abdel Malek (see above, Section C) was transformed into the *Temple of the Lord*, reflecting biblical traditions about the hallowed nature of the site and the memorable Foundation Rock *(Even Hashtiya)* of the Temple. They erected an iron fence around it, visible to this day, and crowned it with crosses beneath and over the splendid Islamic dome. Equally radical changes occurred at the El-'Aqṣa mosque, which was designated as Solomon's Temple *(Templum Solomonis)*.

First it was the palace of Baldwin I, first Latin King of Jerusalem, then it became the headquarters of the Knights of the Temple (Templars) whose name was derived from their new abode. This appellation has survived somehow in Jewish lore under the name "Halls of Solomon." The Knights of the Temple adapted the 'Aqṣa to domestic uses, even fencing drill, by adding porches and bays and extending the main structure by massive vaulted galleries. The present Women's Mosque and its extension into the Islamic Museum are the principal survivals of these activities. A contemporary coin struck by Baldwin I portrays on one side Jerusalem's outstanding edifices: the Church of the Holy Sepulchre, the citadel and the Templum Solomonis.

b. The Renovated Solomon Stables

With the approval of Baldwin II, the Knights of the Temple took over most of the southern sections of the Temple Mount area including the underground Stables of Solomon which covered an area of 600 square yards (500 sq. m.). The great vaults were supported by eighty-eight pillars resting on massive Herodian blocks and divided into twelve rows of galleries. The lower portions of the walls in the halls are also Herodian in design and date. The Templars renovated the huge halls which had been used in Herodian times as storage vaults of the Temple, and added a network of new arches over the ancient supporting pillars, thus enlarging the vaults. They used the space for stables and stores. The Triple Gate a short distance away was apparently blocked by the Crusaders.

3. THE COMMERCIAL ACTIVITY OF THE CITY

Trade in the city centered in the cobbled market streets in the middle of the town, chiefly around the Church of the Holy Sepulchre, and at the northern end of the Tyropoeon valley thoroughfare (today's El-Wad Road). Trade prospered as increasing numbers of Christians visited the city, and many settled there. Foreign currency was exchanged for coins minted by the Kingdom of Jerusalem, and western and eastern goods as well as "antiques" and religious souvenirs were sought and sold in great quantities. Business was brisk in the large market place — the *fonda* — situated north of the Citadel, or in the Jewish Quarter close to the Mount. The cattle mart was near the "Tanner's Gate" believed to be in the vicinity of the present Dung Gate (close to our excavation sites). Though the ban against them was not lifted, Jews, particularly cloth dyers, began

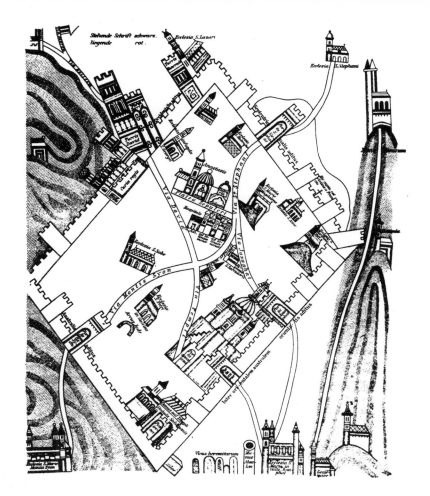

A drawing of Jerusalem of Crusader days. It emphasizes Christian holy places and strongholds, notably the Templum Domini or Temple of the Lord (lower center) and the Curia Regis (palace of the Crusader kings of Jerusalem) and the adjoining Turris David (the Citadel, upper left)

to drift back and live in their quarter in the twelfth century. A larger number immigrated there in the following century, especially after the great scholar, Moses ben Nahman (known as the Ramban or Nahmanides) had settled in Jerusalem around 1257 and built the first medieval synagogue.

4. THE SEAT OF POWER

The Crusaders' principal military force was stationed at Herod's old Citadel which was called *Turris David* (Tower of David; see Part II, F, 3). Their defense strategy for the city was based on the same topographic and military considerations which governed Herod's plans. The Turks maintained this strategy long after the Crusaders. This traditional stance on the part of the Crusaders accounts also for the fact that the arrangement of the western city walls was left unchanged. Several Crusader buildings were discovered by C.N. Johns in the course of his excavations in the court of the Citadel above the levels of the Hasmonean and Herodian fortifications and towers (1934–40). Even more important Crusader remains, however, were uncovered by Magen Broshi south of the Citadel. He found the southern end of their royal palace, the *Curia Regis* built above Herod's Palace. In the process, the Crusaders removed every trace of that vast structure except its foundation podium (see Part II, F, 3, a: Herod's Palace).

The Crusaders built the large Tancred Tower (Kasr Jallûd) at the northwestern corner of the Old City in the early twelfth century; it measured 115.5 × 115.5 feet (35 × 35 m.).

5. THE CRUSADER CHURCHES

The churches built were the visible expression of Christian devotion and attachment to the traditional holy places. The different religious orders erected a plethora of churches, monasteries, hospices and homes, at the same time eliminating older Islamic structures.

Their principal work was the restoration of the Church of the Holy Sepulchre which had fared badly at the hands of the later Arab caliphs. Only the Byzantine Rotunda of the Church of the Anastasis was preserved in its former magnificence. Other holy sites near the Anastasis were marked by small oratories. The Crusaders conceived the idea of uniting these scattered sanctuaries under one roof. The specific nature of the architectural changes could be determined more clearly in the course of the surveys carried out in 1933–1935 by M. Harvey and, more recently (in 1960–63) by V. Corbo, in connection with recent restoration work (see illustration of Baldwin coin.).

To the Rotunda, the Crusaders added a basilica on the east consisting of four naves resting on pillars and columns. The arms of the transept were extended to contain the enlarged chapel of Golgotha (Calvary) at the southeastern angle, as well as other oratories in remembrance of the events of the Passion, and everything was brought under one roof. Finally, the magnificent entrance and triumphal arch were added to the restored church on the southern side; these replaced the older magnificent Byzantine entrance on the east side. Contrary to the accepted tradition, the entrance, since then, is on the east. The edifice, which was completed in A.D. 1149, combined old and new elements in evident disharmony, spoiling its ancient beauty. Nevertheless, the rebuilt cathedral massively conveyed its focal character and vital importance to Christendom. The main structure persists to this day although it has been disfigured further by additions and deplorable restorations made by the Catholic, Greek, Armenian, and other co-occupants of the church since the Middle Ages.

Many remarkable churches and monasteries were erected in other parts of the city and its immediate vicinity. Outstanding among them and still in existence is the *Basilica of St. Anne* in classic Romanesque style, with three naves and imposing entrance, on the site of the former fifth century basilica of St. Mary. It commemorates the traditional birthplace of the Virgin, and is situated on the northeastern border of the Temple Mount, near the Pool of Bethesda (see Part V, B, 1: Simon's Works in Jerusalem).

Recent excavations have added valuable information on other religious buildings of the period, such as the ruined church and monastery of *St. Mary's of Mount Zion* served by the Augustine fathers. Its entrance was uncovered, as well as other interesting features, at the beginning of this century, when building was in process as the foundations of the Basilica of the Dormition were being laid in 1910. Greater interest was aroused by the Crusader *Church of St. Mary* founded by the Teutonic Knights, west of the southwestern corner of the Temple Mount. This was discovered by N. Avigad in the course of excavations in the Upper City (see Part I, G: Interesting Discoveries in the Upper City). One of the two wings served as the church, while the other housed a hospital and hospice for pilgrims. The edifice has now been restored and has become a tourist attraction. Yet, only a few years ago, the old building with its arches and domes served as a stable for donkeys in the abandoned Jewish Quarter (the former Upper City).

Notable among churches outside the walled city are the *Church of the Assumption* and traditional underground tomb of the Virgin with its cluster of graves of royal Crusader families including Queen Melisanda. Excavation of another monastery by C.N. Johns in 1937 revealed the remains of a Crusader church which Saladin destroyed in 1187, when he recaptured Jerusalem.

6. RETRENCHMENT OF THE CITY WALLS ON THE SOUTH SIDE

The sloping area situated south of the Temple Mount, namely the Ophel, as well as the southern section of Mount Zion (the former Upper City) remained apparently outside the walled city after Crusader times. We have uncovered the segment of a solid wall, built of huge, mostly reused stones, some 9 feet (2.80 m.) thick, which ran westwards from the southwestern angle of the Temple Mount. The segment is 66 feet long (20 m.) but its further continuation has been destroyed. This was probably the rampart which continued the southern wall and ran, at the foot of the Upper City, in the direction of a bastion later known as Burj Kibrit. It is visible at the top left of our wide picture on pages 12–13.

M. Broshi has recently discovered a tower of the city wall built by the Ayubid Sultan El-Malik el Mu'azzam (A.D. 1212), namely around the more restricted area of the city. This is testified by an Arab inscription over the present-day Zion Gate. We learn from other Arab sources that the Sultan ordered the destruction of the former defenses for fear that the Crusaders might return and entrench themselves behind them. In all likelihood, the wall in question is another fragment of the massive city wall which we discovered below the southern walls of the Temple Mount. The different fragments bear witness to the retrenchment of Jerusalem on the south side.

E. JERUSALEM IN THE MAMELUKE PERIOD

Jerusalem was lost to the Crusaders on October 2, 1187, when it was captured by Saladin (Salah ed-Din) the Ayubid. It was reoccupied temporarily for fifteen years (1229–1244), and then reverted to Moslem administration. Most of the Christians left the city, but a few of the native Christians remained. The new rulers of the land were the Mamelukes. These sultans, of Kurdish, Turkish or Circassian (Caucasian) extraction, were descendants of slaves of the former Moslem rulers, who had enfranchised and taken over their empire. Throughout the days of Mameluke rule Jerusalem was relegated to the role of a provincial city in a province ruled by the all-powerful governor of Damascus. It possessed no outstanding political or economic importance, but it had religious significance in Moslem eyes which enhanced its sanctity and that of the Temple. Another school of thought which had held sway in former days took an opposing pro-Meccan position, as exemplified by the philosopher Taki ad-Din ibn Tajmiya (1328), but Moslem writings "in praise of Jerusalem" *(Fadail al-Quds)* proved more persuasive. Consequently, the Mamelukes, and later the Turks, took great pains to Islamize and improve the city. They erected a religious center around the Temple Mount, which they took particular pains to beautify.

The long wars with the Crusaders had also brought to the fore old memories of the holy sites once held sacred by Christians or Moslems. The years of Mameluke rule were fertile ground for fresh "discoveries" of the tombs of prophets, and for the mushrooming of holy sites in Jerusalem. Many such "finds" were rooted in distorted traditions held by both Christians and Jews.

Pilgrims of all creeds, mainly large numbers of Moslems as well as Christians and Jews, continued to visit the Holy Land. Among the most fervent were *dervishes*, followers of various Sufite Islamic mystic orders. These *dervishes* were held in great esteem by the people, and the sultans built them attractive and comfortable monasteries, known as *zawiyehs* and *ribat* (hospices). Jerusalem in this period was regarded as an accepted place of refuge for court grandees temporarily out of favor with the rulers. It is during this period that the present-day image of the Old City of Jerusalem was formed.

1. GLORIFYING JERUSALEM AND THE TEMPLE MOUNT

The two magnificent Islamic shrines, the Dome of the Rock and El-'Aqṣa mosque, were of course restored to their former glory. Sultans vied with one another to beautify them or to carry out repairs. At the same time, they set in motion plans to enhance the prestige of the sanctuaries and to add fresh structures, large and small, over the Temple esplanade and around it. Endless efforts and a huge amount of money were invested throughout the post-Crusader period to erect prestigious religious institutions in the sacred precincts and in the other sections of the Holy City inhabited by Moslems.

In 1187, the golden crosses that had stood over the Dome of the Rock and the Templar quarters in El-'Aqṣa mosque were thrown down and the crescent restored. From 1194, Saladin Islamized Jerusalem and reinstated its Arab characteristics, a policy followed after 1327 by the Mameluke Sultan Qalaoun and successive rulers. They used suitable imported materials in the restoration work, and employed numbers of Greek, Armenian, Persian and even Jewish craftsmen. Thus, many different styles are evident on the buildings.

In the El-'Aqṣa mosque, Saladin restored the main *miḥrab* (prayer niche) against the southern wall, flanked by graceful little columns and set out in mosaics. Sultan Malik el-Adel had a beautiful ebony *minbar* (preaching stand), inlaid with ivory and mother-of-pearl, brought from Damascus and put up at the right of the *miḥrab*. Several porches were added to the vast mosque. From inscriptions in the mosque, it can be learned that El-'Aqṣa reached its present form in the middle of the fourteenth century.

280

The open-air pulpit or *minbar* built by Burhan-ed-Din in 1325 on the esplanade, illustrates the reutilization of architectural elements from former monuments: Byzantine (capitals at the foot of the stairs) and Crusader (little columns supporting the pulpit)

The Mameluke structures built throughout the enclosure of the Temple Mount and in the areas immediately adjoining it assumed different forms and shapes, most of them beautiful and typifying the Islamic style of buildings; these lent charm to medieval Jerusalem. They comprised:

(1) *Qubbehs* or vaulted prayer niches with a *miḥrab* at their southern ends in the direction of Mecca.

(2) *Madrasas* or colleges devoted to the study of Islamic theology and law, as well as Arabic grammar and lore, and under the direction of renowned scholars recruited throughout the Islamic world.

(3) *Muṣallahs*, paved chapels with a *miḥrab* to the south.

(4) *Manaras* or minarets, from whose top the faithful were summoned to prayer.

(5) *Raḥat* or *Sebils*, installations provided with water for drinking, or for ablutions and purification before prayer.

(6) *Ribat* (hospices) and *Zawiyehs* (monasteries).

One of the most interesting examples of Mameluke construction is the *Qubbeh* called *Kursi Suleiman*, a closed small mosque topped with domes. Its attribution to Solomon, the artful judge, is fortuitous as it was actually erected by another Suleiman, the seventh Ommayad caliph (A.D. 715–717).

2. THE MADRASAS ABUTTING ON THE TEMPLE MOUNT

On the periphery of the Haram es-Sherif enclosure (the historical Temple Mount), the Mameluke sultans competed with one another to erect, between the thirteenth and the fifteenth centuries, a dozen polychromic buildings of great beauty on the northern and western sides of the Temple Mount esplanade. These buildings housed *madrasas*, which were placed behind charming polychronic cloisters or *riwaq* giving access to the main building. Added to the ring of *madrasas* were numerous adjoining mausoleums put up by sultans and noblemen.

A characteristic feature of Mameluke masonry is the system of alternating red and

281

white stone layers, and the carving of stalactite semi-domes and hanging conch-niches, also polychrome, adorning the entrances to the *madrasas*, hospices, palaces and mausoleums crowding the northern and western sides of the Temple Mount enclosure.

A few outstanding examples of extant medieval Islamic art in the area of the Temple Mount should be mentioned here. One is the *Madrasa Arghuniyeh* on Bab el-Hadid street which leads to the Temple Mount from the west. It was built by Arghun el-Kameli, local governor under the Mameluke ruler of Damascus. Facing it is the *Muzhiriyeh* whose entrance has a recessed trefoil arch with eight rows of stalactites. Its windows bear elaborate low relief decorations typical of late Mameluke art. Another building, located on the northern side of the Temple Mount, is the *Jauliyeh*, named after Sanjar el-Jauliyeh, supervisor of the Islamic sanctuaries of Jerusalem and Hebron and responsible as well for the works of restoration in the Dome of the Rock in 1319. The *Madrasa Jauliyeh*, now occupied by the Omariya school, was built in the area of the Antonia fortress of Herodian times, which had overlooked the Temple Mount enclosure and protected it. It is also the site of the First Station of the Cross of the Via Dolorosa, and is the starting point of the weekly procession led by the Franciscans to the Church of the Holy Sepulchre.

a. *Emir Tankiz's Great Monuments*

This Mameluke ruler of Damascus is famed for two important edifices abutting on the Temple Mount. One is the *Madrasa Tankiziyeh* (1329) which stands right over the Wilson Arch (see Part V, D, 1: The Wilson Arch) along an upper part of the Western Wall. This two-story fine example of Islamic art, identified by its conch-shell niche over the doorway and black joggling, was built in the form of a cross with its courts and fountain. In later years it became a hostel for visiting Mameluke princes and finally, in Turkish times, it served as the *Maḥkameh* (Moslem High Court).

b. *Suq el-Qattanin*

An even more interesting example of Emir Tankiz's public works is his exquisite Gate of Mohammed, now known as *Bab el-Qattanin* (1336), which gives access to the Temple Mount enclosure opposite the Dome of the Rock. It stands about 800 feet (240 m.) north of the southwestern corner of the Western Wall and represents a significant northern continuation of that same wall, as is evident from the ancient squared stones on which it stands. The majestic gate leads into the medieval *Suq el-Qattanin* (Market of the Cotton Merchants). Unlike the other bazaars of the Old City whose architectural design dates them to Crusader times, this bazaar is an outstanding example of a whole street built of reused large ancient ashlars apparently taken from the ruined walls and courts of the Temple Mount at this section. The original bazaar probably dates back to Byzantine times, as do the two ancient baths and the underground spring which feeds them since ancient times. The reconstruction of the bazaar by the Moslem authorities has preserved its ancient character and stones. In many respects, this street and its quaint architecture, as well as the imposing arch at its eastern end (see picture) exemplifies a living link that connects the ancient Temple structures and the Islamic buildings and approaches that have replaced them in this area. Due to prevailing conditions, it is impossible at this time to conduct further surveys at the site.

c. Adminstration by the Wakf

After the *madrasas* and other religious institutions were erected by the Mameluke governors and grandees of Islam, they were given over to the care of the Jerusalem notables and doctors of Islamic theology and law, the *'Ulama*. They were maintained through the generosity and goodwill of other dignitaries of Islam. This accounts for the institution of the Jerusalem organization of the *Wakf* (*Awkaf* in the plural) which holds in trust buildings and estates for the maintenance and administration of public institutions, a system which played an ever-growing role in Mameluke and Turkish times. Returns from this property, added to the revenue derived from the large influx of Christian and Jewish pilgrims, represented the major source of income of the Holy City.

3. THE JEWS IN JERUSALEM

It should be noted that the Jewish community began growing by leaps and bounds after the capture of the city by Saladin. The Jews congregated mainly in the Mount Zion area (the former Upper City). This expansion became more noticeable after the immigration in the thirteenth century of Rabbi Moses ben Nachman (Nachmanides; the Ramban). His famous epistle to his son, written in 1268, provides a graphic description of the desolation following the Turkoman invasion. He describes how he transformed an abandoned

Crusader building built on columns into the first synagogue in medieval Jerusalem. For this reason the Arabs called the quarter the Street of the Jews. It served as a focus of Jewish worship for many generations, and has recently been reconstructed.

a. The Western Wall — a New Focus

Worship at the Western Wall (the section formerly known as the Wailing Wall), the main focus of longing, assumed ever-growing importance in Jewish life. The fact that the Moslems claimed it as their property, and its location beyond the confines of the Jewish Quarter, created difficulties for the Jews. We have already seen (Part III, F, 1) that ever since Talmudic times (third–sixth centuries A.D.) the Jews attached greater importance to this wall of the Temple Mount than to the others. People would say: "The Holy Spirit has never departed from the Western Wall," and they spoke of "the Western Wall of the Temple which has never been destroyed."

Sanctity was attributed to the wall in Mameluke times more than ever before, and

Inscription by a pilgrim of the Middle Ages, carved in the Southern Wall near the Double Hulda Gate, reading "Yeremiah bar Gedalia berabi Yosef"

this feeling increased further from Turkish times (sixteenth century). The common people believed that this sanctity was the inherent virtue of the wall since the days of David and Solomon.

b. *The Condition of Jerusalem in Medieval Times*

Jerusalem's increasing importance as a focus of worship and pilgrimage since the twelfth century is attested to by the Jewish traveler, Benjamin of Tudela (1167) and subsequent Jewish and Christian pilgrims who came to the Holy Land. Rabbi Obadiah of Bartenura (1488) wrote: "...Jerusalem is almost wholly desolate and possesses no protective walls. No more than 4,000 of its inhabitants live in houses of their own and only seventy Jewish families, wretchedly poor, have remained... the Street of the Jews... the Jewish Quarter on Mount Zion is large... They had once owned many houses but most of them lay in ruins... No Jew is allowed to enter the precincts of the Temple Mount... The Western Wall which still stands, at least in part, is made of very large stones. I have never seen such large stones in any ancient edifice..."

During this and the following periods, the Jewish population continued to grow through successive waves of immigration, each following one of the medieval expulsions from the Christian states. In 1517 Jerusalem fell to the Turks, whose dominion lasted until 1917, a period of exactly four hundred years.

F. FOUR CENTURIES OF TURKISH RULE

1. RENOVATIONS OF THE TEMPLE MOUNT AND THE CITY WALLS

In the year 1517, Selim, the Ottoman Turkish sultan, became the new master of the Middle East, putting an end to Mameluke hegemony. Jerusalem, together with the rest of Syria and Palestine, became part of the new empire. Though Ottoman rule started off under bright auspices, the Turks were little capable of restoring the lands they ruled to new life. However, the son of Selim, Suleiman I, called "the Magnificent" (1520–1566), took an energetic interest in building projects, thus also greatly benefiting Jerusalem. One of his remarkable achievements was the complete replacement of the fine but fragile mosaics decorating the outer surface of the Dome of the Rock. He refaced the building with tiles of faience, whose predominantly blue color, alternating with white, green and yellow, gives the mosque its characteristic appearance. The dye used in coloring the tiles was a secret guarded by Armenian craftsmen from Anatolia, and their descendants seem to have made good use of the same process when they renovated the tiles in the early twenties of the present century.

Suleiman effected thorough repairs in other parts of the sanctuary as well as in the Temple Mount precincts. He rebuilt the city walls and gates (1539–42), giving them the form and course they have today. The renovations took place mainly along the upper courses or over debris of the earlier walls, rarely reaching the lower courses lying on bedrock. Part of the Western hill sections of the Upper City on Mount Zion as well as the remains of ancient Jerusalem south of the Temple Mount remained outside the city walls, thus partly perpetuating the course followed by the Crusaders and the Mamelukes. He also restored the Citadel as the seat of the garrison (the minaret which adorns it was added in the seventeenth century), and improved the city water supply by repairing the aqueducts bringing spring water to Jerusalem.

a. *The Turkish Walls of the Old City*

The measurements of the Old City walls are (see pp. 206–7):

Southern wall (facing Mount Zion and the Ophel):   3700 feet (1100 m.)
Western wall (facing the new town since A.D. 1860):   2900 feet (875 m.)
Northern wall (facing modern eastern Jerusalem):   4270 feet (1281 m.)
Eastern wall (facing the Kidron valley):   2540 feet (762 m.)

There are seven open gates in the walls today: the Jaffa Gate in the western wall; the New Gate (opened only in the nineteenth century), the Damascus Gate and Herod's Gate in the northern wall; the Lions' Gate (St. Stephen's Gate) in the eastern wall (the Byzantine Golden Gate into the Temple area is walled up); and the Zion Gate and Dung Gate in the southern wall. Suleiman's erection of the Jaffa Gate is attested to by an inscription attributing it to him in the year 945 of the Moslem calendar (A.D. 1538/39).

b. *Jerusalem since the Sixteenth Century*

After the earthquake of 1545, the Church of the Holy Sepulchre was thoroughly repaired. Its various sections were allocated to the different Christian denominations who jealously watched one another and squabbled over areas and places in the building, or over timetables connected with their ritual, often coming to blows and causing imperial or foreign intervention to settle their disputes (see below: The Crimean War).

Several sultans proved their faithfulness to the sanctity of Jerusalem, mainly the Temple Mount and its Moslem shrines. They are remembered for their good works and the erection or repair of pious institutions in the city. Some followed the example of the former Mameluke rulers by erecting magnificent colleges and other public buildings. We learn, for example, from an inscription of Mahmud II (1808–1839) that he renewed the gilding of the inside surfaces of the Dome of the Rock and had its outside tiles and marble restored.

2. THE NATURE OF TURKISH RULE

Palestine enjoyed a measure of prosperity until the death of Suleiman. In later years, however, when the sultans who ruled from Istanbul weakened militarily, their rule over Palestine and Syria began to decay. The sultans nevertheless encouraged the immigration into the Ottoman Empire, including Palestine, of Jewish refugees from Spain, resulting in an upsurge of Jewish population in the sixteenth century. The process was counteracted by a burdensome taxation levied on the poor community, including confiscation of property, until only the poor were left in Jerusalem. The Turkish officials levied a poll-tax, a watch-and-ward tax, a tax on gifts at festivals, a government-aid tax, and a land tax. In the ensuing three centuries, the Turkish regime accorded Jerusalem no particular importance. As its population dwindled, pilgrims were not prepared to face the dangers, and those in power exacted a special protection tax from all who came to the city. The lax and disinterested local authorities offered no suitable measures for the development of trade, industry, or public security. The rule of the city was extortion and universal graft and bribery, and these were the only means by which Jewish and Christian inhabitants could secure any services.

Conditions became intolerable during the second half of the eighteenth century. Powerful Arab sheikhs in certain provinces rebelled against Turkish rule and eventually brought about the intervention of neighboring countries and of the European powers into the affairs of the land. The unexpected result was Palestine's eventual emergence from oblivion. Jerusalem itself had lived in complete somnolence between the seventeenth and mid-nineteenth centuries. Its population had dwindled, and many parts of the city fell into ruins (see below).

The two panthers carved above the eastern Lions' Gate seem to have been the armorial device of the Mameluke Sultan Baybars. The gate was rebuilt by Suleiman the Magnificent

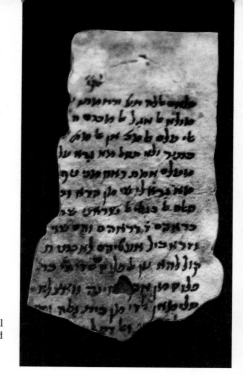

Pious wishes by Jewish masons engaged in restoring columns in El-'Aqṣa mosque in medieval times. They were couched in Arabic and written in Hebrew characters. The parchment was laid under a replaced column

3. AWAKENING IN THE NINETEENTH CENTURY

The first sign of change came at the beginning of the nineteenth century, as Jerusalem and the rest of the country were again afflicted by alternating periods of upheaval and stagnation. Napoleon's military expedition to Egypt, on the pretext of warring against the Mameluke pashas, brought him as far as the walls of Acre where he was conclusively defeated, without ever reaching Jerusalem. This expedition, however, ushered Palestine into the European sphere of interest. The renewed concern of the European powers in the "Eastern question" gained them no profit, but resulted in the fuller assumption of Turkish rule over the whole country. Jerusalem, situated in the heart of the hill district between Hebron and Nablus (Shechem) was administered through the province of Damascus. The main responsibility of the pasha of the province was the collection of taxes, though scant services or public security were offered in return. Rebellions and incursions by Beduin sheikhs were frequent at the time, and in 1825 Sultan Mahmud II was obliged to send Abdallah Pasha, the governor of Acre, to retake Jerusalem. He besieged the city and shelled its walls for two weeks, before it fell into his hands.

a. *The Reforms of Ibrahim Pasha*

In the early nineteenth century, Jerusalem had an estimated population of some 12,000 people, Moslems, Jews and Christians. The city was neglected and lacked the most basic services. A change came in the wake of the invasion of the country by the Albanian, Mohammed Ali, a former officer of the sultan's army, who set his son, Ibrahim Pasha, to rule over Syria and Palestine. Ibrahim Pasha seized Palestine in 1831 and ruled from Damascus for a decade. In the year 1834, a peasant uprising took place. The people refused to pay taxes or serve in the army of the capable general, some of them choosing to cut off toes and fingers rather than be enlisted. Jerusalem, meanwhile, stood in the vortex of the storm and suffered heavily. But history must render Ibrahim Pasha his proper due. His government did introduce progress in Jerusalem in various ways. A city council was set up, restrictions against Jews and Christians were abolished, and

289

comparative security was established. He was the first ruler to openly allow Jews to build synagogues in the Jewish Quarter. As a result, several synagogues with high cupolas were erected with *yeshivot* (Talmudic colleges) attached to them. Jerusalem was slowly emerging from centuries of obscurity and squalor, gradually meeting the renascent west, and attempting to integrate western culture with Jewish aspirations for a national revival. This progress was checked when the city fell to the Turks again in 1840.

b. *Restoration of Turkish Rule*

The agitation against the rule of Ibrahim Pasha finally brought the intervention of the European powers, and with it the renewal of Turkish administration. In 1840, Sultan Abdul Majid once more ruled over Palestine and Jerusalem. Attempts were now made to improve inner organization. Jerusalem became a *sanjak* (district) ruled by an authority subject to the *wali* (general governor) of Damascus directly accountable to the imperial capital (a system which held out until 1897). A certain modicum of order was introduced by means of sweeping reforms and a greater centralization of administrative power. This resulted, incidentally, in a growing expansion of European influence.

c. *European Influence in Jerusalem*

Greater influence in communal affairs was not only wielded by the consuls of Great Britain and France, but also by those of the Russian and Austrian empires and, in the course of time, by the United States consuls as well. The French, as the leading Catholic power, assumed the protection of the Latin community, and the Russians that of the Greek Orthodox. The repercussions of this intervention in local affairs was threefold: 1) Extra-territorial status was secured for the nationals and subjects of the European countries (among whom were many Jews), thus establishing, in a way, states within a state. 2) Modernization was promoted, and the Christian communities strengthened. 3) The foreign intervention provided a strong bulwark and protection to the pioneering scholars intent on investigating the ancient history and cultures of the lands of the Bible (see Part I, C, 3–6).

The true setting, however, may be gathered from the impression conveyed by a contemporary visitor, Cardinal A. S. Stanley who wrote in 1852: "The city is in ruins. One can hardly discern among the shambles…an ordinary street, a neat European house… but as a whole it looks more like a city gutted by fire." (*Sinai and Palestine*, 1864; 183).

4. THE CRIMEAN WAR

The seething rivalry in Palestine between Great Britain and France on the one hand, and Russia on the other, came to a head in 1853 when the former two nations set out to protect the Turkish empire, then dubbed "the sick man of Europe," against Russian aggression. Religious issues were prominently involved in the dispute as France insisted on retrieving its former hold over the Church of the Holy Sepulchre and the Church of the Nativity in Bethlehem. Russia, for her part, claimed the rights established after the Moslem capture of the country, when the Greek Orthodox Church represented Christendom in the Holy Land as heir to the Byzantine empire.

The peace treaty signed after the Crimean War in 1856 consolidated western influence over Palestine, since it granted special privileges to non-Moslem communities. This benefited Jerusalem first and foremost, for it attracted Jews and Europeans to that city. The population grew, and pilgrim traffic increased considerably. In order to accommodate Russian pilgrims, the Russian Hospice was built in the Russian compound outside the walls of the Old City. New churches and hospices were erected including, among others, monasteries, schools, orphanages and residences. The new expansion was strongly in evidence in the Jewish community, which began to spread out and settle in new quarters outside the walls. Living conditions in the Old City proper and outside it were greatly improved by the benefactions of Sir Moses Montefiore in the course of his frequent visits. He established the first Jewish quarter outside the walls of the Old City, *Mishkenot Sha'ananim*, in 1860, thereby setting the course for future expansion.

The first highway connecting Jerusalem with Jaffa and the coast was built only in 1867; next came the road to Nablus in 1870. The Turkish authorities improved the water supply to the Temple Mount reservoirs by reinaugurating the flow in the aqueduct from the springs of Artas, whereupon a great celebration was organized to memorialize the event. The city wall near the Jaffa Gate was breached to facilitate traffic; the act itself was occasioned by the visit of the German Kaiser Wilhelm II in 1898, who was thus enabled to enter the Holy City by horse-drawn carriage.

5. A JEWISH ATTEMPT TO ACQUIRE THE WESTERN WALL

Jews had tried repeatedly to secure permanent rights over the section of the Western Wall and the court facing it, their traditional place of worship. This could be effected either by formal order from the Sultan, or by negotiation with the local *Wakf* (Moslem trustees of religious properties) who claimed ownership by right of conquest. Estates of this character are only transferrable through an exchange for another equivalent property. As far back as the middle of the eighteenth century, Rabbi Abdallah of Bombay had tried to purchase the Western Wall section from the *Wakf*, but the negotiations had failed. Baron Edmund de Rothschild proposed an exchange in 1887, and undertook to build a new living quarter for the residents of the adjoining slum area, which would be administered by the *Wakf*. The attempt failed, and in the wake of Jewish interest, the Western Wall became a focus of Moslem molestation of Jewish worshipers. This culminated in serious anti-Jewish riots in 1921 and 1931. After 1948, when eastern Jerusalem and the Old City were separated from the rest of the city by the cease-fire lines set up after the Israel War of Independence, Jews were not allowed admittance to the site, despite the fact that the terms of the Israel–Jordan Armistice Agreement provided for rights of access.

The desolate area to the south of the Temple Mount continued to be the forgotten corner of Jerusalem. The only change there was the erection of an Arab school over the buried ruins of the great Ommayad palace described above (Part VI, C, 2, a). The Jordanian authorities were not even aware that such a palace had once existed there. The reunification of Jerusalem in June 1967 brought about the resumption of the historical Jewish presence on the premises.

6. THE DAWN OF A NEW ERA

Several quiet revolutions which occurred in Turkish-dominated Palestine at the end of the nineteenth century presaged the final emergence of Jerusalem from its long slumber. The most important was the launching of the Zionist program in 1897. This program resulted in successive waves of Jewish immigration to the country and to the Holy City, as well as a steady westernization and the dynamic restoration of Jewish life in various sectors of the city and the land. This was paralleled at the beginning of the century by a slight relaxation of Turkish domination. Turkish rule came to an end in the course of World War I, when Jerusalem was captured by the British army under General E. Allenby in December 1917, and a British Mandatory administration took over the authority for Palestine and Jerusalem.

Since that time, there has been an ever-growing wave of archeological research (as described in Part I, D). Our present expedition, however, could only take place in a reunited Jerusalem after 1967.

292

The Arab Jordan authorities, who had no special interest in Jerusalem's past, had put up a school building (center) before 1967 at the southwest corner of the Temple area walls. They were not aware that they had thereby covered the site of the Ommayad palace, as well as Byzantine and Herodian remains (see Part VI, C, 2, a)

بسم الله الرحمن الرحيم

An Arabic writ allowing Christians the right of entrance and use of the Church of the Holy Sepulchre after the Crusades

7. UPSURGE IN JERUSALEM

Towards the end of Turkish rule, new life and new aspirations began to invigorate the Holy City, altering more and more the antiquated character of the city. It was symptomatic of the changed conditions that the Moslem taboo prohibiting non-Moslems from entering the esplanade of the Temple Mount was abolished, with a corresponding improvement of conditions in the Christian holy places. For instance, bells had been forbidden in the churches since the time of Saladin; their use was now restored. Public services and new institutions gradually introduced a new era in building. At the beginning of the twentieth century, nearly the entire population of Jerusalem lived within the Old City walls. Turkish soldiers would open the gates at sunrise and close them at sunset, admitting latecomers only through a wicket. However, the exodus to the new quarters had gained strength, so that the city's population quadrupled from about 15,000 in 1844 (7,000 Jews, 5,000 Moslems and 3,000 Christians) to 60,000 (40,000 Jews, 13,000 Christians and 7,000 Moslems) in 1905. It grew to 263,000, nearly 200,000 of them Jews, when eastern and western Jerusalem were reunited in June 1967. The total, incidentally, comes close to the city's population in the late Second Temple period, though the city then covered a far smaller area. By the beginning of 1975, the population of Jerusalem was close to 350,000.

A PLACE OF HUMAN HABITATION

There is a saying of the Jewish sages that the Holy City must be a place of human habitation and not merely a sacred ruin. This saying has been vindicated in the course of the ages, as viewed from an objective historical approach.

In truth, no town in Israel could be like Jerusalem. It is a city in which the Jews have persisted, sometimes in very small numbers and against almost insurmountable odds (as related in this book) for nearly two thousand years after the fall of the Second Temple. They always believed that they were but regaining what had been taken from them by force. It is a fact that under alien domination, Jerusalem was never a great city; on the contrary, it tended to diminish in size and population. Only under Israel rule did it expand and its population, Jewish and non-Jewish, increase.

APPENDICES

APPENDIX 1

The Kings of Judah

David	approximately 1005–965 B.C.
Solomon	965–928
Rehoboam	928–911
Abijah	911–908
Asa	908–867
Jehosaphat	867–846
Jehoram	846–843
Ahaziah	843–842
Athaliah	842–836
Joash	836–798
Amaziah	798–769
Uzziah (Azariah)	769–733
Jotham (co-regent with his father, Uzziah)	758–733
Ahaz	733–727
Hezekiah	727–698
Manasseh	698–642
Amon	641–640
Josiah	639–609
Jehoiakim	608–597
Jehoiachin	597–
Zedekiah	596–586

(Several of the kings were co-regents during the last years of their fathers' reigns)

CHRONOLOGY

Initial stages of the City of David	approx. 1000–965 B.C.
Co-regency of Solomon, approximately	967–964
Beginning of Solomon's construction of the First Temple	964
Division of the United Kingdom	928
Fall of the Kingdom of Samaria (Northern Kingdom) to the Assyrian emperor, Sargon II	721
Sennacherib's campaign against Judah	701
Josiah's death at Megiddo	609
Nebuchadnezzar's accession to the throne of Babylonia	605
First siege of Jerusalem by Nebuchadnezzar	598
Capture of Jerusalem, Jehoiachin's exile to Babylon together with the leaders of the land, the craftsmen and the smiths	597
Beginning of the last siege of Jerusalem	588
Destruction of Jerusalem and the First Temple by Nebuchadnezzar	586

The Years of the Restoration

Cyrus' Edict	(Ezra 1:1)	1st year of Cyrus' reign	538 B.C.
Beginning of the rebuilding of the Temple, and return of Zerubbabel	(Haggai 1:14–15)	2nd year of Darius' reign	520
Completion of the Temple	(Ezra 6:15)	6th year of Darius' reign	515
Ezra's going up to Jerusalem	(Ezra 7:7–8)	7th year of Artaxerxes I	458
Nehemiah's arrival	(Nehemiah 2)	20th year of Artaxerxes I	445
Completion of the restoration of the walls	(Nehemiah 6:15)	20th year of Artaxerxes I	445
Nehemiah's return to the Persian Court	(Nehemiah 13:6)	32nd year of Artaxerxes I	433
Nehemiah's return to Jerusalem	(Nehemiah 13:6)	32nd year of Artaxerxes I	432
End of Persian rule over Judah, followed by the hellenistic rule			331

APPENDIX 2

Archeological Periods	Date	Historical Periods
Early Bronze	3150–2200 B.C.	Early Canaanite
Middle Bronze	2200–1550 B.C.	Middle Canaanite
Late Bronze	1550–1200 B.C.	El-Amarna period; Late Canaanite
Iron Age I, periods	1200–1000 B.C.	Israelite (Judges and Early Monarchy).
Iron Age II, periods	1000–586 B.C.	United Kingdom and the Kingdom of Judah
Persian	586–332 B.C.	
Hellenistic I	332–152 B.C.	
Hellenistic (Hasmonean)	152–37 B.C.	
Roman Herodian	37 B.C.–A.D.70	
Roman II, III	A.D. 70–324	
Byzantine	A.D. 324–640	
Early Arab	A.D. 640–1099	
Crusader	1099–1291	
Mameluke	1291–1516	
Turkish	1516–1917	

B.C. = Before Common Era

A.D. = C.E., Common Era

GLOSSARY

Acropolis, royal citadel, often an elevated part of an ancient city.

Antiquities, abbreviation of "Antiquities of the Jews" by Josephus Flavius, published originally in twenty "books" and subdivided into chapters. Our quotations indicate the book and page numbers.

Architrave, main beam resting directly on the upper slab of capitals of columns.

Basilica, used as the court of justice and administrative center in Roman times. It was generally a long rectangular building with two rows of pillars or columns dividing it into a central nave and two aisles. The design of the basilica influenced that of the Royal Portico on the Temple Mount, and that of synagogue and church architecture, giving the characteristic nave and aisle form.

Bronze Age, the period characterized by the use of bronze for weapons and implements. It corresponds to the Canaanite period in Palestine (3000–1200 B.C.).

Capital, head or cornice of a column or pillar.

Corinthian, a Grecian decorative order having a bell-shaped capital with rows of acanthus leaves, a style adapted to Jewish architecture.

Debir (devir), Holy of Holies.

Epigraphy, the branch of archeology concerned with the study of inscriptions.

Essenes, a religious communalistic brotherhood which existed in the latter part of the Second Temple period, and was distinguished by its mystical tenets and abstemious way of life. Source of the Dead Sea Scrolls.

Hasmoneans (Maccabees), name of a priestly family and dynasty in the second-first centuries B.C. until the days of Herod.

Hassideans (Hassidim), Jewish religious sect which came to the fore in the second century B.C. with the rise of the Hasmoneans; distinguished by their rigid observances, frequent prayer and the dauntless courage of their convictions. They apparently merged later into the Pharisee brotherhood.

Hechal (hēkhal), the sanctuary of the Temple.

Hellenistic, Jews or other orientals who used the Greek language and manner, but were not Greeks. Hellenism could be regarded as a symbiosis of Greek and oriental culture in the near east.

Ionian (Ionic), a decorative Grecian order characterized by two lateral volutes of the capital. The style was known in Palestine as far back as the ninth or eighth century B.C., and was of Phoenician or Egyptian origin.

Iron Age, the period in which the use of iron superseded that of bronze. It heralded a major agricultural and economic revolution, an upward surge in the standard of living, and a marked difference in social organization. It corresponds to the Israelite period (1200–586 B.C.) in biblical times.

Loculus, one of the separate cavities in a burial cave or a rock-cut tomb; plural = **loculi.**

Mishna, codified body of precepts of the Jewish elders (c. A.D. 200), containing the core of the Oral Law, i.e. the Pharisee interpretation and tradition of the Written Law (the Torah or Pentateuch ordinances) and supported by the majority of the population of Palestine. It formed the ultimate basis of the Talmud. Divided into six main orders and sub-divided into tractates, chapters and paragraphs, as quoted in this book.

Nazir, Nazirite, a Jew who had taken vows of abstinence; not to be confused with Nazarene or Nazarean, natives of Nazareth.

Ostracon, ancient inscribed potsherd.

Pilaster, rectangular column, especially one engaged in a wall.

Pillar, vertical stone structure used as support or ornament.

Ptolemies, Ptolemaic, rulers of Egypt from the death of Alexander to the days of the Roman empire.

Sadducees, members of the Jewish sect or party in Second Temple days who observed strictly and literally the traditional Law, denied resurrection of the dead and the existence of spirits; recruited among the priesthood and aristocracy; opponents of the Pharisees and Essenes.

Samaritans, adherents of the large Jewish sectarian community of Second Temple days who lived in central Palestine and were centered in Shechem. Their script is analogous to archaic Hebrew.

Sanhedrin, the assembly of ordained scholars which functioned both as a supreme court and as a legislature, from the century before the destruction of the Temple to A.D. 425.

Sassanids, rulers of the Persian empire, A.D. 211–651.

Seleucids, rulers of Syria after Alexander's time, c. 312–64 B.C.

Stratification, an important concept in archeological research: the strata or layers which are above other strata are more recent. In excavation, it is assumed, in the absence of evidence to the contrary, that any objects found in the upper strata are later in date than those found beneath.

Stylobate, continuous basement supporting a row of columns.

Talmud, body of Jewish law, homiletics and legends (comprising the Gemara, the commentary of the Mishna), codified in recensions in Jerusalem c. A.D. 400 and in Babylon c. A.D. 500. Divided into six main orders and subdivided into specific tractates, chapters and paragraphs, as quoted in this book. The numerous dissertations and references to the life and history of Second Temple days supply important testimony on the period. The fact that many of them are contemporaneous underlines their significance.

Tell, ancient mound in the Middle East, composed of remains of successive settlements.

War, abbreviation of "The Jewish War" by Josephus Flavius, published originally in nine volumes, comprising seven books, subdivided into chapters. The references quoted are from the Loeb edition (Harvard University Press) giving the book and page numbers indicated there.

Zealots, group of Jewish resistance fighters in the wars against Rome.

Vocalization

Hebrew words, appearing in inscriptions or in the Hebrew text of the Bible, are transliterated by the appropriate consonants and occasional vowel letters. These offer an approximation of the actual pronunciation, which was known to the ancient reader, and can be reconstructed on the basis of tradition and linguistic analogy: e.g. šlm represents Shālēm (šalem); yrwšlm = Yerūshālēm (Jerusalem).

Consonants

' (Aleph a laryngeal unvoiced stop (or plosive) as in 'Aqṣa

' (Ayin) a laryngeal voiced fricative (friction of breath in narrow opening) as in 'En, 'Apiru

ḥ (heth) pronounced like the 'ch' in the Scottish *loch* or German *ich*; in Hebrew: Ḥel, ḥeber

ś (śīn) = as in *so*

š (shīn) = as in *shell*

ṣ (tsadde) = as in *Tsar*

Vowels

ā = as in the English *father*; the Hebrew šām

ē = as in the English *cake*; the Hebrew bēth

ō = as in the English *core*; the Hebrew ṣinnōr

ū = as in the English *boon*; the Hebrew Yehūd

Signs

[or []: indicates missing letters or words of an inscription. It also may be used as an insertion in a quotation to clarify its meaning.

INDEX

301

ACKNOWLEDGMENTS

The author is deeply indebted to Professor D. N. Freedman, Ann Arbor, Michigan, and to Gaalyah Cornfeld, Tel-Aviv, for their valuable help. Professor Freedman read the entire English manuscript, making constructive observations and suggestions on both text and style. Gaalyah Cornfeld translated the Hebrew manuscript; he gave inestimable help and editorial guidance, and planned the overall design of the book.

The editors are equally grateful to Hassia Ben-Harari for her comprehensive copy-editing and styling of the English manuscript, and to Eli Gilad for the graphic layout.

Picture credits are due to: Professor Benjamin Mazar, Director of the Archeological Expedition of the Hebrew University and the Israel Exploration Society near the Temple Mount; to the Department of Antiquities and to the Archeological Museum, Jerusalem; to G. Cornfeld's photographic collection; to photographers Garo Studio, Jerusalem, and B. Carmasin, Tel-Aviv.